The Trust Factor

The Trust Factor
Negotiating in SMARTnership

Keld Jensen

palgrave
macmillan

First published in 2013 by
PALGRAVE MACMILLAN®
in the United States—a division of St. Martin's Press LLC,
175 Fifth Avenue, New York, NY 10010.

Where this book is distributed in the UK, Europe and the rest of the world,
this is by Palgrave Macmillan, a division of Macmillan Publishers Limited,
registered in England, company number 785998, of Houndmills,
Basingstoke, Hampshire RG21 6XS.

Palgrave Macmillan is the global academic imprint of the above companies
and has companies and representatives throughout the world.

Palgrave® and Macmillan® are registered trademarks in the United States,
the United Kingdom, Europe and other countries.

ISBN: 978–1–137–33225–7

Library of Congress Cataloging-in-Publication Data

Jensen, Keld.
    The trust factor : negotiating in smartnership / Keld Jensen.
        pages cm
        ISBN 978–1–137–33225–7 (alk. paper)
        1. Negotiation in business 2. Trust. 3. Partnership. I. Title.
HD58.6.J46 2013
658.4'052—dc23   2013022913

A catalogue record of the book is available from the British Library.

Design by Newgen Knowledge Works (P) Ltd., Chennai, India.

First edition: December 2013

10 9 8 7 6 5 4 3 2 1

Printed in the United States of America.

Contents

Figures and Table

Figures

Table

Acknowledgments

Many people from all over the world have contributed to the development of the content that forms the sum and substance of this book. Some of these ideas had their germination years ago but did not come to full fruition until recently when I came to understand that trust is in fact the keystone of successful commercial transactions. It would not be possible for me to recognize everyone who played a role along the way in the formation of these ideas. Much of the content here was inspired during presentations, training sessions, advisory services, and by the writings of scholars and thought leaders in the field of negotiation, behavioral economics, and conflict resolution. As a result, I began to explore what happens at the intersection of these disciplines when the goal is good outcomes for everyone at the table. Other break-through moments happened following friendly debate with my peers or after debriefings held at the conclusion of difficult negotiation sessions. All of the material in this book, however, is the product of hundreds of hours of solitary reflection, where I tried to identify the variables that made some deals work and others a disaster.

There are several individuals who deserve special recognition for their contributions to this project. I want to first acknowledge my gratitude to Laurie Harting and the management team at Palgrave Macmillan for recognizing the universality of the concepts I have developed. I am particularly appreciative of the involvement of Kate Vitasek, without whom I would not have met Laurie. My Palgrave editorial team made the manuscript process as painless as possible and offered exemplary suggestions for readability: Erin Ivy, Lauren LoPinto, and Ginny Faber.

I have numerous professional colleagues in Europe, Asia and the U.S. who have provided support and wise counsel along the way: Tim Cummins from IACCM, Dr. Karen Walch of the Thunderbird School of Global Management, Dr. Dan Shapiro of the Harvard Program on Negotiation, and Andre Bisasor, of the Harvard Conference on Leadership and Negotiation and Chairman of the Global Summit on Negotiation, Verner Worm, professor & director of the Asian Institute at Copenhagen Business School, my PA Charlotte Nielsen, Dr. Denis Leclerc—professor at Thunderbird School of Global Management, and last but not least, Jørgen Jacobsen for staying by my side.

I am very fortunate to have a stellar team in Boston who provided research and editorial assistance on the early drafts of this manuscript: Michelle Lim, Luke Messecar, Genevieve Kim, George Kasparian, Lois Hager, Madeline Rau, and Jack Patterson. Ian Nichols and Taz Sugajima brought their artistic talents to the illustrations interspersed throughout the text. Paige Stover has partnered with me from the beginning on this project and played an invaluable role providing structure to my thinking, developing ideas, and adding her own insightful perspectives to the development of the content.

Lastly, I want to thank my daughter Nadine. Anyone who is a parent understands that the first twenty or so years of your child's life are one continuous study in the art and science of negotiation. I freely acknowledge that she has been my most instructive critic and my least objective teacher. She is also the light of my life.

This book was truly created in the spirit of SMARTnership.

Preface

There *is* such a thing as a free lunch.

One evening, you're sitting at home when the phone rings. A complete stranger introduces himself and invites you and your spouse or partner to dinner at NOMA, his treat. NOMA, a small restaurant in Copenhagen, Denmark, has been ranked the world's best restaurant for the last three consecutive years by *Restaurant* magazine. NOMA's dining experience is near perfection, as are its 386 Google reviews. NOMA is completely booked for the next year, and the earliest reservation you can book is 14 months out.

Forget that distance is an issue. How would you react? Would you excitedly respond, "I would be delighted to join you?" Or would you be highly suspicious and decline the opportunity because you have no idea who this guy is and you think he might be up to something? Turning down a free meal at NOMA would be considered borderline insanity.

Yet, when Steven Htet, associate professor of biology at Northern Virginia Community College, sought to invite a low income or elderly couple to dinner at NOMA in 2012, he was met with nothing but awkward silence and rejection. While planning his trip to the Scandinavian countries from his home in Virginia, Htet searched Google for "elderly people" and "nursing homes." He called the Ministry of Social Affairs in Denmark and inquired whether they would be able to refer him to an elderly couple who would like to eat at the world's best restaurant as his guests. The head of the press department was speechless with astonishment and said that he could not help Htet. Quite simply, no one trusted him or his incredible offer.

Htet continued his search and contacted numerous companies that provided elderly housing and even communicated with a Marriott Hotel in Copenhagen. Everyone was skeptical; no one was willing to accept his unusual offer. In a final attempt, he called a company that built houses for the elderly. A startled employee gave the phone to his boss, who hesitantly gave Htet the number of his in-laws.

Htet rang them up immediately, and despite their reservations, they said yes to his offer. Two days later they met at the restaurant in Copenhagen. The dinner went seamlessly as they had wonderful conversation and became friends. All three savored the unusual food and unique dining experience. The couple quickly discovered that Htet's intentions were pure; he had only wanted to meet new people and spread kindness to others in the hope that they would pay it forward.

Certain situations require caution; no one wants to be naive. But as in the case of the couple who accepted Htet's incredible dinner offer, the opportunities created by trust vastly outweigh the outcomes caused by doubt and distrust. This story is just the latest example of a growing global concern. Convert this story to the twenty-first-century business world, and we must observe that confidence in the commercial marketplace is correspondingly low. Research from the World Economic Forum, based on 15,000 people in 20 countries, indicates that confidence in global companies has nosedived in recent years.[1] The perceived trustworthiness of leaders across many sectors is also on a decline. Too often, businesses begin a commercial relationship with high levels of distrust, requiring enormous amounts of time and resources to create sustainability with a trading partner. When trust is low, it increases transaction costs and lowers profit. Conversely, high levels of trust lower transaction costs and increase profits. I call this concept Tru$t Currency™.

Four Big Ideas That Could Change the World

About 15 years ago, I was the CEO of a public company in Scandinavia. We were a successful mid-sized company with suppliers and clients working with us on both a long- and short-term basis. I had risen through the corporate hierarchy from sales, through marketing, into management without a single minute of training in the science of negotiation. I thought that since I had been through thousands of negotiations, I must be pretty good at it. Since I was CEO of the company, I concluded I was probably even an expert.

I can tell you now, I was unconsciously incompetent. I did not know what I did not know. I was blind to the fact that I was not equipped to develop cooperative relationships with employees, suppliers, my board of directors, and customers. What is more, I was completely results oriented and clueless as to the importance of business culture and the process of company management. I threw myself into sales situations, delivery meetings, management meetings, board meetings, and employee interviews without identifying what was being negotiated in any one of them.

Then I was introduced to the ideas generated by Iwar Unt. He established a consulting company, in 1976, with one purpose—to train people in negotiation techniques. Iwar was way ahead of his time—in fact, his company was founded prior to the Program On Negotiation (PON) project at Harvard University. Harvard actually came to Iwar in the early 1980s and asked for his assistance, but he wanted to work on his own. He subsequently was given the title the Father of Negotiation in Scandinavia.

Iwar introduced me to the importance of negotiation in the organization I led. He showed me the immense amount of value we failed to create in our commercial transactions. He opened my eyes to the fact that everything from production to governance is about negotiation.

Since my initial meeting with Iwar and the revelations that occurred, I have been obsessed with telling the world about the enormous potential of cooperation. Regardless of whether you negotiate with your life partner, your child, your self, your manager, or your employees, bank, insurance company, or tax authorities, there is value hidden in the transaction that is rarely, if ever, identified. Good opportunities are lost.

In the last 15 years, I have researched and studied thousands of companies. I have looked under the petticoats and found that some are more successful than others. Not surprisingly, I continued my study and looked into their collaboration scenarios to see how big or small the share of their success (or lack thereof) was attributable to this variable. I found that the companies that were doing better in cooperative situations, whether it was buying, selling, project management or otherwise, succeeded because of mastery of four fundamental concepts:

- They have a defined negotiation strategy.
- They closely monitor the financial consequences of Tru$tCurrency™.
- They articulate the Rules of the Game before undertaking bargaining.
- They practice NegoEconomics™.

When I first became a consultant to the business community, I thought the big obstacle to commercial success was lack of negotiation competency. I jumped in as a negotiation specialist and tried to show the world that I could solve many problems if executives improved their negotiation skills. After several years of working with some of the top companies in the world, I decided that the big problem was not negotiation, but lack of communication competency. I then wrote several books on communication and added communication training in my consulting business to improve communications skills in the negotiation environment. Five years ago, I came to the realization that neither of these is at the root of the dysfunction. The real problem is the lack of trust and the failure of business executives to understand the behavior of their counterparts.

I have written this book in an effort to heighten the business community's awareness of the extraordinary impact the Trust Factor could have on international business transactions. You may not agree with all that you read here, at least not initially. I am compelled to challenge some deeply held concepts that are pervasive in the business cultures of North America and Europe.

People tend to buy and read books that support their belief system. They choose not to be challenged in their mindset. My hope is that this trend does not carry over to business books. My hope is that you will be intrigued by this book because it challenges an approach and a mindset that are no longer delivering the expected results.

My experience working in the world of international business indicates that the heavy-handed, combative, win-lose techniques that at one point may have consistently delivered effective results, are no longer producing the success business leaders demand. Globalization of the commercial marketplace, which has in turn introduced other approaches to problem-solving, has reduced the effectiveness of zero-sum tactics. It has also diversified the marketplace so that negotiators who no longer see the advantages of playing by the old rules have other alternatives, allowing them to do business with organizations that demonstrate values more closely aligned with their own.

The feedback I am hearing from my colleagues is that they are becoming aware of the need for another approach, but they have not found a suitable replacement in the current literature.

Why Negotiators Still Aren't "Getting to Yes"

I wrote my first book back in 1998. It was published in Denmark, and I thought that I had produced a piece of art that would live forever. About a year ago, I picked up my first book from 1998 for the first time in more than ten years and started to read the book again. I was

shocked. Most of the content was rubbish. I was in strong disagreement with the majority of the conclusions delivered in 1998. But was
the book that bad in 1998, or has the world moved forward, meaning
that the advice presented on negotiation in 1998 is not valid in 2013?
I hope and believe the latter. I was amazed to learn that the fields of
collaboration, cooperation, and relationships has changed that much
in less than 15 years.

One of the all-time best-selling books on negotiation is *Getting to
Yes* by Roger Fisher and William Ury. Millions of people have purchased and read this masterpiece for its tremendous insights and academic perspective on deal-making. Many corporate organizations are
trying to use the Fisher-Ury techniques and have adopted its teachings
as their strategic "bible." Unfortunately, there's one major problem
with this classic title: It hasn't worked. It simply has not translated
into the down-and-dirty world of corporate deal-making.

I agree with many of the powerful bargaining strategies articulated
in *Getting to Yes*. At the time of its publication, 32 years ago (no
cell phones, no Internet), in 1981, it was a groundbreaking text that
provided fresh ideas on cooperative problem-solving. The book origi-
nated the concept of entering negotiations with a BATNA: best alternative to a negotiated agreement, an idea that remains fundamental
to preparation before any negotiation.

Yet, no matter how many people have read the book with yellow
highlighters in hand, it has failed to change how they approach commercial negotiation. Despite the success of this best-selling title, it
failed to change the executive mindset or the American culture of the
negotiation table. It did not solve the unproductive negotiation tactics
that we use with our coworkers, family, friends, vendors, customers,
employees, suppliers, and competitors.

While cooperation is something we all say we desire, business
people end up in combative or zero-sum negotiations over and over
again. The compulsion to win comes at the expense of the other
person. As a European living in the United States, I have observed
American business's obsession with sports and sports analogies
in the workplace. One of the fundamental notions of team sports
around the world is that one team wins and the other team loses. In
American business, all the talk is about winning, or defeating the
opposition, or emerging victorious—all very combative and polar-
ized ways of looking at business problem-solving. Most significant
is the fact that this attitude is exactly opposite of the underlying
mutual-gain approach suggested in *Getting to Yes*. My perception is
that many corporate organizations are pledging one approach and

in fact doing something quite different when you closely examine their actions.

Clearly, there has been a breakdown. Why is it that everyone has read and endorsed this best-selling business book as one of the greatest negotiation texts ever written, yet so few actually follow it?

My intention in writing this book is to shift your thinking about the most effective approach to deal-making and then give you the toolbox to get the job done. I am a strong believer in SMARTnership™. Not only because it sounds good, but because it is a nice way to treat other people and because it will make you more profitable without hurting your counterpart.

I am a strong believer because I see that it works. It works not only in the laboratory and in the theoretical realm, but with my many international clients that are rejecting the traditional choice of zero-sum games and choosing to negotiate in SMARTnership. Creating mutual gains is the way of the future and the right path in order for the world to become a more rewarding place to conduct business.

In a SMARTnership negotiation, you will need to be open, honest, and willing to cooperate at a different level than ever before, but without becoming naive. At the same time, you will need to be an efficient negotiator and have the skills to split the additional value you have created, which, previously, was not even an aspect of the deal. The zero-sum negotiator never gets to the added value. The naive negotiator gets punished, and does not benefit from the value discovered.

In this book, I will show you how to accomplish both the creation of trust that serves as the keystone of SMARTnership and NegoEconomics, and how to efficiently divide the value once it has been identified.

In my world, optimized negotiation outcomes are achieved atop a three-legged stool. The legs are:

• Trust
• Negotiation competency
• Behavioral economics

If you master these three aspects of business relationships, you will see a dramatic improvement in the results you are able to achieve. But perhaps more significantly, you will make a meaningful contribution to the culture of the commercial marketplace that transcends individual performance. You will join forces with a growing number of colleagues who are committed to the restoration of trust in the international business community. If you believe that the values of trust, honesty, and fair dealing are important factors that contribute to the success of your business and your industrial sector, do not lose sight of the fact that you can make a difference. The reinsertion of trust in commercial transactions is a grass-roots movement. Somebody has to be the first person to act. It all starts with you!

Thank you for accompanying me on this journey. So far, I have been on the road for 15 years, and I feel like I just got started.

PART A

The 3-Legged Stool: Trust, Behavioral Economics, and Negotiation Competency

CHAPTER 1

A New Paradigm for
Commercial Relationships

You enter the conference room and take your seat across the table from a guy who has something you want. It could be cash, or services, or widgets. You have an expectation in your mind of the probable outcome of your negotiation with him based on your past experiences with similar people. Before you even begin the bargaining, you are pretty clear as to what you will leave the table with, give or take a percentage point or two.

Your vision of what you might come away with isn't big enough. Take that figure and double it. Triple it! The traditional rules governing negotiation in commercial transactions don't work anymore. If you stay on the familiar path, you may be losing out on millions—not because of increased costs, but through lost opportunity. You have failed to take advantage of a potential in the transaction that you can't even see until you get on the alternative route—the third road (Figure 1.1). The third road is called SMARTnership—it is a toll road. The toll is paid in trust.

The Roadmap for SMARTnership

Here is the roadmap to SMARTnership:

- Operate from a position of mutual trust, honesty, and fair dealing.
- Bargain constructively, using open, transparent, two-way communication.
- Leverage the differences between you and your counterpart.
- Cooperate to reduce risk and improve the utilization of resources.

Figure 1.1 There is a third road on the list of strategic options: SMARTnership™.

These elements sound simple, but they make serious demands on the delegates, and failure to follow them has enormous costs. According to studies by the Copenhagen Business School, businesses forfeit as much as 42 percent of the total value of a transaction because both sides fail to bargain for hidden variables—variables which may allow for an alternate solution that enhances the relative value of the transaction for both parties.

The SMARTnership Opportunity

Billions of dollars are left untouched in business dealings across the planet because the current culture of business negotiations measures success through a win-lose or zero-sum transactional model. If this model is abandoned in favor of the SMARTnership/NegoEconomic model, billions of dollars of added value will be infused into the global economy. The formation of a SMARTnership enables negotiating parties to expand the potential that lies within a commercial transaction and broaden the vision of what is possible for the business relationship.

My research shows that $3.25 trillion would flow into the US economy if that lost 42 percent of revenue from commercial transactions suddenly became manifest. How did I get that number? I looked at the total revenue of the one thousand biggest corporations in the United States, and identified the portion related to negotiations, whether that portion is the result of procurement or sales, and calculated 42% of that amount. Over three trillion dollars is an enormous amount of money.

Are you shocked? Don't believe my calculation is correct? Then let's assume, for the sake of argument, that the researchers working on this project were not the brightest in the world, and that the real number is only $2.5 trillion. Isn't this number still large enough for you to want to explore the potential?

Still not convinced? Let's pretend that the researchers were drinking when they did their calculations, and that the real number is only $1.5 trillion. Are you suggesting that you would not be interested if you were the CEO of one of the top one thousand largest corporations in the United States? This number would represent at least an additional $1.5 billion per company in profit annually.

How Does NegoEconomics Work?

A Bigger Pie Means More to Share

Think of the total value of a commercial transaction as a pie. A freshly baked, right-out-of-the-oven, cherry pie. You feast your eyes on its perfectly golden-brown crust and smell the sweetness of the cherries. You are hungry, and you want the biggest piece for yourself. The value of the deal is like this cherry pie. Everyone wants the biggest slice possible for himself—or, if the delegate is really greedy, he wants the whole thing. What most negotiators fail to realize is that there is a way for each of the delegates to get more pie.

Two parties can divide a small pie equally, or they might agree to some other ratio, say one-third/two-thirds. But if both parties mutually pursue the additional value in the deal, then the pie becomes larger, and both can net more than the value of their original half. NegoEconomics is the active pursuit of that additional value through cooperative deal-making; in other words, it is a mutual effort to increase the size of the pie and expand the room for negotiation (Figure 1.2). The added—or *asymmetric*—value that results from NegoEconomics can come in a variety of forms: It may come in the form of money, reduced competition, increased inventory, intellectual capital, or brand awareness. Once the asymmetric value has been located, all that remains to negotiate is how to divide it.

The objective of NegoEconomics is to establish a creative and constructive dialogue that will improve the conditions for finding a distribution that is acceptable to both parties. The sharing of the value does not have to be a 50/50 split. One party might take a significantly greater portion of the value by agreement. The parties might negotiate a 90/10 split. A 90/10 split can be perfectly within the spirit of SMARTnership if the party receiving the 10 percent is satisfied with the outcome.

Figure 1.2   Negotiators can unlock up to 42 percent more value by abandoning distrust and a zero-sum mindset. Source: MarketWatch Centre for Negotiation.

Who Has the Lowest Cost of Ownership?

NegoEconomics distributes tasks to the party who can perform the function at the lowest cost. If one side's costs are higher than the other side's, the task is allocated to the party who has the lowest cost of ownership.

NegoEconomic value shows itself when a supplier who offers to shorten his delivery times bears lower costs than the net gain accrued to the buyer. By making the extra effort the supplier can increase the quality of his services or products. If the benefit accruing to the buyer exceeds the costs incurred by the supplier, NegoEconomic value is created for both parties.

Example: Leveraging the Cost of Capital

Nathan is a supplier running a small company with very little cash on hand. He is signing a $10 million contract with a manufacturing company named Blossom. Blossom is a very successful company, with loads of cash. Blossom's negotiators want to pay him only at the time of delivery, which is six months in the future.

This puts Nathan in a difficult situation. His subsuppliers, on whom he depends to be able to fulfill the order to Blossom, are demanding an up-front payment from him to deliver the parts he needs to build the components Blossom is buying from him. The subsuppliers all require 30% up front on the total order value, which adds up to $3 million. This is money Nathan doesn't have.

Nathan has two options:

1. He can go to his bank and ask them for a loan for $3 million.
2. He can ask Blossom to pay $3 million up front.

He opts for option 2. Blossom's lead negotiator tells Nathan that the up-front payment is out of the question and adds that if he requires it, the negotiator will cancel the contract and search for an alternative supplier.

Nathan's only remaining alternative is to approach his bank and ask for a loan. The bank approves the loan but charges him interest in the amount of $150,000. This, of course, reduces his profit on the deal by $150,000.

Blossom's cost of paying Nathan the $3 million up front is $60,000. Why? Their cost of capital is lower than Nathan's.

Blossom's negotiator believes he won a strategic victory by not paying Nathan anything up front. Nathan knows he did not handle the negotiation well, but in reality both parties lost. Both parties lost the potential of creating NegoEconomic value by leveraging the terms of payment variable.

What NegoEconomic potential was lost in this transaction? The difference between Nathan's cost and Blossom's gains:

$150,000
– $60,000

$90,000 was lost between the two parties.

What should Nathan and Blossom have done instead? By figuring out the difference between their respective costs of capital they would easily have discovered that by utilizing this difference, they created $90,000 of NegoEconomics to divide between them. Imagine if Nathan reduced his price by $120,000—Blossom would make an additional $60,000 and Nathan would save $30,000. A win for everybody (with the exception of the bank—who is not part of the deal)

Money costs money. Actually, money is a commodity just like this book you are reading, a computer, a car, a table or a house. We can put value on money, on people, and on organizations. Look at your credit card statement. Are you paying 15 percent or 19 percent interest on your balances or more than that? That percentage quantifies the value to you of using American Express's financial leverage.

When I present this very simplified example of NegoEconomics to executives, some will tell me they do not have the time to focus on $150,000 when they are working on a $10 million deal. Then I ask them if they personally make more than $150,000 an hour? Most people I meet tell me they don't. Then I respond that in a negotiation that has a total value of $10 million, they will easily find 200 or 300 variables each having the potential to deliver $150,000 in NegoEconomic value.

In the last few years, I have noticed a trend stemming from corporate management who have directed their procurement departments to generate positive cash flow by expanding their credit from suppliers. Prior to these new directives, the typical credit term might have been 30 days. Under the new directives, it is often 60–90 days.

Who do you think typically has the lower cost of capital—a major publicly traded company or a local supplier with 50 employees? It always costs the smaller company more to obtain financing. A large corporation generally has the lower cost of capital. With these new directives coming from the procurement department, the small supplier with the higher costs is picking up the bill for the huge company with the lower cost of capital. This makes very little sense by anyone's standards.

The Trust Factor

Trust is the key ingredient that enables the development of a SMARTnership which, in turn, unlocks the benefits of NegoEconomics. The Trust Factor can best be described as a cocktail of trust, honesty, and cooperation, flavored with good intentions that your loyal opposition fully benefit from the deal you are making. Delegates expand the economic potential of a business relationship through the discovery of mutual gains that only become apparent in an environment based on openness, honesty, transparency, fairness, and trust. A SMARTnership is formed when the parties agree that they will allow trust to govern the interpersonal dynamic and their decision-making and that they will share the information necessary to bargain with the intention of creating gains for both. By negotiating creatively and openly, delegates will be able to access benefits that were not originally in play, and increase the value of the transaction for everyone involved.

Building a SMARTnership requires you to understand that there are negotiation strategies other than zero-sum or partnership (Figure 1.3).

The Zero-sum Game Leads to Low-quality Solutions

Zero-sum games dominate most negotiation climates because of the eternal struggle for survival. The strongest individuals have learned to seize most of the limited resources for themselves. At the negotiation table, zero-sum games are the results of shortsighted strategies,

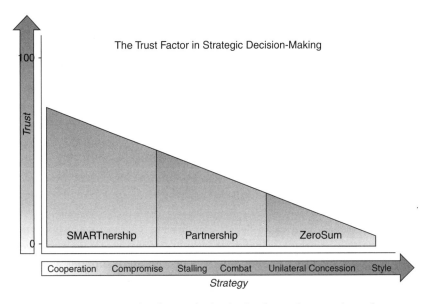

Figure 1.3 A SMARTnership features higher levels of trust than a traditional partnership or a zero-sum negotiation. It allows parties to share information and increase the potential value in the deal.

a fear of opening up and listening, poor preparation, and insufficient insight into how the alternative method of cooperation works and what results it may yield.

Unfortunately, in zero-sum games, it is common for negotiators to work with solutions that are unnecessarily costly. The ability to be rational is restricted if and when the parties are emotionally affected by the negotiations. Threats, insecurity, and stress are countered with a fight-or-flight response—a knee-jerk reaction which has been given little to no serious thought. This irrational reaction causes the resources to disappear into thin air and shuts down any opportunity for leveraging them. Neither party benefits from a share in the expanded value.

Example: Negotiating to Dig A Ditch

Kevin and Ramona are doing a project together. They have been hired to dig a ditch. Kevin's costs are $50 per yard, while Ramona's are $30 per yard. If Ramona digs the entire ditch, the two of them will save $20 per yard. If Kevin digs the entire ditch, as opposed to sharing the task 50/50, they will save $10 per yard.

In a zero-sum game, Ramona and Kevin will disagree about who is going to dig the ditch. If the partners cooperate, however, Ramona will do the digging at her lower cost rather than Kevin. Then they will share the added value generated, so that Ramona is paid $35 per yard.

While this solution may appear simple, it is actually quite complex because, typically, negotiators are trapped in the zero-sum game. A zero-sum negotiation may result in the party with the highest cost digging the ditch on his own. Using threats and manipulations, one negotiator can make the other party undertake all the work: *It won't take long to dig this ditch. You won't have to dig very deeply. The ditch is only a hundred yards or so, and the soil is easy to work with. If you want your money, the ditch must be finished by tomorrow afternoon!*

In this zero-sum negotiation, openness and trust are in short supply. The parties waste energy fighting. As long as they think that a "victory" in the bargaining process will lead to good solutions, they will continue to battle. This assumption is generally flawed or yields only short-term positive results.

In zero-sum games, the negotiators use a combination of four strategies: combat, concession, stalling, and compromise. Important components of zero-sum games are

- withholding information,
- bluffing,
- making power plays,
- using tactical moves to try to create stress and insecurity in the other party,
- dishonesty,
- decisions that are made with great uncertainty,
- giving priority to short-term gains,
- status ploys—the parties do not treat each other as equal partners,
- manipulation.

Zero-sum Games, Partnership, or SMARTnership

In NegoEconomics, the three primary negotiation methods are zero-sum games, partnership, and SMARTnership. The question to consider is not: *How can I use these methods to get the best possible result?* An effective negotiator might combine SMARTnership, partnership, and zero-sum games and use each strategically to optimize the negotiation outcome. She uses cooperation to strengthen relationships and intensify the Trust Factor. Zero-sum games could be used to negotiate the division of the increased value that materializes during the NegoEconomic process. The way in which these two approaches are combined will vary from case-to-case depending on the circumstances of the transaction and the interpersonal dynamic in play.

Defining a Negotiation Strategy

Open a new document on your computer and describe your company's negotiation strategy to achieve cooperation from your trading partners? I do not mean your sales or supplier policy, but the strategy for how cooperation is initiated and implemented regardless of whether it is short or long-term. My guess is that you are staring out into space and wondering what I mean. Do not worry, you are not alone. More than 96 percent of the surveyed companies, governments, and organizations doing business internationally have no negotiating strategy.

Why do you need a strategy? You must decide what you want from a trading relationship. Do you want zero-sum, partnership or SMARTnership? My experience is that when asked this question, many people respond that they work toward partnership, when in fact all their tactics are zero-sum. The majority of the world's organizations unconsciously conduct most of their negotiations using the zero-sum strategy. They are unconsciously incompetent and do not know the alternative.

CASE STUDY: The Merger of Disney and Pixar

A great example of NegoEconomics and SMARTnership was the merger between Disney and Pixar.

The merger of these two companies was a match made in cartoon heaven. Disney let Pixar retain both its name and creative control of its projects, and two years into the partnership, the newly merged company was releasing box-office hits like *Wall-E* and *Cars*. The success of this merger was centered on both companies' willingness to cooperate with each other. Prior to the deal being settled, many people had reservations about the success of the merger. Many feared that Disney would be unable to rein in the audacious personalities that made Pixar great. Those at Pixar feared a loss of creative license under Disney management. However, when both parties came to the table, they were united by the same goal: to produce quality animation for the next generation.

The success of this merger speaks volumes about the advantages of employing NegoEconomics and SMARTnership to a negotiation strategy. The opposing cultures at Pixar and Disney—Pixar being more laid back (having released only six films between 1995 and 2005), as opposed to Disney's much greater productivity (having releasing 24 animated features between 1995 and 2005)—could have initially posed a problem. Instead, these oppositions ended up working positively for both companies. Shortly after the merger, Pixar enjoyed a spike in productivity and released two films in the following year while Disney benefited by expanding their audience to capture the Pixar market as well.

By playing to and taking advantage of each company's strengths they were able to increase the size of the pie and leave the table with more than they had originally thought possible.

The Trust Factor and the Rules of the Game

What became of the "good old days" when an agreement was a gentleman's agreement and was finalized with a handshake? How were deals made before we had employment contracts, confidentiality agreements, and teams of lawyers with boxes of documents? It is true that these legal tools help safeguard our interests. But attorney-drafted contracts and agreements cannot ensure personal trust and the preservation of ethics and morality. The chapters that follow will show you that a shift in thinking and an abandonment of traditional approaches to deal-making will lead to greater success for you personally, as well as in the attainment of your business goals. It begins with the Trust Factor. Failure to make the Trust Factor the foundation of your Rules of the Game will render your aspirational goals impossible to attain. The miraculous thing about the Trust Factor is that it requires nothing more of you that a shift in attitude. The only thing you need to know to get the ball rolling is that it all starts with you!

Take aways

- SMARTnerships requires trust.
- The Trust Factor is a cocktail of trust, cooperation, and honesty.
- Trust starts with You and must be at the foundation of your Rules of the Game.
- $3.25 trillion dollars are not being capitalized in the USA alone.
- Define your negotiation strategy: zero-sum—partnership—SMARTnership.
- A bigger pie means more for everyone to share.

CHAPTER 2

Behavioral Economics in Deal-making

Optimized Outcomes Are Achieved
on a Three-legged Stool

In commercial transactions, optimized outcomes are measured financially—more gross revenue, increased profit margins, greater percentage of market share, and so forth. In personal relations, optimized outcomes are measured in better understanding, less conflict, and more collaboration. Regardless of the kind of transaction in which you are involved—as a CEO, a procurement officer, a sales director, or a dad or mom—the optimized outcomes are achieved atop a three-legged stool (Figure 2.1). The legs of that stool are:

- Trust
- Negotiation competency
- Behavioral economics

Behavioral economics is simply a fancy way of saying *the way people make decisions*. For many years, social scientists based their assumptions on the reasoning that people always make rational decisions. In the late twentieth century, the academic community confirmed that the opposite is in fact true. People most often, or even always, make irrational, emotionally driven decisions that are largely unpredictable. Decisions are made based on emotions and documented subsequently with facts! The future seems far more secure for sociologists and psychologists than for economists.

The interpersonal dynamic of the delegates at the negotiation table is as important to the outcome of a commercial transaction as negotiation competency and trust. If any one of these is not accounted for in the process of preparing for a negotiation, the outcome will be suboptimal.

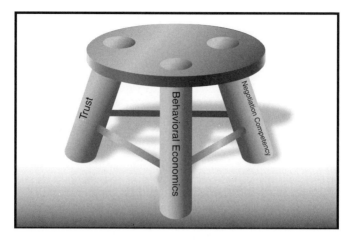

Figure 2.1 This three-legged stool represents optimized negotiation outcomes. What would happen if one leg were shorter than the other two? The deal would be suboptimal.

You're Not As Smart As You Think You Are

Look around where you are sitting—lamps, chair, computer, remote control, mobile phone. Then, think of an airplane, the space shuttle, a car, or an oil rig. Is man not a fantastic creature to have created all this? One technological achievement after another. We must be brilliant!

However, despite all these accomplishments, you forget your car keys. You cannot remember where you parked the car. You lose your glasses. You gain and lose weight in a never-ending cycle. You smoke when we all know it causes cancer, and you drink too much alcohol. You are late for meetings.

You are not as smart as you think you are. It has been proven scientifically that people generally think they are smarter than they actually are. You also believe that you make sound decisions and reach rational conclusions when you are deciding something. Neither of these is the case. You make irrational decisions constantly, which actually are quite unreasonable.

You Can't Trust Your Memory

For years, researchers believed that the human memory system worked like a hard drive. It recorded everything that was sent to it and stored it for retrieval. This is partially true; however, the memory system in your brain manipulates your sense of reality.

Read the following words, and then close this book and try to write down all the words on a piece of paper: roof, floor, windows, door, kitchen, garage, garden, bathroom, bedroom, ceiling, basement, bedroom, hallway, driveway, staircase, air conditioner.

How many did you remember? If this exercise is presented correctly, a majority of people will have written the word "house" as well. The word "house" is not in the list, so what is happening here? The brain is manipulating the data it receives and filling in the missing pieces of the puzzle.

Your Emotional Brain

Your emotional brain is an interesting contrast to your rational brain. The processing by your rational brain has obvious limitations. Your emotional brain, however, can handle far more complicated tasks, like cycling, dancing, drumming, or gymnastics. These operations appear to be simple, but break them down into individual orders from the brain, and there are hundreds, if not thousands, of data feeds.

When you make decisions during a negotiation, to purchase a product and do business with someone, it is more often than not feelings that are the cause of the commitment. When you choose Company A over Company B, in many situations it is the result of an irrational decision-making process, in which you cannot quite put your finger on the reason for preferring one over the other. You cannot justify the decision because your subconscious mind has made

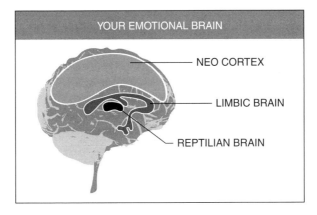

Figure 2.2 Although most people will never admit it, our decisions are often made using emotions instead of logic.

the decision, and therefore your rational brain is not even aware of the process.

This behavior is physical. People basically have three brains: the reptilian brain, the limbic brain, and the neocortex, or the rational brain (Figure 2.2). The reptilian brain was the first to develop, and it is many millions of years old. The limbic brain is feeling oriented, and acts on instincts. The neocortex was the last to develop, and is the most rational. We might call it the orthodox economic brain. The decision-maker of the three brains, the limbic brain, is the part of the brain that sits at the front. Experiments have shown that people who have had an injury following an accident that has affected the anterior part of the brain—the limbic—become unable to make decisions. The neocortex sifts through the data in order to make a decision, but the decision is actually made in the limbic.

The Orthodox Economic World

Man has for many centuries been regarded as homo economicus—the sensible rational person who lives in an orthodox economic world and always makes rational decisions and good choices. Brain research has been able to document that we do not make good decisions and we are not rational in our conclusions. We do not live in an orthodox economic world, but in a behavioral economic world. It is a world that economists do not like because, suddenly, it is impossible to predict what is happening. In a behavioral economic world, we do not do what the scientists expect.

Daniel Kahneman's Research

Professor Daniel Kahneman received the Nobel Prize in Economics for his research in behavioral economics, a slightly unusual result for someone who is not an economist. He is in fact a psychologist! Kahneman was actually the first noneconomist to receive the Nobel Prize in Economics.

Kahneman concluded in his research that people are completely irrational. The rational person does not exist, in his view. People prefer to do business with someone whom they like and trust, who has an inferior product, at a higher price, than to do business with someone whom they do not like and have little confidence in, but who has a better product at a cheaper price. These conclusions do not support the assumptions upon which most economic predictions are based. In a rational economy, subjective factors like sympathy and confidence are not included on a spreadsheet of economic variables.

Kahneman further concludes that people's decisions are all based on emotions, regardless of whether we are buying a new car, choosing a new job, selecting a supplier, or choosing a life partner. After we make a decision based on emotional factors, we reach out for facts that support the decision we have already made. Decisions are made on emotional criteria and validated, subsequently, with facts[1].

Many corporate executives strongly resist the notion that they are indeed deeply irrational. Yet few people recognize their irrationality and, in fact, there seems to be an attitude in the world that it is taboo to be irrational, as if it is a mind disease. But we all must accept that there is a new world order. You are irrational, and so are all the people you meet and negotiate with. If we believe that Kahneman is right, we are suddenly in a new situation. Product, price, quality, and delivery time are now secondary factors in negotiation. The most important criterion in the negotiation process is you. The person is more important than the facts and details of the transaction. People create relationships, and relationships and trust are more important than product and price.

The older we get, the more entrenched we become in our attitudes. You may have already become irritated with me as a writer if you do not agree with the positions I have taken so far in this book. You may even have considered dropping the book and refusing to read further. Is this irrational nonsense?

But stop for a moment. This behavior is actually what we often do. We choose to read material that supports the views we already have. And we choose not to read material that is contrary to what we already know. We do not like to be confronted with contrary views, but rather, we want to reinforce what we already believe. We read material that supports our existing knowledge base and avoid material that challenges our knowledge and beliefs.

An interesting experiment was conducted during the 2012 US presidential election that documented these preferences. The researchers surveyed people who had bought books about Barack Obama on Amazon. There were books critical of Obama and books that supported and explained Obama's thinking and behavior. The interesting finding was that books critical of Obama were bought by voters who would not vote for him, and the supportive books were bought by voters who had already decided to vote for him. So in this case, the purchase of the book supported a decision that already had been made.

Immediate Gratification

Procrastination is one of man's great challenges. We live in a microwave society. This means that results must come quickly, and often we choose a quick bad solution rather than a solution that will take longer but that is better!

In the 1960s and '70s, Walter Mischel of Stanford University conducted experiments in which he offered children marshmallows, cookies, or a pretzel. The children were seated at a table with a bell on it. The children were told that they could choose to eat one of the goodies right away or wait a few minutes and then they could have two goodies. If they waited, they could double their reward. If they could not wait, they had to ring the bell, after which the researcher would stop the experiment.

Some of the children lacked self-control and ate one of the treats immediately. Others stared at the treats, wrestled with themselves, and licked the marshmallows, until finally they relented and grabbed one of the treats. Many writhed in frustration, rubbing their hands together, wiggling, trying to look at other things in the room, obviously in great internal conflict. Some made funny noises. The final results showed that 33 percent could not resist the temptation and ate one of the goodies rather than waiting to double the reward.[2]

The results of the study are a very interesting comment on human nature. The conclusion has to do with thinking about thinking, which is a key factor in success. The struggle is between need versus want. Westerners as a whole are generally not good at deferring gratification.

Mischel followed the children who participated in this experiment through college and into their adult lives. An interesting conclusion he drew was that the children who were able to postpone gratification and resist temptation were not more intelligent. They were, however, more disciplined and able to exercise self-control so that they consistently made decisions that were in their best interest. During the experiment, these were the children who looked elsewhere in the room while they waited, rather than focusing on the treats. They looked up at the ceiling, out the window, or stared at the wall. The wait was torturous, but those who could resist their impulses got a greater reward. Those who could not resist the temptation of the goodies exhibited greater character flaws and behavioral difficulties throughout their lives. Those who deferred gratification scored, on average, 200 points higher on the SAT exam and were able to perform better later in life.

Money—Sex—Power: The Three Super Motivational Factors That Drive Most of Us

I frequently ask people I meet through my work the odd question "What motivates you?" It is a strange question to get from a person you have just met. I receive an enormous variety of answers. Everything from family, career, freedom, my boat, horseback riding, and music, to the more exotic, like travel to Mars.

When we return to our most fundamental drivers, I have found that there are three main motivators for most people. Everyone is not driven by all three, at least not at the same time. The three factors that drive most people are money, sex, and power. My observation is that in order to obtain one or more of these factors, you must negotiate. Want a pay raise? That requires a salary negotiation with your boss. In a debate with your supplier or customer, you must negotiate to retain the account or get the terms that you want. If you want to spend more on holiday vacation travel, you must negotiate with your partner about a larger share of the household budget. If you want to increase your credit line at the bank, you must negotiate for more credit.

If you want more power, or influence, this also requires negotiation. I meet people who claim that they do not have power or influence. But every time you want to convince someone else that your idea is the best, you are exercising power and influence.

The last of the three motivational factors is sex. People sometimes wonder where I am going with this when I launch into this part of the discussion. But appreciation, admiration, connection, and a relationship of some sort are necessary to find a sexual partner.

I have a colleague who made an observation that is brilliant. He believes that if you have plenty of one of the three—money, sex or power—you will get the other two. I think he's right! If you have plenty of money, you will undoubtedly find your way to power and sex. If you have great sex appeal, there is a good chance you will have money and power.

Psychological Needs

Negotiations are intended to meet different needs, which are tangible and partly psychological in nature. The needs are measured and expressed in monetary terms, through market share, production quality, utilization of production capacity, and supply security. Superficially seen, the negotiation seems to be centered on purely tangible needs. However, the psychological needs of the negotiators are just as important.

Abraham Maslow's hierarchy of needs is very useful when it comes to a discussion on the psychological needs and motivations of a negotiator. Maslow's pyramid consists of five tiers that break down the quintessential elements of human motivation.

- *Self-realization:* wanting to meet the budgetary targets, conquer new markets, and try out new techniques, and having the freedom to go one's own way.
- *Social recognition:* wishing to gain other people's respect, recognition, and approval. This can be achieved by reaching tangible results, by appearing to be the winner, by arriving at an agreement, by not losing face, by demonstrating skill, and by making new friends at the negotiating table
- *Security:* seeking to avoid technical and commercial risks, new technology, untried suppliers, and incentive agreements. Finding contentment in staying within budget rather than going for maximum gains.
- *Retaliation:* wanting to get even.
- *Self-assertion:* desiring to be bigger, stronger, and more clever, and wanting to rule and manipulate others.

Be Aware of Your Drivers

Usually we do not have insight into our own conscious and subconscious needs and desires, and this leads to conflict that we attribute to the other party. Without being conscious of it, we are led into situations where our subconscious actions trigger conflict. Only when you have become aware of these drivers and have learned to see the linkage between our conscious and our subconscious action, will you achieve the maturity required to tackle certain types of cooperation. Be in tune with your tendencies, and do not be afraid to adjust the tempo of the interpersonal dynamic.

Tru$t Currency™

I have conducted research with more than 3,000 people who were confronted with a simple task: you must buy plastic bottles of water for your staff. For the last five years you have purchased bottles of water from Angie, whom you really like. You have a great relationship with her—you laugh at the same jokes, you communicate well, and the trust between you is complete. Angie's price for a bottle of water is thirty cents per bottle.

A new supplier, Burt, approaches you and says that he can deliver exactly the same product, an identical bottle of water, with no difference in content, packaging, or quality at a price 2 percent lower than Angie's price. You have never met Burt before, and there is something about him you just don't trust. You cannot put your finger on it, but the personal chemistry is not there. You do not communicate well and have difficulty understanding each other. Who are you going to do business with?

My respondents had no difficulty deciding to continue to do business with Angie when the price difference was only 2 percent. Things began to get interesting, however, when I increased the difference in price in 1 percent increments. I wanted to know at what price point would the test subject decide to stop doing business with Angie and switch to Burt, in spite of the fact that he or she did not like or trust him.

My research showed that for most people, the threshold of pain was a 10–20 percent price differential. Some test subjects went as far as a 30 percent price difference before they chose to switch to Burt. But the majority of my test group agreed to pay 10 percent more for an identical product and continue to do business with a supplier in whom they had confidence and who had higher likeability.

I also speculate that the higher the complexity of a service or product, the greater the importance of likeability and trust.

Testing the Bounds of Rationality

Consider the following stories. Think about how you would respond to these situations and then compare your behavior to the research results. All the examples are actual research experiments using thousands of volunteers.

Scenario #1

You have just had dinner at a restaurant in a city and a country where you are absolutely certain you will never come again. Do you give the waiter a tip? Tipping is an altruistic act, something you do for others and not yourself. Under traditional, orthodox economic principles, there is no reason to tip in this fact pattern. However, are there other considerations that might cause you to leave a tip?

Scenario #2

What would you rather have? $50 today or $100 tomorrow? Seventy-two percent of subjects choose $50 today.

What would you rather have? Fifty dollars in 30 days or one hundred dollars in 31 days? Suddenly, the majority of test subjects say that they would rather have $100 in 31 days. Can you explain this behavior? When we ask respondents to choose between today or tomorrow, the majority select today. Yet, when the choice is between 30 days or 31 days, 82 percent agree to wait one more day to get $100. The different results in these two cases are irrational.

Scenario #3

You are employed by a company that has market growth of 12 percent this year. The company is profitable, and yet it provides a salary increase of only 7 percent annually. Is this fair or unfair?

You are employed by a company that has market growth of 0 percent. The company is unprofitable this year, and reduces wages across the board by 5 percent. Is this fair or unfair?

Which of the above two examples do you think is most unfair?

If you think that the example of wage reduction is more unfair than the example of the pay raise, you are irrational. In both examples, the employee is at a disadvantage—and a disadvantage that is financially equal.

Scenario #4

You are on your way to the theater. When you arrive, you discover that you have lost the ticket, which is worth $100. Will you buy a new one or go home?

You are on your way to the theater with the intent to buy a ticket costing $100. When you arrive at the theater, you discover that you have lost $100 in cash on the road. Will you buy the ticket anyway or go home?

People react very differently in these two situations. In the first scenario, 69 percent of respondents who lost the ticket indicate they would buy a new one. But in the second situation, where they have lost $100 in cash, the majority of subjects say that they would go home! What is the difference between the two situations? Both involve the same loss of a value of $100.

Scenario #5

You walk through a town, and when you get home you discover that you have lost $25. Too bad. The next day, you are out walking again and once again discover you have lost $25. You are amazed at your clumsiness.

Another scenario: You are out for a walk, and when you get home, you discover that you have lost $50. Annoying.

Which of the two situations do you prefer? Losing $25 over 2 days or losing $50 in one day?

New situation: You are out for a walk, and you find $25. You think that it is your lucky day! The next day, you walk again and find another $25.

New situation. You're out for a walk and find $50.

Which of the two situations would you rather experience: finding $25 twice or finding $50 once? Think about your answer.

In the situation related to lost money, most people preferred to lose $50 once, rather than $25 twice. Presumably, they want to feel the impact and the pain and irritation immediately. In the found money situation, it is quite the reverse. People prefer to find $25 twice. They want to spread the joy and satisfaction over time.

What we learned: when we lose something or are being "punished," it is better to get it over with in one blow. When we are being rewarded or having a windfall, it preferable to spread it out in several stages.

Think of companies in financial crisis that have made a series of cutbacks in several stages, rather than taking a larger, more significant action in one big move. Reflect also on the situation in which you as the supervisor give an employee a promotion and simultaneously provide a pay increase. It would be more rational to give the promotion in one month and provide the pay increase in another month. This would give the employee more psychological satisfaction. Rational, though? Hardly.

Scenario # 6

One of the most famous experiments is the Prisoners Dilemma. Connor and Melinda are the test subjects. Connor is handed $100 in $1 bills. Melinda is told how much Connor has been given. The rules are the following: Connor must share the $100 with Melinda. Connor will determine how the distribution is made. However, the rule is that if Melinda rejects the amount Connor offers, they lose the entire $100.

If you were Connor, how much would you offer? 10 percent? 30 percent? 50 percent? 70 percent? The results of thousands of repetitions of this experiment are that if Connor gives less than 20 percent, Melinda will reject the offer, and both participants will have lost everything! This is highly irrational behavior, because something is better than nothing. Why does she reject the offer? Melinda rejects anything less than 20 percent because she feels she is being treated unfairly and she wants to punish Connor. I have conducted this experiment among 2,000 of my students and confirmed the results.

This experiment has been modified so that Connor pretends to be a business person as opposed to an ordinary person of no defined professional position. He wears a suit and arrives carrying a briefcase. When Connor is dressed as a business person the minimum requirement of fairness for the distribution is increased over the amount required when Connor is dressed specifically as a "civilian."

Scenario # 7

You are working in your office late one night when the phone rings, and it is your wife asking you to bring home some colored markers and some copy paper from the office. She is under the gun to produce a project for her job. Should you pilfer office supplies and take them home for your wife to use?

You promise to bring home the items she requested. You go to the supply closet and discover that there are no markers and no copy paper. This is a very poorly managed workplace you say to yourself!

You are certain that your wife will be terribly upset if you do not come home with markers and paper. You remember that on the way home, you will pass an office supply store that is open late. On the way out the door of the office, you discover, however, that you have left your wallet at home so you cannot buy the items she needs at the store. You are very frustrated and look around the office exasperated. You find a solution. Next to the coffee pot is a basket of candy and fruit that is run on the honor system—if you take an item from the basket, you put the designated amount in a little box next to it. You discover that there is enough money in the box to pay for the things she needs from the store. Do you take the cash from the box?

The majority of respondents in this scenario indicate that they would NOT take the money, but that they would take the paper and the markers. What is the difference? Both represent the same value. Either way, it is theft!

This experiment has also taught us something completely different. One of the reasons that trust is in decline in this world is that we have moved away from cash. Most commercial transactions today are conducted without physically touching the money. You write a check, process a credit card, click a mouse, and you have bought something. When we come into contact with cash, we are more honest.

Competence and Awareness

Perceptual Blindness

In 1500, when the first European settlers arrived in the Caribbean, the native people could not see the ships that had transported the Europeans to the island. The natives were terrified at what appeared to be falling clouds, and they believed that the sky was going to fall in on them. They could not comprehend the sailing ship with its enormous sails coming into the bay under wind power. They saw only white billowing clouds. They had no concept of a ship. They related what they saw visually to the only comparable thing in their consciousness—clouds. They had never seen a ship before and therefore perceived it within their view of the cosmos. They could not see anything else because they had no contextual framework.

The same thing happens to twenty-first-century people when we are exposed to something we haven't seen before, heard about, or been exposed to. Truly educated and enlightened people understand what they do not know. They pursue a quest for more information and seek to be life-long learners. Amateurs think they know it all, and often they just don't see it!

Where Are You on the Competency Scale?

Most negotiators will not admit that they do not know how to do their job. In fact, ask anyone, and he or she will not readily admit to incompetence. The majority of people believe that they are at least above average when it comes to competency at what they do. This has been proven countless times when I have opened a new training session on negotiation for managers. I ask the group: "How would you rate yourself on a scale from 1–10, where 10 is the perfect negotiator and 1 is really bad?" The majority responds with answers at 7 or 8 on the scale, which means that they consider themselves to be pretty good!

Two or three days later, near the end of the training session, I repeat the question to the same group. This time the average response is 3 or 4 on the scale of 10. What happened during the three-day training class? Did I manage to make people stupid and cause them to lose knowledge about how to negotiate? Did I remove their motivation and create a less competent group of negotiators? Or had they previously overestimated their competence?

People tend to rate their competency higher than it actually is. This is known as the Dunning-Kruger effect, a cognitive bias in which unskilled individuals experience illusory superiority, wrongly rating their abilities much higher than average.[3]

Individuals also generally give themselves credit for their successes, but blame failure on external factors from the outside world. This is called a self-serving bias, or self-serving attributional bias, as studied in 1999 by Keith W. Campbell and Constantine Sedikides.[4]

Is this rational behavior?

Developing Awareness of Where You Are in the Learning Process

The negotiators in my training classes have simply been made aware of mistakes they did not realize they were making. People are sometimes oblivious to the reality that they are lacking skills in an area where they feel they have above-average competence. This is part of the learning process, and there is a definite pattern to the way we learn.

Nadine Learns to Pour

The learning process requires you to go through four levels (Figure 2.3) of competency:

Level 1—Unconsciously Incompetent

Imagine a typical two-year-old girl. This little girl, whom we will call Nadine, has spotted the milk carton on the table during breakfast. Nadine gets the idea that she wants to pour the milk into her glass. She has seen mom and dad do it many times, and it looks easy. Her first few attempts are stopped by her mom and dad to prevent a flood of milk from splashing onto the kitchen floor and the table. Nadine is unconsciously incompetent. She does not realize that she is physically incapable of pouring milk into her glass without assistance.

Many video-recorded negotiations exemplify similar situations in which the negotiators do not realize they are fruitlessly attempting to come to a solution until they see themselves on the playback.

Level 2—Consciously Incompetent

Nadine is not the type of little girl who easily abandons an idea. Mom's and dad's backs are turned, and she is suddenly presented with an opportunity. She grabs the milk carton—and—SPLASH! The

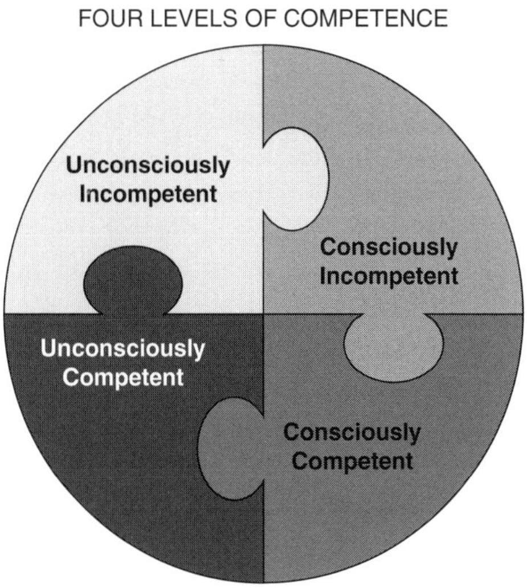

FOUR LEVELS OF COMPETENCE

Figure 2.3 Negotiators are oftentimes unconsciously incompetent. They are unaware of their inability to negotiate effectively.

carton slips from her tiny hands and falls to the floor, spilling milk everywhere. Nadine has suddenly gone from Level 1 to Level 2. She now realizes that she is unable to pour the milk on her own without creating a mess.

You find yourself in this situation when you see yourself on video and realize you are not performing effectively. You become aware of your mistakes and the areas in which you require improvement.

Level 3—Consciously Competent

Nadine practices, under the guidance of her father and mother, until she is able to pour the milk on her own without a disaster occurring. Nadine is now aware of her new skill, but she still requires full concentration and attention in order to pour the milk on her own.

Level 4—Unconsciously Competent

Nadine is now 6 years old. She can bike, climb trees, and swim. She pours her own milk several times a day without thinking about it. Through habit, she has acquired a new skill.

This is how learning to negotiate works. A delegate begins with limited theoretical and practical knowledge and develops competence until eventually, these techniques become second nature.

Executive Competence

Great demands are made of people at the top in the business world, and they are now finding themselves in the limelight more than ever before. The competition for success has intensified, and there are people who choose to resort to bad or unethical behavior in order to succeed.

Demanding jobs at the top have become more and more complicated. A job that ten or fifteen years ago involved 400 tasks related to work and responsibility, may now involve 600 tasks. The demands on the top executive's ability to perform have also increased, and competition for these jobs has intensified. Research shows that typical job complexity has increased by approximately 50 percent over the last 20 years, and at the same time, motivation to perform the job has reduced by 10 percent (Figure 2.4). Higher complexity and lower motivation are not a good mix when you are looking for excellence.

Previous social-scientific theories about leadership tried to measure universal traits that would characterize executive competence. Top managers were interviewed, evaluated, and put through psychological testing, but attempts to identify common characteristics of a proficient executive were completely inconclusive.

Each efficient and competent executive had a unique combination of attributes and characteristics that made the individual the right person for the particular role at a given time. It was the right person, in the right place, at the right time rather than any predictable group

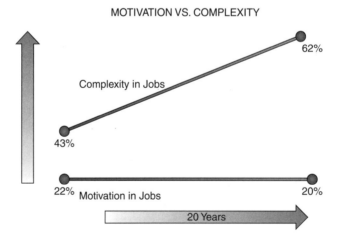

MOTIVATION VS. COMPLEXITY

Complexity in Jobs — 62%
43%
22% Motivation in Jobs 20%
20 Years

Figure 2.4 Technology has allowed us to delegate simple jobs to computers. People are now in positions of increasing complexity, yet personal motivation has decreased.[5]

of criteria. Many of the qualities that seemed most important were also subjective, qualities like charisma, leadership, and likeability.

If two people with the same education, the same qualifications, and from comparable backgrounds were to submit identical presentations regarding a given problem, invariably it would be the person with the greatest authority, self-confidence, and credibility who would be most successful at putting his or her ideas across.

It is not just the terms of the business world that have changed. What has also changed is the experience of top company executives. There are some CEOs who have been regarded almost as celebrity pop stars—think of Bill Gates, Mark Zuckerberg, Carly Fiorina, and Meg Whitman. Some of these CEOs are now under incredible scrutiny, as their performance is evaluated in markets and by investors who distrust them, and are critical of their personal motivation. These corporate leaders are trying to optimize shareholder value in an environment of increasing requirements for openness with a hyperfocus on company revenue and management bonuses.

Relying on Technical Superiority as a Corporate Strategy

Many negotiators, particularly those working in technical or engineering enterprises, are completely locked into their computers and the nuts and bolts of technology. They assume that they will achieve results at the negotiating table using factual data and technical reasoning. These negotiators are strong and rational as long as the negotiations are centered on technical specifications and performance.

When the technical negotiations are over and the transaction enters the bargaining phase, however, the engineers are out of their comfort zone. They are disinterested in the commercial or business aspects of the negotiation. They do not think these variables are of any real importance. Their personal objectives are to stay within the boundaries where they are comfortable and competent. Instead of negotiating their way to the optimal solution, the engineers give in as soon as they bump up against the limits of their competency. The confidence they exude, as long as the discussion concerns technical issues, evaporates entirely.

Businesses can do well for a while because of a strong negotiating position that comes with a superior product that dominates an industrial sector. As long as the company can dictate terms and conditions, because of the company's market dominance, its executives do not have to have strong negotiation skills. In the long run, it is dangerous to build corporate success on technical superiority. As soon as the bargaining equity is reduced, negotiation skills become vitally important at the bargaining table. Suddenly the executives are experiencing competition. They watch their market share shrink when their technical superiority disappears. The transition is difficult to manage because the leadership has not learned how to negotiate.

Not Everything Can Be Measured in Currency or Tech Savvy

Not everything can be measured in dollars or in terms of technical performance. You will experience meetings where you suddenly do not understand the opponent. As far as you are concerned, he has stopped functioning rationally, and his decisions no longer make sense to you. Value judgments that you have difficulty understanding and accepting seem to be more important than money and measurable facts.

Decision-making cannot be illustrated or explained exclusively by means of fact-finding calculations of an economic or technical nature. There is an additional dimension that cannot be measured and that often can be difficult to understand. A delegate must learn to see more than one dimension in a negotiation situation and seek to understand the irrational.

Example: The New Model

Ramon, the supplier, wants to sell Violette the most recent model of his product, the one that demonstrates his technical superiority. He is very proud of the cutting-edge design and the fact that his product is state of the art. Yet much to Ramon's surprise, Violette wants to purchase the model he launched five years ago. Ramon thinks he has a very strong case for convincing Violette to take the most recent model. Its performance is superior, and his calculations will show Violette that the newer model is highly profitable. Nevertheless, Violette insists on purchasing the old model.

Violette's decision is irrational to Ramon. He thinks she is stupid and does not know what is best for her. Ramon tries to show Violette that she is making a bad decision. In Violette's eyes, however, Ramon is being an obnoxious supplier who does not take the least bit of interest in what she wants and needs.

Violette's choice of the five-year-old model can be seen as a correct choice against the background of her needs and market requirements. She does not require the newest technology; she does not have a staff that is trained for it; and she might not even be in a position to take advantage of its finer points. What you consider to be rational arguments might be pure nonsense, seen from the other person's point of view.

Irrational Negotiators

Negotiators are irrational. Negotiation is a game in which people try to fulfill their psychological and material needs. The thoroughly rational negotiator does not exist.

The fact that you prefer doing business with people whom you like, whom you trust and feel a sense of identity with, rather than focusing on what is appropriate for your technical and financial needs, may seem irrational. Psychological needs outweigh your commercial objectives, and from your point of view, your decisions are completely rational.

Example: The Cost of the Superior Brand

On the same street, there are two hotels a few hundred meters apart. They both offer the type of service that business people generally require. Both hotels make comfort and safety a priority. The price for a room differs between the two hotels by more than $100. Both hotels have a high occupancy rate. Many of the people who have chosen the expensive hotel could not imagine choosing the cheaper alternative. Why? There are many different answers:

- The cheap hotel does not have the same atmosphere.
- Some people felt that the cheap hotel's profile did not fit their image. They did not want anyone to associate them with a low-priced alternative.
- They had had a bad experience at another franchise of the cheaper hotel, and since then, they have always associated the company with bad food and poor service.
- The more expensive alternative is part of a well-known hotel chain that invests in its brand. The expensive hotel works hard to convey the image that the rich and beautiful stay there, and many people choose the expensive hotel to be included in this demographic.

In companies where new rules have been introduced that direct employees to stay at the low-price hotel, many executives will likely object. This is difficult for the rational finance manager to understand. He does not share the others' value norms. It is difficult to measure and objectively assess atmosphere and image, which only further aggravates the situation.

There is no such thing as a single objective truth. Your perceptions and assessments are no more correct than those of the other party. There are different views of how to describe and evaluate past and future events. However, in order for your decisions to be perceived as rational, your assessments and experiences must be in keeping with those of the other party. Negotiators are always working from different maps, but you must share an identical perception of the reality about which you are going to negotiate.

Take aways

- A solid understanding of trust, negotiation competency, and behavioral economics is essential for all negotiations.
- Remember that you are not as smart as you think you are, so prepare even more than you might previously have thought sufficient.
- Avoid an emotional response in a negotiation. It will cost you potential gains.
- What drives you?
- Value the value of trust and add it to your spreadsheet.

CHAPTER 3

The Trust Factor: The Keystone of NegoEconomics™

Trust Is Basic to Business

This past summer, I was dining at an outdoor restaurant in Copenhagen. When I ordered my food, the waiter told me that I had to pay in advance because they had experienced a growing number of guests who left without paying the bill. I was curious and asked to speak with the owner. He came out and confirmed the issue about paying the bill. I then asked him, "If you do not trust me to pay the bill, why should I trust that I will receive my food after I have paid?" While I did stay for the meal, I will not be returning to a restaurant that does not trust me. Other guests will feel the same, which will lower the restaurant's Tru$t Currency.

> *A man who trusts nobody is apt to be the kind of man nobody trusts.* British Prime Minister Harold MacMillan[1]

Trust is absolutely essential in any important long-term relationship, whether you are selling, buying, resolving conflict, or negotiating solutions. It is difficult to establish an effective business framework if there is no trust between the parties seeking to work together. Very few people want to do business with a supplier whom they cannot trust, even if the supplier offers the lowest prices. Likewise, very few people want to work with a colleague on whom they cannot rely.

My company carried out an Internet-based survey in which more than 5,000 Europeans were asked about their attitudes toward ethics, morality, and trust on a number of different points. Everyone agrees that trust is central to all relationships and to every positive transaction between individuals. At the same time, more than 60 percent of the respondents believe that trust is something that can be created in a few hours, and one-third believe that trust is something that can be created a few minutes after meeting the other person. How can this be?

Demonstrating Trustworthiness

Despite corporate adherence to economic measures of success, all the research indicates that people would rather do business with a person whom they trust, whose product is slightly more expensive and slightly inferior, than they would with a person whom they do not trust, whose products are on the cutting edge and less expensive. Yet, very few companies attempt to compete based on trustworthiness. They are product focused, and measure success only in financial terms.

Consider the people with whom you prefer to do business. What about them makes you feel secure and comfortable? In all likelihood, you have come to trust these people.

Trust Is Money™

Recently the consulting firm A. T. Kearney carried out a study that confirmed the central role of trust in negotiations. A direct link exists between trust and profit. The more trust you are able to bring to the table, the more money you are likely to take away. This means, provided you continually share information with your negotiation counterpart in an honest and open manner, not only will trust increase considerably, but so will the quality of the agreement—the potential for optimizing the result and the financial prospects. The ability to build solid, trustworthy relationships is increasingly seen as a vital competitive advantage.

Numerous studies carried out in Europe and the United States indicate that lack of trust is a direct cause of unprofitable agreements and the loss of business opportunities. There are plenty of examples of the difficulties created when trust and respect are absent from a negotiating environment. Good relationships lay the groundwork for a profitable future. The more an agreement is based on trust, the greater the likelihood it will be implemented. Without trust and understanding, the parties have no more than an empty agreement that may, or may not, translate into a productive business relationship.

The most profitable negotiations for both parties are those in which mutual and absolute trust are paramount. Commerce would run more smoothly if our capacity for developing cooperation and building trust were more advanced than it is currently. If your point of departure with other people were trust instead of distrust, imagine the difference it would make to your daily life. Imagine the infusion of capital that could be pumped into the global economy if trust and honesty became an understood prerequisite to the commencement of a commercial transaction. Can we quantify how much money is wasted because contracting parties do not trust their business partners, or their attorneys, to conduct business fairly, honestly, and with transparency?

Conveying a sense of trustworthiness to others through negotiation is key to making certain that your counterpart becomes enthusiastic about exploring potential business opportunities with you.

In order to ensure that you are perceived as trustworthy, you must first identify why trust is present in your existing relationships. Why do your friends confide in you? Why do you have credit at your local cafe? Why does your most loyal customer continue to do business exclusively with you, despite the variety of other options in the marketplace?

In order to gain your counterpart's trust, knowledge, awareness, and a willingness to cooperate need to be communicated from your side of the negotiating table. Trust in other people is a prerequisite for being perceived as trustworthy. In particular, when you establish a new relationship, you should be open and willing to take chances. Trust is based on a certain willingness to assimilate risk. However, trust is necessary to ensure that information may be shared from both sides of the negotiation table. Trust is the best, and, in all probability, the only way forward, if you want your deal to materialize the way you envision it during the negotiation process.

Trust always starts with you. You need to trust yourself before you can trust others. If you do not trust your own evaluation of other people, you can very easily misread your own compass. If you cannot count on yourself and are not responsible for your actions, no one will rely on you. People's ability to count on others is commensurate with their ability to count on themselves. If you believe yourself to be a person who is reliable and trustworthy, other people will be more willing to trust you.

Case History: Chancing Your Arm[2]

A couple of years ago, I was in Dublin on a business trip, and I had an afternoon free to be a tourist. I find it easiest to get the feel of a town by just strolling about. By chance, I walked past Saint Patrick's Cathedral, one of the biggest and oldest cathedrals in Dublin. I went in and admired the fascinating architecture and the enormous vaulted ceiling. Suddenly I found myself in front of an old door that was placed on an exhibition platform. This door was large, oval at the top, and had a hole in the middle. The sign above the door said that this was "The door of reconciliation."

Naturally I was curious, as there must have been a story behind why this door hung there. The story is as follows: in 1492, this was the main door to the cathedral. At this time, two Irish families were in the midst of a bloody feud. They were the FitzGerald family and the Butler family, two large clans. They waged war, and they fought as if there was no tomorrow. Many were seriously injured or killed. When the fighting had been carrying on for some time, the Butlers closed in on the FitzGerald family, who sought refuge in the cathedral. There was amnesty in the sacred space, and occupants were not allowed to lay hands on any sacred object. In an act of strategic brilliance, the Butler family formed a ring around the cathedral and waited for the FitzGeralds to make the next move.

The chieftain and the wise men of the FitzGerald clan discussed the matter and concluded that the feud had become ridiculous. No one won; everyone lost; there were dead and wounded on both sides. What could they do to stop the bloodshed? The problem was that these two families did not trust each other at all. There was no basis from which to re-establish trust.

The chieftain of the FitzGerald family cut a tiny hole in the cathedral door. He did not dare open the door for fear of being killed with an arrow. Through this small hole he peeped out in search of the chieftain of the Butler family. By chance he spotted him right in front of the door to the cathedral and shouted: "Let's have a ceasefire and discuss how we can live in peace and harmony. This feud is destructive for both our families." The chieftain of the Butler family responded to the offer of ceasefire by saying: "I don't trust you and your people. You have attacked us relentlessly for years. What you have thought up is a crafty plan to outmaneuver us." The offer to discuss a ceasefire was dropped due to lack of trust.

What now? FitzGerald understood what lay behind Butler's refusal. Then, he had an idea. He cut an even bigger hole in the cathedral door, one that was big enough for him to stretch his right arm all the way out. When he had finished making this hole, he extended his right arm as far out as he could. When his arm was completely out and vulnerable to the Butlers, he shouted at the top of his voice: "Look—this is my sign of trust to you. Will you do the same for me by entering into a conversation about a ceasefire?"

How could this have been a sign of trust? It would have been easy for the Butler family to take an ax or a sword and cut off the chieftain's arm. Apart from it being his weapon-bearing arm, he would have died of loss of blood back in 1492. The Butler family accepted this as a sign of trust and laid their weapons down.

Case History: Air Travel Post 9-11: Distrust Costs Money

High trust lowers transaction costs and increases profit. When trust is high, we do not need 100-page contracts, dozens of advisers, or a whole firm of lawyers checking and rechecking. When parties do not trust each other, they need to introduce control procedures to avoid incurring losses and prevent fraud. All these measures cost money. Vladimir Lenin said that trust is good, but control is better. The Soviet Union did not survive, and its demise left in its wake generations of people living with the consequence that it was a society without trust between the state and the citizens.

Remember September 11, 2001—the day that forever changed the world? Planes collided with the World Trade Center, and thousands lost their lives. Justified or unjustified, the world went into panic. Strict security procedures were introduced in airports around the world. Airport security was tightened, and passengers were now required to show up earlier than ever before. Business travelers now lose hundreds of hours a year waiting in airports. The incident also required the introduction of extensive new safety procedures in airports. Thousands of people were employed with no other purpose than to screen passengers. Enormous investments were made in safety equipment—scanners, X-ray machines, conveyor belts, and plastic bins. Billions of dollars were spent to ensure the safety of the public.

Simultaneously, passengers became afraid to fly. Fewer seats were sold, and the airline industry suffered a huge economic setback.

Imagine what air travel would look like today if we could trust every airline passenger who boarded a plane. Prior to September 11, 2001, we trusted our fellow passengers. Domestic flights in many countries had no security procedures. International flights required a simple process where you walked through a scanner and that was it. You could arrive ten minutes before departure, walk straight through the airport, and board your flight. Airports would save millions of dollars by eliminating security screening. Airlines would likely see a spike in bookings and experience economic growth as the obstacles to and hassle of flying would be removed.

When I present this idea in my presentations around the world, and especially in the United States, people say to me "But you're terribly naive—that kind of trust is not possible anymore!"

The distrust of air travel is slowly but surely spreading to other parts of the business world. Today we have less trust, higher transaction costs, and lower profit than we had in many prior years. Trust can be correlated to economic success on this issue!

The Decline of Trust in the Marketplace

According to the Edelman Trust Barometer's survey on the state of trust across 25 countries, public distrust in government all over the world declined massively in 2011, making government only slightly less trusted than business.[3] The global trust in government was near 51 percent, while trust in business was only slightly higher at 53 percent.[4] These statistics show the fragility of public opinion. The decline of trust in the government was attributed to the "policy paralysis" in the US government's drawn-out debates over the debt ceiling, as well as the behavior of the Eurozone governments. Trust in business, of course, had already imploded in the wake of the earlier failures of Lehman Brothers and AIG (Figure 3.1).

My company conducted a survey of 1,800 executives, in which they were asked whether they had "absolute trust" in leaders in various spheres and whether they thought those leaders made morally acceptable job-related decisions. The result was shocking:

Table 3.1 Trust Levels for Selected Occupations

	Percent that had the public's complete trust
Senior managers in international conglomerates	5%
Elected politicians in counties, local authorities or the parliament	4%
Film and TV producers	7%
News journalists	8%
Small business owners	13%
Clergy	16%
Teachers	19%

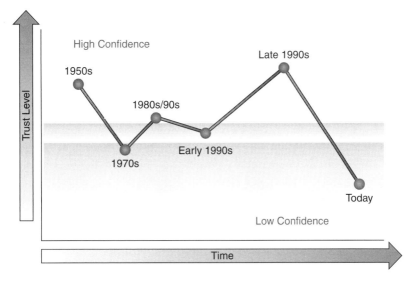

Figure 3.1 Confidence in business leadership has declined significantly between the 1950's and today.

Source: MarketWatch Centre for Negotiation.

The good news is that teachers, the people in whose hands we put our most treasured possessions (our children), have the highest trust score—19 percent. Certainly, this is an issue in need of attention. What drives this lack of trust? Why is trust in the business community so low? These are questions in need of answers.

As scandals across major corporations have increasingly diminished the public's trust of the business community, there is evidence that this trend can be reversed and that businesses can regain consumer trust. Even major scandals can be turned around to create more trust. Johnson & Johnson, the drug manufacturer, encountered a crisis in 1982 that could have cost the company its continued existence. One of their products, Tylenol, which accounted for 15 percent of the company's revenue, contained cyanide in certain bottles, and several people died after taking the drug. The senior management tackled the issue efficiently, ethically, and morally, recalling millions of units of the product. Further, they refused to put the product back on the market until every detail of the internal breach had been scrutinized and every unit checked for safety.

In another case related to trust, in January 2012, the *New York Times* began a series of exposés entitled "The iEconomy." The articles questioned some of Apple's business practices—including Chinese labor conditions and the company's refusal to return outsourced jobs to America. In response, Apple, in conjunction with their Chinese contract manufacturer Foxconn, pledged improvements, including reducing the number of hours worked in a day, improving safety, and upgrading the housing conditions of workers[5]. What is most important for Apple's public image is its transparency. Many have argued that consumers love the brand so much that as long as Apple is transparent about its practices, the company will be able to retain the value of its brand. The global supply chain is difficult to manage, and it is hard for Apple to keep a close eye on the practices of its labor suppliers. But as long as Apple maintains an ethical stance on its labor standards, openly tackling problems as they emerge rather than hiding them, it will likely maintain the public's trust.

Everyone is tired of workmen who do not turn up when they say they will, the repair bill that is larger than promised, the colleague who promises to complete a project but fails to do so, the boss who promises a raise but is not forthcoming, and the supplier who promises the goods for Friday, but does not deliver until the following Wednesday. Investors and analysts are frustrated with this general lack of trust, and unease about those on whom they can rely. This problem is not solely confined to the business world. In the political arena, nepotism and corruption are becoming ubiquitous. Everyone is tired of this moral fog and the inability to trust the people with whom they are doing business.

Distrust and the Internet

The Internet has contributed to a decline in the level of trust among buyers and sellers. Many transactions lack any personal contact, and business is conducted without the parties ever having spoken to each other. These virtual business relationships often remove the human element from transactions. There is no effective way for parties to demonstrate their trustworthiness. It is easier to cheat someone whom you have never met than it is to cheat someone with whom you have an ongoing relationship.

Why Is Nobody Talking about the Decline in Trust?

If trust is so important to commercial relationships and is in fast decline, why isn't more done about it? I don't ever hear my colleagues or clients talking about it. Why don't we acknowledge its importance? Why isn't this issue discussed in business schools? It appears that the decline in trust has not been widely acknowledged either in the business or the political arena.

Trust is a delicate matter: Trust can easily shatter into fragments. Trust can take a long time and a lot of work to generate, but it takes a very short time and a single action to ruin. Many people put more energy into focusing on when and why trust has been destroyed rather than how to establish it. People tend to publicize adverse accounts about lack of trust far more frequently than they do positive stories about trustworthy people.

Trust is a complex trait: Trust is a complex human trait that can be difficult to understand and pin down. Far more advanced research has been done on scientific and technological development than on the study of human relationships. Left-brain logic dominates the analytical process. As straightforward answers evaluating trust are few and far between, people tend to cling to the immediately obvious.

Dr. Pat Lynch, President of Business Alignment Strategies, Inc., clarified in simpler terms. "Unlike other values, trust is very personal," he said. "That is, we put ourselves in a position of vulnerability when we trust others, so our well-being rests partly in their hands. In effect, because we cede control of some part(s) of our lives to those individuals, we have a vested and personal interest in the outcome. Our hope is that their actions will justify the faith we have entrusted to them, and that they will live up to our expectations."[6]

Trust requires an investment: You know whom you can count on and whom you cannot trust. If you become more observant about the presence and absence of trust, you will realize that it is one of the first things you consider when you meet a new person. In order to generate trust, you must constantly invest in things that maintain trust. If trust is lost, you must make an even greater investment in order to get it back.

The Trust Factor Makes SMARTnership Possible

The Trust Factor is a cocktail of trust, honesty, cooperation, and fairness, flavored with good intentions that your loyal opposition will fully benefit from the deal you are making. When the Trust Factor lies at the foundation of a transaction, a SMARTnership is formed and the NegoEconomic potential in the deal is optimized.

The Architectural Arch

Arched doorways have been part of the architectural landscape since before records were kept. We are unable to credit the thoughtful man or woman who engineered the physics of constructing the 180 degree (or thereabouts) masonry arch that tops passageways all over the world. The tricky part of engineering the arch was how to make the damn thing stay in place. I can assure you the inventor who solved this puzzle understood geometry and physics, although it is unlikely he or she used those words.

The secret to the stability of the arched doorway is the keystone (Figure 3.2). The keystone is the wedge-shaped brick that sits at the center of the top of the arch. When the keystone is inserted into the arch it locks the other bricks in place, based on principles of physics. If the keystone is removed, the entire arch collapses.

The Trust Factor is the keystone of optimized commercial relationships and the business transactions that flow from these relationships.

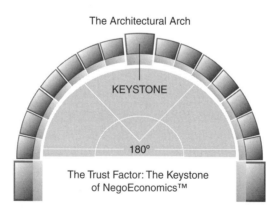

Figure 3.2 Without trust as your keystone, the entire structure collapses, and NegoEconomics is rendered impossible.

The Pursuit of Mutual Gains

For NegoEconomics to work, negotiators must be generous with their counterpart and demonstrate a willingness to share gains. The negotiator who attempts to keep too large a share for himself leaves no room for creativity, risk distribution, or wholehearted efforts to find optimal solutions.

A commitment to optimize the NegoEconomic potential in a transaction may yield new solutions that can easily meet the requirements of both parties. If you have a bigger pie to share, it is more likely that you will be able to find a way of dividing it that is acceptable to both parties.

Finding the right combination of openness, firmness, pressure, and concession is not easy. A certain approach may yield the desired result in one area, but at the same time it can run counter to your original objective. It is up to the individual negotiator to realize how best to proceed in a given situation. Allowing the Trust Factor to govern your decision-making at the negotiation table requires courage, skill, and judgment. The ability to infuse the Trust Factor into the interpersonal dynamic at the table is an invaluable attribute, and will certainly result in more frequent and successful negotiations.

Cooperation Is NOT Consensus

Some negotiators believe that cooperation at the bargaining table requires them to weaken their bargaining equity, resulting in transactional objectives built on a consensus with which all parties are comfortable. The more cynical negotiator may also believe that cooperation will inevitably lead to a clean 50/50 split of transactional assets, and, consequently less profit from the deal for the party who might otherwise have held the stronger bargaining equity. Neither case is necessarily true.

Even if cooperation does lead to an unequal distribution of assets, NegoEconomics will increase the number and value of those assets, so that both parties gain more than they anticipated from the transaction. The Trust Factor allows delegates to more fully examine the matter at hand, discover unforeseen value, and build a foundation on which future deals can be based. When the Trust Factor is absent, negotiations become battles, where delegates work against each other, arguing endlessly over price and quantity. This style of combative negotiation ultimately inhibits the infusion of trust, damaging future business prospects.

It Takes Two to Tango

The Trust Factor is not an attribute of a single delegate. It will only materialize when both (or all) of the delegates at the table agree to allow trust, cooperation, and the quest for mutual gain to govern the interpersonal dynamic. A single delegate can make overtures in an effort to infuse the Trust Factor into the transaction, but it does not form until both parties have embraced the Code of Conduct that underpins it. In order for the parties to optimize the outcome of a negotiation, the Trust Factor must be included as part of the Rules of the Game exercise.

This Code of Conduct is based on a set of values that determines particular rules of play:

- honesty
- full and fair disclosure
- respect for the dignity of the others
- ethics and morals

Morality almost always comes into the picture when discussing trust. As Søren Kierkegaard, the philosopher, emphasized: "one cannot assign responsibility to a group. Responsibility is always individual by nature."[7] However, he also says that at the end of the day, it is up to the individual—your morals and my morals—whether the organization we work in is ethically responsible. As delegates, we are the public face of our organization. Our actions are assumed to reflect the values of the organization we represent. We sit in a fiduciary role that must find a balance between the brand equity of the company we represent, our goals related to the transaction on the table, and our individual approach, or style, to negotiation.

In rhetoric, the concept of *pistis* (demonstration, trust, credibility) is used to describe the generating of a sense of trust and credibility.

Create a Positive Negotiating Climate
So the Trust Factor Can Emerge

SMARTner Tip™

The delegate who seeks to create a positive negotiation climate and infuse the Trust Factor into the interpersonal dynamic of the transaction will:

- listen actively,
- answer questions with transparency and full disclosure,
- demonstrate openness with words and body language,
- express interest in the counterpart's needs and requirements,
- respect the opponent's opinions.

Prerequisites for the Formation of a Cooperative Negotiation Climate

There are a number of basic prerequisites to the formation of a cooperative negotiation climate. The presence of these elements will ensure that the proper environment for a cooperative negotiation is developed. These are the factors that enhance the probability that the Trust Factor will be successfully infused into a negotiation:

1. Personal Chemistry
2. Generosity
3. Creativity

Personal Chemistry

If there is no personal chemistry between the delegates, trust will not emerge. Personal chemistry is demonstrated through humility, mutual respect, trust, and openness. Though critical, these attributes are not always sufficient. Enthusiasm and a positive attitude also play a major role. Deals are made between people. People require an interpersonal dynamic that facilitates openness and a free flow of information. If the signals customarily sent by people who want to establish good rapport—such as eye contact and inclusive gestures—are absent, it is almost impossible to build a foundation for the infusion of trust.

A negotiation dynamic governed by the Trust Factor is built on trust, cooperation, open and honest communication between the parties, and a willingness to listen to and understand each other's needs and requirements. When the negotiator's actions are inconsistent with her words, the other party loses trust and becomes reluctant to continue the bargaining process. Lack of personal charisma and a reluctance to engage socially and emotionally can also create failures in communication. When they face these personality types, delegates will have to work particularly hard to facilitate constructive dialogue and build a foundation for cooperation and trust.

Lack of sympathy, understanding, and respect for cultural differences can also limit the space for success in negotiations. For instance, Eastern negotiators may assume Western negotiators will be combative and operate primarily using a zero-sum strategy. It is important that Western negotiators dispel this preconception, in order to generate a cooperative environment.

Generosity

Many people find it difficult to be generous. Their own assessment of what constitutes fair compensation or a fair price is, more often than not, non-negotiable. They become indignant and are influenced by the classic who-do-you think-you-are attitude. If you try to eliminate your opponent's ability to turn a profit, you are cutting off your nose to spite your face. Your counterpart will come to resent you and the organization you represent. When it comes to future transactions, he will likely look for another partner.

CASE STUDY: Be Generous With Your Partner

My friend and business client, Thomas, is a really tough negotiator. When he is representing his organization, he consistently achieves an optimized outcome. A few years ago, Thomas was negotiating to purchase a company being sold by a Swede. The negotiations took place over a period of several months through various meetings, emails, and telephone calls. As the months went by, Thomas noted that his Swedish counterpart became more and more inattentive; he lost his focus. The Swede made mistakes when providing the details that supported his own arguments and suddenly started to unconditionally accept all of Thomas's proposals.

Many negotiators would have taken advantage of this situation. They would have sensed an opportunity and asserted themselves in order to take advantage of the Swede's vulnerability.

Thomas decided to confront his Swedish counterpart about his unusual behavior. To his amazement, the Swede opened up completely, tears came to his eyes, and he disclosed that his wife had been diagnosed with a malignancy and was receiving treatment. Thomas could have closed the deal with an extraordinary result of more than $260 million, but chose to delay negotiations. He accepted the balance for a smaller amount and closed the agreement once his Swedish counterpart had made a profit.

Thomas made the deal. But he got more than that. He gained a life-long friend and partner.

What would you do if you did not have enough money? What would you do if you had plenty of money? Would you actually take stock of the situation? Would you go by your gut feelings when it came to distinguishing right from wrong?

Very few people make a conscious decision to be dishonest, but then no one wants to lose. As shown with the case of Thomas, never take advantage of your opponent. You should make a point of bringing your opponent around so that he sees you as a human being, someone with whom he feels at ease.

A ship in port is safe—but that is not what ships have been built for.
William Shedd[8]

Insist That Your Supplier Make a Decent Profit

The relationship between buyer and seller should be one of mutual benefit. Neither can succeed without the efforts of the other. The incompetent purchaser says, "If the supplier has earned money from the deal, we have *not* done our job." Smart purchasing professionals recognize this and allow their suppliers to earn money. Really smart purchasers go one step further and demand that the supplier make a healthy profit on the transaction.

NegoEconomics requires that you demonstrate generosity when it is time to share the gains that have emerged in the course of the negotiation. Such behavior will enable you to earn Tru$t Currency and ensure the likelihood of future business with your counterpart. Keeping your allies alive and financially successful is just as vital as succeeding yourself. However, such generosity can be difficult to practice, as the following example demonstrates.

Example: A Mediator Proposes to Share in a Good Result

Client: Would you be willing to mediate a dispute that my colleague and I have failed to settle? My colleague has demanded that the dispute be settled in court. If we can't reach an amicable settlement, it's likely that we'll lose $200,000. Would you like to at least try mediating so that we won't have to take the matter to court?

Mediator: I must be given a free hand at the negotiating table so that I can make a proposal that would cost you less than $200,000.

Client: How much do you charge per hour?

Mediator: I do not charge by the hour. It is possible that my mediation efforts could fail. If you do not get any positive result from my mediation, then I will not charge anything.

Client: OK, I agree on the principle: no results, no charge. But if you are successful, what is your hourly rate?

Mediator: I do not charge by the hour. If I succeed in getting an agreement of $140,000, that would leave us with a $60,000 advantage. This money we will split down the middle, which means that you will pay me $30,000 for the mediation.

Client: Are you seriously suggesting that it would cost us $30,000, even if you got an agreement in the course of a single afternoon? That just isn't reasonable!

Instead of realizing that he would save up to $30,000 and avoid going to court, the prospective client was annoyed by the mediator. The fact that he would gain the same amount was of no importance to the client.

The client rejected the deal out of hand rather than allowing the mediator to make a $30,000 fee, even though his own gain would have been the same. He ought to have investigated whether the 50/50 split was negotiable: whether or not a ceiling could be put on the mediator's compensation.

The client wanted to purchase hours; he did not want to pay by the result. Hours can be checked and an hourly rate can be compared with the hourly rates of other mediators. The client could have accepted the payment of a high hourly rate and a large expenditure of hours on the assignment without any demand for a guarantee of success. The important thing to the client was that the hourly rate should be compared to other hourly rates. Feelings, not rationality, governed the client's way of thinking.

Creativity

NegoEconomics can only work if traditional assumptions are altered. The creative forces required for this shift in perspective are up against:

- the conservative person who opposes any change,
- the person who wants to avoid conflict, settles too quickly, and thinks she has done her job,
- the person unwilling to consider a full range of options,
- the combative opponent who has no interest in creativity.

As a frequent negotiator you may encounter difficulties trying to build on and improve previously existing business relationships. Often your counterpart may hold onto the old adage "if it ain't broke, don't fix it." Similarly, you may encounter those who are unwilling or unable to think outside the constraints of the price/quantity-focused model.

Reinventing and improving preexisting relationships is key to building trust. Creativity is particularly critical when you face a troubled economic climate. The negotiator who thinks creatively will find value hidden in previously existing relationships and develop innovative ways to generate value through new relationships.

Increasing the Flow of Information

A troubling issue for all negotiators is being the first one to demonstrate trust. Trusting the opponent can be risky and requires a good sense of timing, especially if you are dealing with a delegate who has not tried this approach before. Negotiators are understandably hesitant to reveal their own requirements and motives to their opponent until they see evidence that the opponent is trustworthy. However, some degree of transparency is necessary for the Trust Factor to emerge.

I'm OK, You're Not

Most people do not think that they are the ones with a problem. But they all agree that morality, ethics, and trust are declining in the business world and on the political scene generally. In a survey that I conducted, 76 percent of all respondents said they believe that senior managers and politicians today do not make decisions according to the golden rule, or with a focus on morality and ethics. At the same time, this group finds that senior managers and politicians are responsible for the decline in ethics and morality. In the same survey, 59 percent admit to having cheated in one way or another on an exam when they were students.

The Golden Rule:
Do unto others, as you would have them do unto you.
All 13 of the major religions in the world include this concept as part of their teachings.

Most people swear by their ethical and moral virtue, but they do not generally have confidence in the moral integrity of others. In a 2011 National Business Ethics Survey, 40 percent of all respondents said their direct supervisors don't display ethical behavior.[9] It seems that their attitude is, "I am okay, but you are not okay."

For 20 years, Dr. Karen Walch, of the Thunderbird School of Global Management, has conducted an ongoing negotiation study among her students, asking them to answer questions regarding how cooperative and trusting they are personally, and how they feel about their counterparts. "What we've generally found so far is that 40% of people surveyed believe that they are cooperative and trusting," says Dr. Walch. "Yet, when asked about the counterpart, people generally believe that the other party is just looking to win. It's this type of mentality that causes negotiators to take a defensive strategy, which tends to leave a whole lot of value left on the table." Low trust makes collaboration impossible!

Consider for a moment whether there are times when you are not morally "okay." Have there been times when you did not live up to agreements that you entered into, or you did not keep to what you had promised? Do you take shortcuts? Do you use manipulation to reach a goal? Do you hold information back if you see an advantage in doing so? And do you rationalize unethical behavior if it is to your advantage? Believe it or not, a lack of ethics, morality, and credibility is more pertinent to most people than they actually believe.

Constructive Dialogue and Good Communication

NegoEconomics requires delegates to carry out an unbiased review of existing alternatives. If you want to locate better solutions than the ones currently on the table, or if you want to obtain extra information about the requirements stated, you must create a dynamic that encourages constructive dialogue. A negotiation should be a constructive dialogue through which the parties benefit from each other's experience and resources in order to locate the added value in the relationship.

Cooperating with your counterpart does not mean avoiding contentious issues or disregarding your own needs and requirements. One party should never try to dominate and benefit at the expense of the other. This type of behavior will cause the relationship to fail, or at a minimum, put it on uneven ground. It will also limit future business opportunities.

The primary cause of failure when a negotiator is seeking to build cooperation is poor communication. The results of an effective negotiation depend on the parties establishing good two-way (responsive and receptive) communication. When both parties master the art of constructive two-way communication, synergies arise because more energy is spent on the discovery of mutual gains and problem solving and less on the process. This can only be achieved when negotiators make an effort to recognize and utilize the resources brought to the table by the other party—their experience, creativity, and unique capabilities.

Communicative Competence

Communicative competence includes personal qualities beyond the content of the delegate's statements. It extends to personal magnetism, enthusiasm, the ability to persuade others, being able to sell your ideas, listening actively, and fully understanding what your counterpart is trying to communicate to you. Many negotiators fail just before they reach the finish line. Their intentions may be first rate, but they do not succeed in getting their message across.

When parties are speaking at cross-purposes, their inability to communicate creates conflict that was not initially there. They fail to understand each other, making openness and cooperation impossible. The parties are not in conflict, yet they cannot come to an agreement.

An open, cooperative negotiator does not view demands from the other party as threats. Behind these demands you might find opportunities that can yield added value if properly leveraged. In order to make use of this opportunity, you should use a technique other than resistance, and you should encourage productive discussion.

Congruence

One of the most important factors for generating trust is that there is congruence between what you say and what you do. In many areas there is a discrepancy between what people say and what they do, a discrepancy that is often governed by greed, ego, or dishonesty.

The Importance of Body Language and Nonverbal Communication

Professor Albert Mehrabian from University of California, Los Angeles has performed groundbreaking research that focuses on communicative correlation. In his book *Silent Messages*, he concludes that only 7 percent of the credibility or the value in what we say is reliant on words; 38 percent is reliant on tone of voice; and the remaining 55 percent is reliant on body language. His studies show that 93 percent of the value or credibility of a person's message is decided by how he or she presents him-or herself. When you meet someone for the first time, he or she is more aware of your nonverbal behavior, rather than what you are saying.

Beyond words, communication consists of hand and arm movements, facial expressions, gestures, stance, tone, volume, speed, intonation, and personal habits. When these parameters are adjusted in an optimal way, it creates congruence. When your words and your body language are congruent, you don't merely become credible, you create impact. It is not what you say, but what you *do*!

Incongruent behavior is inconsistency in what you do and say. An example could be a trainer in stress management who bites her nails and habitually twists her hair around her fingers, or a Weight Watchers leader who eats Danish pastries during her break. Most people have a built-in "lie detector" that unconsciously sends signals telling them when something is wrong.

Imagine a CEO of a publicly traded company who reports to investors: "We have had a terrible year and expect greater losses than we previously reported." He says this with a big smile and direct eye contact with his audience, and is self-assured in dress and manner. "But we expect a much better result for next year, as our new sales strategy will be in place." He says the second statement with a wandering gaze while he nervously wrings his folded hands. His inability to maintain eye contact with his audience indicates his complete lack of confidence in his own statement.

Cheating, Bluffing, and Little White Lies

Honesty is a precursor to trust. Cheating is the opposite of honesty, and therefore precludes trustworthiness. The use of bluffing, "white lies," and the belief that "smart people cheat those who are not so smart" appears to be increasing at an alarming rate. In fact, there is a widespread belief that business goes hand in hand with dishonesty, cheating whenever you can get away with it, and bending the rules.

According to Dr. Brad Blanton, a survey of 40,000 Americans reported that 93 percent admitted to lying "regularly and habitually in the workplace."[10] Another early study surveyed 14 lawyers representing a diverse group of civil practices, and found that respondents considered low-level deception to be part of the negotiation "game," and were comfortable having only a cursory knowledge of the operative ethical rules.[11] Additionally, a 1997 survey of lawyers at an American Bar Association Annual Meeting found that 73 percent of respondents admitted to engaging in "settlement puffery."[12]

Research at my company shows that up to 50 percent of the people surveyed believe that they *ought* to bluff just a little bit in a negotiation. The problem is that when people start down the path of cheating or bluffing, it becomes an endless spiral. The boundary between the permissible and the nonpermissible begins to shift, slowly but surely.

A study carried out at the University of Virginia by Dr. Paul Ekman shows that one-fifth of every ten-minute conversation consists of lies.[13] However, if you only look at participants from the educated middle class, lies are told more frequently than that: on average with this group, one in every three conversations consists of lies. It is thought that this difference has a lot to do with the fact that the better a person's education, the larger his or her vocabulary. Along with that, the educated person tends to be self-assured, making it easier to lie. People with a higher level of education can more easily see the advantages of a well-placed fabrication, which is why they are more likely to elaborate on the truth. This research also shows that men in 68 percent of cases lie or cheat at a job interview, whereas 62 percent of women would do the same.

Studies conducted by Dan Ariely, a professor of behavior economics at Duke University, have persuasively shown that cheating is much more widespread—and *infectious*—than we commonly believe. An anecdote Ariely shares in a *Wall Street Journal* article quotes a locksmith, who quips that "one percent of people will always be honest and never steal. Another one percent of people will...always try to pick your lock and steal your television.... The purpose of locks is to protect you from the 98 percent of mostly honest people who might be tempted to try your door if it had no lock."[14] In the studies Ariely conducts, which typically entice people to cheat by showing them potential financial gain in doing so, he claims that he "lost hundreds of dollars to the few big cheaters in our experiments—but lost *thousands* to the many little cheaters." The picture that emerges from these studies is that, it is not merely Madoff-like characters who lie and steal and damage the global economy—it is rather the countless dishonest acts that 98 percent of us commit. Ariely claims that as long as we can convince ourselves that we are basically honest when we look in the mirror, that is, as long as we don't go *too* far with our lies, we will continue to commit little dishonest acts here and there.[15]

Ariely believes that these little acts only reinforce others' bad behavior, building a culture of dishonesty. The variables that increase dishonesty include knowing others are behaving dishonestly, an easy ability to rationalize, and previous dishonest acts. The more a person excuses himself, the more he damages others through insidious little white lies.[16]

If the business community committed to a policy of total honesty (and increased practices such as honor codes, moral reminders, and signature requirements), we could reinforce overall practices of ethics and fair dealing in the business world, creating a new culture of honesty.

Bluffing may yield good results, but the decision is always uncertain. The person who subsequently discovers that his partner is a liar will not be forgiving.

The short-term gain that you have achieved through bluffing may turn into a painful defeat in the long run. In negotiations, things are rarely black and white. Carefully assess the facts before you claim that you are better than the other party. More often than not, negotiators function in a grey zone.

Individuals, industries, and cultures impose different limits on the acceptability of bluffing in the course of negotiations. Be responsive and do not cross the line of what is acceptable, especially if you think there is a chance your bluff will be called.

Corruption and Bribery

Corruption and bribery are more insidious problems in the global commercial marketplace. In many countries, you simply cannot do business without bribing government officials or other people who are the gatekeepers of required resources, permits, or social approvals. These abuses of power are among the greatest obstacles to commercial development in developing countries.

Daniel Kaufmann, governance director of the World Bank, has stated that global corruption is a bigger issue than global warming.[17] The Global Agenda Council on Anti-Corruption 2012–2013 report published by the World Economic Forum states: "Estimates show that the cost of corruption amounts to more than 5% of global GDP (US$2.6 trillion) with more than US$1 trillion paid in bribes each year."[18] The report also states that corruption increases the cost of doing business globally by an average of 10 percent. Of the 183 countries in the Corruptions Perceptions Index, 134 are ranked as corrupt to a significant degree, and 72 are ranked "very corrupt."[19] New Zealand is perceived as the least corrupt country, and Somalia and North Korea as the most corrupt.[20] The United Nations, the Organization for Economic Cooperation and Development, the World Economic Forum, and other international organizations are working to increase regulations and penalties, but the Council report observes that "the most effective solutions are often collective. They involve public and/or private sector solutions at country, regional, or global levels or at industry or cross-industry or multi-stakeholder levels."[21] The clear message underlying this report is that the real solution must come as a cultural shift. Corruption and bribery have to stop being acceptable ways to conduct business or enter a new market, and the business community must unite in a refusal to participate in these practices. Absent a unified resistance movement, the powerful will always be able to profit through greed and dishonesty.

Assess Trust in Others

Has there been a time when you distrusted a person and missed out on a golden opportunity? On the other hand, has there been a time when you trusted a person too much and you were abused? How did you feel about that? How do you know when you can count on a person? And how can you trust others so that you generate promising, profitable, successful results?

When you are involved in relationships with others, trust is a foundation for progress and an indicator of success. However, it seems that when trust is discussed, there are two extremes—distrust is one extreme, and naivete the other. Regardless of which you adopt, you will not get much out of a relationship built on either extreme.

Some people are more inclined to be distrustful than others. They hold their cards close to their chest, do not believe that people should rely on others, and claim that they only rely on themselves, when in actuality they do not. You also come across people who are naive and have complete trust in everyone they meet right from the start. This is a dangerous approach to life, as it increases one's chance of being exploited and taken advantage of in both social and professional interactions. The overly trusting individual does not consider ways of protecting his or her own interests.

The Four Types of Negotiators

I have, through research on more than 25,000 negotiations, identified four personality types who share common characteristics that determine their willingness to trust others (Figure 3.3). The four types are identified as follows:

The Naive Negotiator: The naive negotiator is abysmal at assessing how much trust he should show. In negotiations, he is alarmingly submissive, which usually results in a costly outcome to the organization he represents. He has blind trust in his counterpart, and is vulnerable to every kind of persuasion.

THE FOUR TYPES OF NEGOTIATORS

The Naïve Negotiator	The Submissive Negotiator
The Analytic Negotiator	The Distrustful Negotiator

Figure 3.3 There are four types of negotiators. Which category best describes your style?

The Submissive Negotiator: The submissive negotiator is the relatively unprepared amateur who is not aware of what is required in analysis and preparation. He may display openness, but in doing so does not have a particular goal or intention in mind. Generally speaking, trust is absent for the submissive negotiator, and he is not strategic about which matters to be open about and how to demonstrate his trustworthiness. He is invariably indecisive, uncertain, and taciturn. In negotiation situations, counterparts tend to find his unpredictable behavior confusing and extremely irritating.

The Analytic Negotiator: The analytic negotiator is the type of person who knows how to incorporate trust as a factor in the interpersonal dynamic. This approach is a combination of gradual trust paired with sensible analysis of opportunities and risks. This is also the type of person who tends to be good at assessing situations and evaluating the traits and behavior patterns of the person with whom he is dealing. He pays heed to his gut feeling and draws on his experience. His instincts and intuition assist him when summing up people. He does not necessarily rely on everyone. For him, the starting point of a trusting relationship tends to be based on careful analysis, rather than blind faith.

The Distrustful Negotiator: This person is the wary type of negotiator who does not count on anyone—at times, not even himself. Distrust looms large with everything he does—he is completely unforthcoming. At the same time, this person risks overanalyzing. He believes that going into detail and analyzing every single item minimizes the risk of being cheated. The end result is that everything drags out interminably.

The Naive Negotiator, the Submissive Negotiator, and the Distrustful Negotiator incur substantial risk for the party whom they represent. The Analytic Negotiator does not involve quite as much risk.

Which personality type do you think creates the greatest risk? Lack of insight, preparation, and analysis leave much to be desired with the Submissive Negotiator, and the Naive Negotiator is a hazard, due to his complete trust in everyone. Surprisingly, neither of these types gets the worst results in negotiation. The personality type with the worst results is the Distrustful Negotiator, who takes the fewest risks. He is extremely well prepared, but refuses to open up. The distrustful person is critical and suspicious, and never reveals himself. One of the many reasons why the Distrustful Negotiator comes out worse than the three other categories is time. This person spends too much time analyzing the details and reduces his opportunities for both collaboration and accessing the added value. A holistic picture of the overall potential in the transaction is missing for this person. The result tends to be limited perspectives, bad relationships, and lost opportunities.

Why do so many people adopt the behavior of the Distrustful Negotiator? Possible explanations include: perfectionism, fear of losing, too much focus on detail, and low emotional intelligence. Perhaps these people believe that they are better than others and trust only themselves. Perhaps they were badly burned early in their life, and they do not want to repeat the bad experience. Or perhaps they have found that no one is willing to trust them!

Risk and Naivete

When you are negotiating, this dilemma poses a distinct challenge: you must be open and display trust in order to achieve the best result, but you want to avoid being naive and openly displaying too much trust. How do you find the ideal middle ground? How do you avoid exposing yourself to unreasonable risk?

Life is full of risk, and the aim is not to avoid risk—that is impossible. Every business, every relationship between individuals, contains a certain amount of risk. Risk is a central part of life. Opportunities and risk go together. By analyzing the situation sensibly, you can find a balance—or the ideal middle ground—without ending up on the losing end if things go awry.

A combination of risk taking and careful analysis of both the interpersonal dynamic and the substance of the bargaining process is the ideal way to make progress. You must display trust and create credibility without becoming naive. Proper analysis can help to ensure that if a transaction does go badly, you will be fully protected and secure in your position.

Integrity: Living by Your Maxims

The integrity of a trustworthy person is like a rock: solid, firm, and completely unshakeable. Principles are underlying rules for conduct based on one's moral code. They are not nice slogans. They are fundamental values. When these values are challenged, the trustworthy person has the moral courage to stand by his or her values. Integrity consists of actions rather than just words. With trustworthy people, the very idea means something, and ethics are associated with a set of personal values that influence the whole of a person's life.

Keeping Agreements: Acting on Your Commitments

When you think about a person whom you find trustworthy, you think about the agreements and the promises this person has kept. This is the way in which most of us evaluate trustworthiness. However, trustworthiness goes far deeper than keeping agreements and reaching your goals. It means that your word is your honor and that you demonstrate loyalty toward others.

It All Starts With You

Consider the real meaning of trust and the responsibility that goes along with it. You can speak about credibility, write about it, and sign confidentiality declarations, but they are not worth the paper they are written on unless everyone involved can be considered trustworthy.

The constant striving for cheaper and discounted products and services is like a vicious spiral that, unfortunately, has its ultimate effects in increasingly low morals, poor ethics, and undermined trust. There is no doubt that the business community needs to stop and look at traditional values, which say that a person's word is their bond and one does what one promises. Financial goals must not trump trust and the value of business relationships. Greed must never replace ethics and morality.

Take aways

- Trust is money.
- Trust is the keystone to any relationship. Without it, the relationship collapses.
- Finding the right combination of openness, firmness, pressure, and concession is crucial.

- Cooperation is not consensus.
- Generosity is a requirement of success.
- Insist that your counterpart makes a profit.
- Communicative Competence is fundamental for negotiation success.
- One out of five people lies in every 10-minute conversation.

PART B

Defining the Rules of the Games,
Articulating a Negotiation Strategy,
and Making the Pie Bigger

CHAPTER 4

Rules of the Game:
Defining and Setting Expectations

The first item of business in any negotiation is for the parties to decide how they are going to negotiate. The Rules of the Game must be articulated and agreed to before any conversation takes places regarding the merits of the matter to be decided or the deal to be made. Who are the teams? What are the rules of play and the conditions for termination? This process can be time consuming. In fact, it can sometimes take more time than the actual negotiation, but establishing the ground rules prior to commencement of the bargaining saves a lot of time down the road, avoids misunderstandings, and enhances the prospects for cooperation.

Talking about How We Should
Negotiate before We Negotiate

Imagine you are on your way to a tennis match. Your racket is in your bag, and you are looking forward to a good game of rally, volley, and service. You are tremendously surprised when you arrive at the tennis court, and your counterpart has set up two chairs and a table on one side of the net. On the table are a chessboard, knights, rooks, and pawns. He looks expectantly at you and says, "Are you ready to play."

This scenario plays out every day in millions of cases worldwide. Not with a tennis racket and a chessboard, but in a negotiation. One side comes to the table with an understanding of the rules of play, and their opponent arrives with a completely different set of assumptions. Many of my clients over the years have been amazed when I open with the question: *Shall we talk about how we are going to negotiate?*

The Rules of the Game must include an agreed-upon agenda, the selection of a negotiation strategy, and agreement on the Code of Conduct:

- Should we negotiate in zero-sum, partnership, or SMARTnership?
- How do we divide the NegoEconomic value if we are negotiating in SMARTnership or partnership?
- Who will open first for the exchange of information?
- How do we establish trust?
- How do you present all the variables? Who lists them?
- Who takes care of the whiteboard and visual aids?
- Must breaks be agreed to, and when should they be?
- Do all delegates have the authority to conclude? And if so, what is their mandate?
- Should we articulate a lack of trust and openness?

Failure to define the Rules of the Game is the same as letting a football team play a game without agreeing to a common set of rules. Exciting game, but nobody understands how to score points, and the players do not know how to win.

Articulating a Negotiation Strategy for the Organization

Successful businesses have a strategy in place for virtually everything they do. They expend huge amounts of resources creating, developing, and fine-tuning a marketing strategy, a product development strategy, a human resources (HR) strategy, a communication strategy, and a research and development (R&D) strategy. Can you imagine Apple or Toyota operating without defining these strategies or setting a budget? It's almost unthinkable.

I have asked countless audiences of business leaders of all cultures, generations, and genders, whether they have articulated a negotiation strategy for their organization. The results never change: almost no one has a defined negotiation approach that governs how they transact business with their partners, suppliers, customers, or other stakeholders in their organization.

The vast majority of negotiators have no strategic consciousness. They negotiate with their "gut" and allow emotions to drive their demands. Consequently, it becomes nearly impossible to develop open, honest, and transparent partnerships that allow for the creation of asymmetric value. Despite the fact that "all business is human," almost never is there a policy in place that instructs the organization and its employees in how to deal with their strategic partners. This is the equivalent to not having a communication strategy, a legal strategy, a market strategy, an HR strategy, or even an annual budget—unthinkable in most organizations. As a result, the relationships and connections that the company builds are not operating at optimal levels of openness, trust, and profitability.

Why a strategy? You must decide what you want from a trading partner. Do you want a win-lose, zero-sum relationship that has little or no long-term prospects? Do you want a partnership in which you share just enough to allow the relationship to function, but you keep enough distance so as not to reveal your hand? Or do you want a SMARTnership where you share your needs and desires in order to build a long-term relationship that withstands the ups and downs inherent in commercial transactions? Even the United Nations has never defined an international standard for negotiating. The result is that the concept of negotiation is envisioned very differently from delegate to delegate.

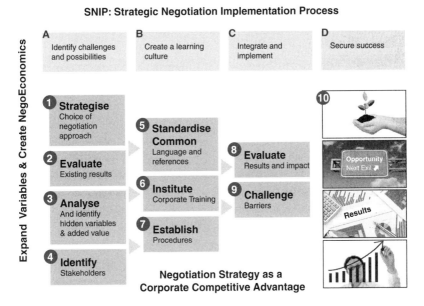

Figure 4.1   It would be absurd to think of a Fortune 500 company without a marketing, R&D, or customer service strategy. Why have so few established a negotiation strategy?

My experience tells me that most negotiators, when asked this question, respond that they are looking for a partnership, but they conduct themselves in a way that renders zero-sum results. The majority of the world's organizations unconsciously, through the culture embedded in the company, have opted for a zero-sum negotiation strategy. The business leaders in these organizations are unconsciously incompetent and do not know they have alternatives.

With a well-developed negotiation strategy, companies will find it easier to create relationships based upon informed cooperation (Figure 4.1). By managing the personal chemistry and improving the flow of information, it becomes possible for two negotiators to achieve a partnership that makes problem solving more attractive than combat. This creates added value, increases co-innovation, and allows for long-term stability in relationships.

Thinking through the Transaction Ahead of Time

Before every negotiation, the following questions should be asked and decisions made as to the approach the delegation will take when these issues are in play:

- What are the negotiation variables, times, prices, performances, and payment plans that will be discussed?
- What is the scope of the negotiation on all these points? What is our threshold of pain?
- Are we willing to take on greater risk if we have an opportunity for greater margins of return?
- What are the consequences if we do end up making concessions? What will we ask for in return?

These elements must be taken into consideration in the preparation stage, as well as speculation as to what the other party's answers might be. Depending on the circumstances of your transaction, there may be many more questions that need to be addressed.

If you start the negotiations in the proper way, you can often get your counterpart to help you achieve your objectives and meet your requirements.

Negotiations rarely go as planned. Subconscious wishes, personal agendas, irrationality, and emotions always distort final outcomes. But by taking the lead and coming to the table with a negotiation strategy, companies can put themselves in a far better position to achieve more value than they had originally thought possible.

The Negotiation Code of Conduct

A Negotiation Code of Conduct can be used to create a cooperative climate as well as serve as a tool to implement strategic choices. This code establishes the rules of behavior that guide the company through even the most challenging situations. It includes statements of what employees will and will not do, under all circumstances, in order to preserve the honesty and integrity of any negotiation, internal or external, undertaken by an employee. Every staff member in the organization should sign the Code, regardless of his or her position or role in the company.

In my business, I take this concept even further. Whenever I sit down at the table to negotiate with a trading partner, I ask them to sign it too. It sets the right climate for open communication and creates a positive environment.

I have developed a Negotiation Code of Conduct that can help you and your business partners establish rules of behavior to guide you through even the most challenging situations. This code includes statements of what we will and will not do, under any circumstances, in order to preserve the honesty and integrity of the negotiation. Use our list as a basis for your own Code of Conduct, share it with your business partners, and reflect back on it when the stress levels rise:

We will not:

- We will not lie / bluff.
- We will not intentionally put any pressure on the counterpart, including time pressure.
- We will not make inflated offers.
- We will not practice emotional manipulation.
- We will not employ aggressive and hostile negotiation strategies and tactics.
- We will not hold back information.

We will:

- We will put forth our best efforts to keep the trust level in negotiation as high as possible.
- We will restrain from attempts at spying, bribing, and infiltrating.
- We will walk as we talk and will fully observe our agreement, if one is concluded.

- We will be open about variables and values, and share the information on an equal basis.
- We will behave fairly and share the added value generated during the transaction equitably.

We believe:

- We believe that working together outperforms winning at the expense of the counterpart.
- We do believe in the power of ethics and morality in negotiation.

Please inform us immediately if you find that we are not observing our negotiation Code of Conduct. At the end of the day, openly adhering to a common set of moral and ethical guidelines buoys company morale while assuring your business partners that you are a fair dealer.

Crafting Your Own Code of Conduct

If you and your colleagues conceptualize and write your own code of behavior, it will be easier to stand by your word and view any negotiation, no matter how challenging, through a lens that optimizes productivity and honesty. Encourage your employees and trading partners to enforce your own Code of Conduct, and emphasize its importance during even the most difficult transactions.

Develop an Awareness of Your Unconscious Motives

As soon as you become aware that you are about to enter into a negotiation, you begin a mental preparation process—some of it conscious, some of it unconscious. Be aware of the irrational behavioral that impacts your decisions. Although most of us try to stand on firm ground, and collect and assess facts, there are always subconscious and repressed needs, motives, fears, and hopes in the background. They govern us. It's important to be aware of these subconscious needs. The goal is to become aware of your own desires, intentions, and emotions in each situation—to lower your defenses so that you become conscious of your impulses and know how to control them.

When you are preparing to make a deal, internal negotiations take place between your conscious and your subconscious minds. Most of us know very little about our subconscious mind, and many people deny that it has any impact at all on the way we negotiate.

However, without your becoming aware of what you are doing, your conscious and your subconscious minds begin cooperating with each other and you start to rationalize. Focusing on your objective, you tell yourself how easy or difficult the coming negotiation is going to be. You consider what the opportunities and constraints will be. You assess the strength or weakness of your bargaining position, such as:

1. *There is no reason to ask for a raise. There is no money this year.*
2. *They will not give me a discount, because this model just came out and it is very popular.*
3. *I don't think I will ask her out to go see a film. She doesn't go out with guys like me.*

Only you can determine whether you are painting too rosy or too gloomy a picture in the anticipated negotiation. If you do not have sufficient insight into how you are inclined to behave, how will the other party across the table be able to understand, predict, and react correctly to your signals and decisions? You have a need for power, security, and acceptance. You do not want to lose face. You want to achieve good, tangible results, or you want to get even and retaliate.

You do not always have a complete and clean overview of your own objectives, assessments, possible alternatives, decision variables, and the previous chain of events. Often you pay no attention to some of the alternatives, but pick one associated with previous experience. At least you know what you are doing and you are working with familiar information, but very often you are governed by intangible needs. Often, you are not conscious of these needs and, even if you were to become aware of them, you would not acknowledge them.

Preconceived Notions

It is important to understand that you will sometimes fall victim to your own preconceived notions. Sometimes you have not set the bar high enough, and your level of expectation is too low. If you view things from an angle that is too limited, you may prevent yourself from reaping certain benefits.

It is not a good idea to enter negotiations with negative expectations:

- *They are never going to accept this.*
- *Cooperation is senseless.*
- *The other side is prepared for combat.*

If you are anxious when you enter a negotiation and have negative expectations, these feelings will be apparent throughout the process and reflected in the end result. As long as the negotiation continues, anything is possible.

Your assessment of the circumstances behind a negotiation is always based on incomplete information. The information gaps are filled in by your preconceived opinions of the other party. Your opinions are based on experience and expectations. Despite this uncertainty, the only thing that you can truly depend on is that your assessment will not tally with the reality you will encounter at the negotiating table.

Example: Ambushed by the Buyer

Elger gets a call from Biyu, one of his most important customers. Biyu wants to check a number of details concerning the forecast for the following year. Because Biyu is the head of production, Elger expects the conversation to be about technical details. Every year at this time, Biyu prepares the next year's forecast and always double-checks details with Elger. When Elger arrives at the meeting, it turns out Biyu wants to discuss terms, delivery, and financing. Elger was not prepared on these variables, so he enters into an agreement with which he is not happy.

When Elger returns to his office, his boss calls and asks how things went. He replies: *There was no way I could have known that the production manager wanted to discuss terms, delivery, and financing with me. She normally never does that until the end of the year.* In Elger's opinion, Biyu is at fault. She did not do what she usually does, and he feels that she tricked him.

When Biyu called the meeting, Elger should have asked: *What are we going to talk about, and who will be at the meeting?* If he had done this, he would have been prepared on the variables she wanted to discuss.

Never forget that time is negotiable—Elger could have asked to take some time to process his questions and schedule a follow-up call for the next day, after he had time to prepare.

Time Is Negotiable

Do not begin a negotiation when there is not sufficient time to complete the process, for instance, just before you are about to leave on a vacation. Postpone finalizing the negotiation rather than submitting to a rushed conclusion, which probably is not your best work. You can always negotiate about where and when to meet. If you have very little time, suggest a new time frame for the negotiations, so that you will be able to prepare. If you are forced to negotiate without being allowed to prepare, take things slowly. Limit yourself to listening to the other party. Do not make decisions on the spot. Instead, collect information, familiarize yourself with the issues, and give yourself time to evaluate and reflect.

Reschedule So You Are at Your Best

On short notice, you are called to take part in a negotiation. You schedule the meeting, book your flight, and reserve a hotel room. You put the important papers into your briefcase and hope to prepare while you are traveling or the night before in your hotel room. You already know that your preparation plan will not work, but you see no other solution since you were called in at the last minute.

If the other party has set the schedule, timing can be made a subject of negotiation. Your response to your counterpart should be: *I would really like to come, but I can't make it before Wednesday.*

It is a good practice not to make consequential decisions or sign important documents within the first 24 hours after a long journey. The stress of international travel and jet lag reduces your ability to make good decisions.

Example: The Cruise Ship Leaves Tomorrow, But There Is No Deal in Sight

Imagine that you are negotiating in a foreign country. Negotiations are taking more time than anticipated, and no agreement is in sight. You and your family have booked a wonderful vacation cruise, and you are anxious to get home. The day you are scheduled to fly home has arrived. The agreement is not concluded. These are your alternatives:

Option #1: Cancel your family holiday and continue to negotiate unrushed.
Option #2: Lower your expectations and force an agreement before the end of the day.
Option #3: Face the fact that you are not going to succeed and go home.
Option #4: Discuss the matters that the other party wants to take up, but postpone your decision. Request that you be allowed to come back to finalize the agreement.
Option #5: Do not accept a deadline set by the other party. Never inform your counterpart of the date of your return flight. If she

knows that you have an external deadline, she can purposefully delay the negotiation in order to put you under time pressure. Do not let the other party force you into closure because of the need to catch your flight.

Option #6: If a deadline has been set with the purpose of putting you under pressure, you may try to dodge it:

I don't know how we can solve this. Break off the deliberations in order to see how the other party will react. He may be under pressure to meet his own deadline, and, consequently, will attempt to speed things up. Stay cool and put the other party to the test: *If you insist on having an answer today, it will have to be no, but let me have another day, and I just might be able to give you a positive answer.*

Working with an Agenda

An agenda can be a very effective tool. Your ideas are stated in an orderly arrangement, and matters can be discussed in a structured manner. The negotiation will be more organized and more efficient if you discuss one issue at a time. Be careful not to reach a decision on any particular item. Avoid making decisions or reaching conclusions until you have an overview of the whole situation and are in possession of the requirements of the other party.

Examine what it is the other party intends to get from the negotiation, which questions may come up for discussion, and who will participate. The agenda specifies the issues that will be taken up for discussion and the sequence in which the conversation will take place. Your agenda will govern the expectations and preparations of the other party and the composition of their negotiation delegation.

If your opponent prepares the agenda, insist on a copy in advance. You will acquire valuable information about how the other side is viewing the negotiation. You can prepare your delegation. and you will avoid surprises. Do not build your bargaining strategy on your ideas alone. You will be in a stronger position for your decision-making when you know what your opponent hopes to gain from the negotiation.

Seek out a representative from the other party a few days in advance and clearly state your desire to work on a meeting agenda *with* him. This step ensures that there will be no surprises on the day of the meeting, as each party will have had the opportunity to familiarize themselves with the key points in advance. Such preparation eliminates the possibility of being pressured into a deal or being blindsided by unexpected terms.

You can discuss an agenda internally. It helps you keep the negotiation structured so that you do not skip around between the various issues. The members of the delegation stick to their roles at the negotiating table, and you can avoid the confusion that ill-prepared negotiators can fall into if there is an unclear distribution of roles.

SMARTner Tip for the Advanced Practitioner: An Agenda Is Unsuitable in Some Cases

You should note that some negotiators might become very uneasy when you present them with an agenda. It can have a negative effect on the other party and make him feel manipulated. There are situations in which an agenda can lock down negotiations in an undesirable manner. Some negotiators will resist using an agenda, and if you encounter this attitude, it is best to let it go and work without one. Even without an agenda, both parties will undoubtedly arrive with their own objectives in mind and work toward these in their own style. In other situations, it becomes an obstacle to the creativity that is required to move the negotiation forward. An agenda will have no advantage at all if the individual who prepared it does not follow it.

Look at the Other Party's Requirements

Before you can present your own requirements and begin advocating for them, you must understand the requirements of the other party. Do not assume that the other party has stated all his needs in the initial position statement. In his initial position statement, you will undoubtedly find a description of the technical and financial requirements, but the background for those requirements may be missing. Therefore, you cannot tell which needs the other party wishes to have met. The personal psychological needs are never apparent in the initial bids.

In order for the solutions and arguments that you present to be accepted by the other party, and for them to exert influence on him, they must be perceived as relevant. The solutions you offer must correspond to the needs of the other party.

Determine Your Bargaining Equity

Knowing the strength of your positions and your arguments enables you to work from a position of confidence during the bargaining process and opens the way to full cooperation with the person or delegation on the other side of the issue. When you are self-confident, you tend to be in a rational state (as opposed to an emotionally charged state) as to the facts, and you are best able to function from a place of honesty, transparency, and full cooperation.

Assess the Relative Strength of Your Bargaining Equity Ahead of Time

In any negotiation there are issues on which one or the other party is in a stronger position because of their ability to control the distribution of resources or produce a required outcome. Your bargaining equity is the degree to which you have the upper hand at any given moment during the transaction, and is measured by the degree to which you control the outcome.

As you prepare your plan of how to accomplish your objectives during the negotiation, think of the process like a tennis match. Either you or the other party puts each new issue or requirement on the table with a "serve," and then it is "volleyed" back and forth until a cooperative resolution is achieved. Your bargaining equity may shift several times in the course of the negotiation. You may have the stronger position on one issue, but have less control or ability to produce the required result on the next issue. It is important to remember, however, that you do not lose the game just because you gave up a point along the way. Recover quickly from your losses and keep your focus on the overall game.

Understanding your bargaining equity at every step of the transaction will help you understand the interpersonal dynamic. Being confident in your position enables you to explore the NegoEconomic value in the transaction.

Advancing your bargaining equity requires some back and forth with the loyal opposition—the dance of determining what the opposite party truly values in the transaction and then discovering what they are willing to give in order to get what they want. An effective negotiator uses his counterpart's value base (below her value base, your opponent is not willing to give anything in return) as the point of beginning to delve deeper into the deal in order to expose the asymmetric value hidden in the transaction.

Example: When Rockefeller Wanted to Sell His Company

John D. Rockefeller had a business that J. P. Morgan, the financier, wanted to buy. He contacted Rockefeller and asked whether the business was for sale. Rockefeller did not know why Morgan was interested or how he intended to use the enterprise, and therefore he did not know what it was worth to Morgan.

The men met and talked about the weather, the business trends, and other neutral matters. The story goes that after a while, Morgan became impatient and said to Rockefeller: *You know why I'm here. Let's get cracking. On what terms would you be interested in selling this business to me?*

Legend has it that Rockefeller remained silent for quite a while, and then looked at Morgan and said: *I think you've misunderstood the situation, my friend. I'm not here to sell, you are here to buy.*

Rockefeller decisively sent the ball into the other man's court. Rockefeller needed information in order to assess his own bargaining equity. He did not want to present any negotiation terms at that juncture. He chose to negotiate from a position of strength, forcing the other party, who was in the weaker position, to show his hand.

Take aways

- Negotiate the negotiation prior to the actual negotiation.
- Create an individual and corporate Code of Conduct for negotiation.
- The agenda is the law of the land for the negotiation. Prepare and negotiate the agenda.
- Be proactive and show initiative.
- Remember to look at the counterpart's interests.

CHAPTER 5

Preparation and Analysis Prior to Bargaining: The First 5 Phases of the Negotiation Process

Negotiation is a process that requires both time and experience to be truly effective. Almost no one is a born negotiator. Since each negotiation involves difference circumstances and each counterpart is unique, the more you prepare, the better the chances for optimized outcomes for everyone at the table. The important thing is to be able to recognize, at any given point, where you are in the process and be able to assess your objectives and make a proper judgment call about your next step. This breakdown of the phases is a tool to help you think strategically about the process so that you are working toward the mutual gains that lie inherent in the transaction. Breaking the process down into phases can help anyone experience a better outcome. There are ten phases to this process. They are not necessarily linear. Each phase relies on the others.

In this chapter we cover the first five phases, which is the preparatory work that must be done prior to the actual bargaining. In these early phases, you are focused on cooperating with your loyal opposition in order to make the pie bigger. Beginning with phase 6, your focus shifts to dividing the pie you have created and frequently involves style switching in order to optimize your personal objectives from the transaction.

The Ten Phases of the Negotiation Process

These ten phases describe the typical sequence of a negotiated commercial transaction:

1. Developing Awareness of the Need to Negotiate
2. Preparing to Negotiate
3. Opening the Negotiation
4. Argumentation
5. Charting the Negotiation Options
6. Bargaining
7. Concluding
8. Confirming
9. Implementing
10. Continued Relations or Divorce

You will not be able to distinctly identify all ten phases in every negotiation. In some situations, an offer is made and bargaining begins as soon as the parties arrive at the table. It is also quite common for phase 4 and phase 5 to be combined into one complex phase. Sometimes a conclusion may be reached without your realizing that you are in the middle of a negotiation. The first five phases, which are the steps prior to structuring the deal, are discussed in this chapter. The second five phases, which are the deal-making process, are addressed in chapter 9.

Phase 1: Developing Awareness of the Need to Negotiate

A need to solve a problem may arise in many different contexts:

- A customer wants a quotation for production of a customized widget.
- Your top sales representative resigns, taking with him your largest customer.
- The state has decided to build a highway exit ramp over your property.
- There is an oil spill in the bay.
- Your boss rejects your budget draft.
- You need a technical expert to relocate to your manufacturing facility on the other coast.
- Your wife wants to buy a second vacation home.

These examples demonstrate that a negotiation may be voluntary or forced upon you. If it's voluntary, it's up to you to decide whether you want to continue or to break off the conversation. Business negotiations are normally voluntary. The most common exceptions occur when you have a dissatisfied customer, a contractual dispute, or government intervention. Involuntary negotiations, though occasionally unpleasant, are sometimes unavoidable. In the case in which a negotiation is involuntary, it is important to stay calm and remain strategic, rather than becoming angry or vengeful. You must do everything possible to keep your cool, remain rational, and strive for cooperative solutions.

When Caught Off Guard, Pause Before You Begin

If you have taken the initiative in the negotiation, you are likely to be prepared before you begin, and you will have an idea about how to frame the issues. If the other party has taken the initiative, it can be a strategic error to rush to a conclusion. Take a moment to consider your options before diving in.

In connection with negotiations over the phone, the party who receives the call will often be unprepared for the conversation. Listening carefully and saying you will get back to the caller doesn't cost anything. Many deals are made over the phone. Taking five minutes to think about an alternative arrangement might be enough to come up with something better than a tacit acceptance of a suboptimal offer.

Example: A Telephone Sales Call

Dante, a supplier rep, phones Lania to offer a special discount on an inventory surplus of spool widgets. Lania purchases a large quantity of this product, and the price Dante is offering is about 15 percent below what she normally pays.

> *Dante*: We have managed to secure a truckload of spool widgets. I can offer you a 15 percent discount if you take a minimum quantity of 100 units.
> *Lania*: That sounds interesting, we go through a lot of spool widgets here. But I don't know how many we'll be able to take. Can I call you back?
> *Dante*: Can I hold while you find out?
> *Lania*: OK, hang on for a minute, and I'll check the warehouse and ask the production manager.

Two minutes later, Lania places an order for 300 units. She is happy with her purchase.

Alternative Scenario: Always Be Ready with an Alternative

Here is an alternative scenario demonstrating how Lania might have made a better decision:

Lania: That sounds interesting. How many do you have?
Dante: I have between 3,000 and 4,000 units.
Lania: And what price do you want if I take more than 100?
Dante: I might be able to increase the discount by a few percent. How many did you have in mind?
Lania: I have to step into a meeting right now. I'll get back to you in half an hour. See what you can do for an order of 500 units.

Lania did not have a meeting to go to, but she needed time to think about the offer without being hurried. It is important to have an alternative when bargaining. What price are the other suppliers offering?

Lania phones a few of the supplier's competitors and inquires about their price. There are a lot of spool widgets on the market suddenly. You now have the information you need. Lania calls Dante back:

Lania: You were going to quote me a new price.
Dante: I can let you have an 18 percent discount on 500 units.
Lania: I have received the same discount from another supplier.
Dante: There is quite a surplus of spool widgets on the market right now, but you should watch out, we have had shortages in the past.
Lania: I am willing to place a larger order, but you will have to come up with a better price.
Dante: I can give you an additional 1 percent.
Lania: Nineteen percent, you say. Well, in that case, I can't take more than 300 units.
Dante: OK, we have a deal.

This example shows how Lania tested the boundaries without being hurried. By doing so, she got a better deal. Lania collected information, assessed the situation, set a goal, and achieved it. Without harming her relationship with Dante and enabling him to secure the sale, she saved her company money.

During the negotiation, Lania also achieved personal gratification. Although the first offer she received was good, she did not passively accept it. Lania assumed there was room for negotiation.

Be on Guard for an End-run Conclusion

An opening-phase mistake that can sneak up on you is when you realize you are in a negotiation only seconds before the other party concludes.

Jane and her coworker Sam share the responsibility of answering the office phones. Jane has an important appointment at the end of the day, and would like to leave work a bit early.

Jane asks Sam: Any plans after work this evening?
Sam: None at all. I need to continue working on this report for much of the evening.
Jane: Good—then I can leave twenty minutes early? You'll have to answer the phones—I have an important appointment that I cannot be late for, and you were planning on staying late anyway.

Jane familiarized herself with Sam's situation and moved directly to a conclusion. Because Jane doesn't reveal the intention behind her initial question, Sam doesn't realize that he is in a negotiation before the conclusion has been reached. This tactic is clever and effective, and is commonly employed by controlling personalities.

Grab the Opportunity When It Falls into Your Lap

You won't always have time to prepare. Sometimes a situation arises in which you must grab the chance in mid-air. If you don't, you won't get another opportunity. This type of situation puts entirely different demands on you.

Example: A Chance Meeting Reveals a Prospect

Several years ago, a colleague of mine participated in a course in London organized by two American consultants who offered training in negotiation techniques in direct competition with Ivan. Ivan is Swedish, and had been told that two other Swedes were among the more than 100 participants at the seminar. Ivan decided to find his countrymen among the attendees, and upon doing so, introduced himself and asked them why they were attending the London seminar. He received the cryptic answer, "A new Procurement Officer has been appointed at our company and has issued an order that all purchasing agents must be trained in negotiation technique." The conversation continued along these lines:

Ivan: But why are you in London?
Swedes: We have been looking for courses on negotiation techniques in Europe. We've been able to find two, and of the two, this is the best one.
Ivan: Oh really, so what are you going to do now?
Swedes: We are trying to hire these two Americans to help us.

Ivan: How do you like the course?

Swedes: There is a lot of useful information in it.

Ivan: Do you want to offer the same type of course back home?

Swedes: We would prefer a course customized for our industry, offered in Swedish. But it looks as though we will have to bring these guys to Stockholm and offer our team the consultants' standard course in English.

Ivan: When do you want to hold the training?

Swedes: We would have preferred to have it this winter, but the Americans can't make it until May or June.

Ivan: What is it going to cost?

Swedes: American consultants are expensive, and there are two of them. We have to pay for the trip from the United States and back for both.

Ivan: Have you already concluded an agreement with them?

Swedes: No, we wanted to hold off signing an agreement until after the end of the day tomorrow.

Ivan realized that he had stumbled into a golden sales opportunity for the training seminar he offered on negotiation techniques. On the spot, he proposed to hold the training in Swedish, customized to their industry requirements, early the following winter, and at a price below what the American consultants were going to charge.

The two Swedish prospects were somewhat taken aback and inquired, "But who are you?"

The Power of Initiative

Ivan won the contract for the seminar. His technique was simple: question, listen, question again, and draw conclusions. Ivan was the active party, the one who took the initiative. If the Swedish prospects had attempted to strike a better balance in the flow of information, they would, most likely, have been able to get a better deal for themselves. Information almost always strengthens your bargaining equity. Ivan was able to suggest a solution that obvious benefits for both parties.

Stall or Delay Until You Get the Information You Need

When the conversation turned in the direction of Ivan's fee, he had to stall, "I can't tell you today. First, we have to look into your goals and objectives in further detail. Then I can quote a price, and I can promise you that it will be lower than what the Americans are asking. What we should do now is schedule a meeting when we get back home and solidify the deal so I can put your dates on my calendar."

Be Bold Enough to Reach a Conclusion

An indirect conclusion was reached that same evening when Ivan booked a time for the follow-up meeting in Sweden where the parties agreed they would fill in the details and create a plan for further action. Ivan's next step was to listen to the Americans' presentation and inquire what they would charge for a course in Sweden that met the prospect's specifications.

Phase 2: Preparing to Negotiate

The Timetable for Negotiations

Preparation is crucial for success when it comes to negotiation. If you start the negotiations in the proper way, you can often get your counterpart to help you achieve your objectives and fulfill your needs while meeting their own needs at the same time.

Do Your Homework

Laying the groundwork ahead of time is extremely important for a successful negotiation. People seem to understand this in theory, yet when it comes time to negotiate, they have typically not done their

Negotiation Example

	Your Company			Your Counterpart	
Variable	Starting Point	Negotiation Scope	Effect of Change of Condition	Negotiation Scope	Effect of Change of Condition
Price	$1,500,000	$1,500,000 down to $1,350,000	−$150,000		
Payment Conditions	10 days net	60 days net	at 10 percent interest: −$21,000		
Delivery Time	1st of August	1st of September	+$60,000		
Guarantee 1	Year	2 Years	Increased risk costs go up by $25,000		
Technical Specification	Upon request	Alternative 1: incorporate more Alternative 2: remove demand	Alt. 1: −$10,000 Alt. 2: +$80,000		

Figure 5.1 Effective deal-making requires you to enter an agreement being aware of the negotiation scope for yourself and your counterpart.

homework. They begin to bargain in an unstructured manner and hope that something will show itself and that they can find an opportunity in the heat of the moment. Their faith in their own ability to improvise is exaggerated. The outcome is likely to be protracted, and decisions will be made too quickly with suboptimal results.

Make Good Use of Your Time

Unprepared negotiators commonly rely on a lack of time as their excuse. However, experience shows that they have not utilized the time available in a constructive manner. They have failed to prepare on the key issues that will make or break the success of a negotiation:

- They have failed to familiarize themselves with the other party's situation.
- They have locked themselves into a certain approach.
- They have overlooked the distribution of roles within their own delegation.
- They have not thought about alternative solutions.

Their preparations are limited to logistics—making reservations with the airline and booking a hotel, compiling a list of supporting documents, and obtaining copies of blueprints, queries, and letters. They fail to have a clear overview of the transaction and get hung up on details rather than creating a roadmap of how the negotiation should proceed. With proper preparation, you can enhance the probability that you and your counterpart will be able to reach a mutually beneficial outcome.

Develop a Roadmap

Preparing does not mean creating a detailed plan that you religiously follow without considering the developments of subsequent negotiations. Preparations are intended to provide you with a resource that gives you your bearings, and the map in turn provides security. The purpose of such preparations is to increase your flexibility and, consequently, your chances of coping with the challenges of the upcoming negotiations (Figure 5.1).

You should be able to get an overview of the possibilities, the obstacles, and the alternative routes. The choice of routes toward your specific objectives should be fairly obvious. When the conversations begin, do not attempt to arrive at your goal by the shortest possible route. First, obtain information about your counterpart's situation:

- What are his requirements?
- What are the needs behind these requirements?
- To which alternatives might he have an open mind?
- How flexible is he?
- What do various changes of conditions mean to him?

Negotiating with Your Own Organization

You want to anticipate scenarios and have internal dialogue prior to the negotiation with your colleagues. If you are the sales rep, you could contact the production department to squeeze delivery times or adjust the specifications of the product. You might see if the finance department can get better terms, and you might have a conversation with your boss to determine the depth of the discount you can give.

Reduce Your Insecurity

If you fail to prepare and analyze the upcoming negotiation, your uncertainty will grow. The stressful situation that might arise will place you squarely within the classical choice of fight or flight. If this happens, you will have surrendered the initiative to the other party. When you become defensive, you increase the risk that you will begin to make unilateral concessions.

Negotiations tend to have a life of their own. Unexpected situations arise and present problems as well as opportunities. Negotiation is not a rational process in which the reactions of both parties can be predicted. In a negotiation, well-prepared actions clash with unanticipated and irrational actions. It is difficult to predict behavior that is not logical. Something that comes out of the blue may requires a swift response.

Understand Your Counterpart

Information about the other party, such as his values and patterns of behavior, makes it easier to understand him and his actions. Such knowledge is particularly important in connection with international negotiations. Unfamiliar norms prevail in other countries. If you have failed to obtain information about the customs, culture, and protocol of any country where you are working, you may be thrown off by unfamiliar practices. You will become insecure, stressed, and prone to making errors.

Don't Lock Yourself into a Single Alternative

Ted and his group are convinced of a particular solution. They go to the negotiating table with a single proposal in mind. Ellen, their counterpart, has locked herself into another solution. Both parties are strong advocates for their preferred solution, and neither is listening to the other. Ted thinks that Ellen is not to be taken seriously because she refuses to listen to him. Ellen feels the same way about Ted.

This kind of deadlock may be due to the fear of listening to something you are not prepared to discuss or because you have locked yourself into a solution that your group has agreed upon. Locking is usually brought on by internal negotiations in which the members of your group have convinced each other that your solution is the only right one. It tends to create polarity and reduces or, in some cases, eliminates the opportunity for cooperation and trust.

If instead of locking, the delegation approaches the negotiation from a position of openness and a free flow of information. Both parties have the potential of a mutual gains solution.

You often see this problem in political situations. The politicians seem unwilling to listen to each other. This is the result of their internal discussions in which they have become indoctrinated into the party line. They also believe it is dangerous to listen to the opposing party. Listening entails a risk. You might be influenced by the arguments of the other party and relinquish your own position. When a brutal reality forces politicians to open their eyes, an alternative approach may then be taken up for discussion within the party. This triggers another problem: how to retreat from the prior position without losing face? A standard political response is: *It was merely an objective; there was no promise.*

Analyze the Negotiation Process

A thoughtful analysis of the negotiation you are about to undertake will make it easier for you to understand patterns of interaction and the potential opportunities between you and your counterpart. Along the way, you may have to modify your objectives and the solutions you have in mind. By reflecting on the psychological dynamic between the players around the table and between your conscious and subconscious minds, you can get closer to your own objectives. Without the perspective provided by this analysis, you will find it difficult to take advantage of the new information that shows itself in the course of the negotiation.

If the negotiation develops differently from what you expected, take a break. With new facts, you need time to prepare. The new information must be analyzed and your previous assumptions reassessed. Do the new facts alter your strategy or your objectives?

Phase 3: Opening the Negotiation

Six Steps for a Successful Opening

1. Develop personal chemistry and build rapport.
2. Summarize the background.
3. Prepare an agenda.
4. Create a positive negotiation environment.
5. Define the interpersonal dynamic.
6. Lay the groundwork for bargaining.

Step 1. Develop Personal Chemistry and Build Rapport

It is rarely a good idea to leap right into things. Spend some time getting to know the other party, build trust, and get him or her to relax and feel at ease. The personal chemistry has to work in order to achieve an optimal result. Building trust is a factor that needs to be built into the negotiation process.

Step 2. Summarize the Background

It is often wise to open by summarizing the history of the transaction. Confirm that you and the other party are in agreement about the reason for meeting and about the issues that have been resolved previously. Then fall silent. Your silence might make the other party start talking. If the supplier summarizes what the buyer has said prior to the meeting and falls silent, many buyers will start talking. The supplier will obtain more, often valuable, information. If things go well, after a while the buyer will ask to buy. The supplier has now completed the argumentation phase, and has arrived at a discussion in which cooperation is the dominant theme.

Step 3. Prepare an Agenda

An agenda can be a very effective tool. Your ideas are stated in an orderly arrangement, and matters can be discussed in a structured manner. The negotiation will be more organized and more efficient if you discuss one point at a time. Be careful not to reach a decision on any particular item. Avoid making decisions or reaching conclusions until you have an overview of the whole situation and understand the requirements of the other party. Evaluate what the other party wants to get from the negotiation, which questions may come up for discussion, and who will participate.

Step 4. Create a Positive Negotiation Climate

The purpose of the opening is to create the proper setting for the upcoming negotiation. Become acquainted with the other party, learn to trust one another, and work toward establishing a constructive environment for cooperation. The interpersonal chemistry will be highly beneficial to impending negotiation.

Example: Shopping for Carpets in Istanbul

Mark enters a carpet shop in Istanbul and asks to be shown a particular carpet. Instead of praising the qualities of his choice, the shop owner asks Mark to sit down and join him for a cup of tea. Mark accepts the invitation and takes a seat. The owner's assistant prepares the tea on a primus stove placed on a tray in front of them.

Mark is intrigued by the small ceremony taking place, and the shop owner explains to Mark how and why his assistant follows a particular ritual. In this way, the owner establishes rapport with Mark and gains his trust.

After a while, the conversation turns to other matters. While they are having tea, the owner obtains some information about Mark:

- *How long have you been in Istanbul?*
- *When will you be leaving?*
- *Where have you come from, and where are you going?*
- *Which hotel are you staying at?*
- *Have you ever been to the bazaar?*

Mark responds that he has been in Istanbul for four days; he is staying at the Hilton; he has come from Bulgaria; and he will be going to Romania the following day. Finally, Mark reveals that he has never been to the bazaar, but has visited other tourist attractions in Istanbul.

The shop owner warns Mark against pickpockets, and he instinctively checks his pockets. The owner knows that he has before him a customer who has little time and much money, and that he is someone who hasn't spent a lot of time bargaining in the bazaar. However, he needs to know more about his customer before negotiations can begin. He asks his assistant to get out the carpet that Mark is interested in. In the meantime, the owner asks if he wouldn't mind being shown a few other carpets.

A little further into the shop, three carpets are spread out on the floor. The shop owner asks: *How do you like these carpets?* Mark looks at them, and his comments immediately reveal that he does not know a great deal about carpets. He makes comments about the colors, and points out that the one in the middle is commonly found in the United States. The owner asks: *How much would such a carpet cost in the United States?* Mark replies: *$700 to $900.*

A little later, the assistant brings out the carpet that initially piqued Mark's interest. At last, the bargaining begins. The owner has all the information he needs to steer the negotiation to a conclusion that is satisfactory to both parties. He has strengthened his bargaining equity by obtaining information from Mark.

You should not view negotiation as a fight to be won by means of slick tactical moves. In every fight, there is a winner and a loser, and the loser will always try to retaliate. If you polarize the situation, the victories you gain may be both costly and of short duration.

Step 5. Define the Interpersonal Dynamic

The more you know about yourself, the better you will understand why you negotiate the way you do and the better prepared you will be for what lies ahead. At the opening of a negotiation, your tone of voice, your choice of words, and your appearance will influence and govern the interpersonal dynamic. The other party's response to these factors will be reflected in their treatment of you.

Test positions and solutions so that you have a clear perception of the boundaries of the bargaining. Be firm on substantive matters. This doesn't mean you should use dirty tricks, bulldoze your way through the day, or resort to personal attacks. Being firm in substance and flexible in form does not preclude a positive dynamic between the parties. Avoid any moves that might offend the other party!

Step 6. Lay the Groundwork for Bargaining

Opening the negotiations can be tough. The following opening remarks are probably familiar to you:

- *Your price is too high. If we are going to do business you are going to have to lower your price.*

- *If you cannot give us a firm price now for the whole order, it doesn't make sense to continue with the negotiation. We might as well pack it in and go home.*
- *All your competitors have reduced their price by 10 percent. A similar reduction on your part is a prerequisite for you to be included in the final round of talks.*
- *We have sent you all our requirements. Please, let us have your offer.*

If you come across this type of opening, just relax and take it easy. Ask questions and postpone any decision. Try to reassure the other party so that she will present her solution. Ask her to tell you what she wants. Do not view demands and threats as risks and costs, because very often they are buying signals and opportunities. If your proposal was really as horrible as she indicated, and if she had other, more favorable alternatives, she most likely would not be negotiating with you at all.

Your job is to get the other party to specify and develop all her requirements. If you meet her demands too soon by making a new and better offer, you will diminish the opportunity for more creative solutions. Analyze the opening possibilities, and ask for a counterbid before making a new offer. If you skip this step, you risk ending up in a situation in which you are making one concession after the other, until you have nothing left to give. A more hesitant and cautious approach will enable you to inch your way forward and get a read on the other party and her intentions before setting your course.

Choosing Tactical Gambits

Your goal is to create a negotiation climate with a view of cooperation from the outset. Some tactics are constructive and lead to greater openness and better understanding; these tactics enhance the Trust Factor. Using these tactics will make it easier for you to find the paths that can lead to NegoEconomic solutions.

There is no such thing as a single tactic that will work no matter what the circumstances. Tactics will always have to be adjusted and adapted according to your objectives, your choice of strategy, your resources, and your knowledge base in contrast to the objectives, strategy, resources, and the knowledge base of your opponent.

As you select a tactic, try to anticipate what reactions and countermoves it might provoke from the other party and determine how you will respond. Put yourself in the shoes of the other delegation.

Consider how you would react to the gambit you are about to put into play and what your countermoves might be. In this way, you can assess whether you are about to put the opportunity for cooperation at risk or the relationship in jeopardy.

If you are uncertain about the tactics of the other party, take it slow and easy and wait until you are better able to read your counterpart's intentions. Be wary of using gambits that the other party might interpret as combative. Such gambits may lead to deadlock and could preempt future cooperation. And never use manipulating tactics in a proven SMARTnership.

Tactical moves must be executed with good sense and caution because clever tactics tend to be double-edged swords. Tricky tactical play may cause the other party to feel manipulated, make him feel insecure, or put pressure on him, which might cause him to surrender a point. These stress-inducing moves may advance your position in the short term, but they tend to ruin relationships, trust, and openness in the long haul. If the other party sees through your intentions, a clever countermove may enhance your opponent's bargaining equity and leave you scrambling to regain yours. It is very important for a delegate who attempts a tactical trick to know exactly what his next move is going to be if the ploy is not successful. Absent planning for the fallback position, the door slams shut and the added value is lost.

Sometimes it is difficult to determine in advance whether one tactic is superior to another or whether clever gambits and moves will do more harm than good. Only when the negotiation has been completed will you know whether your style choice or tactical strategy was the right one. However, you never know what the outcome would have been if you had chosen another approach.

When making your style choice and choosing your tactics, adapt to the norms of your market. Be mild in manner and firm in substance. The objective is to get as much as possible from the negotiation without being perceived as a combative negotiator.

Phase 4: Argumentation

In the argumentation phase, each party attempts to clarify their understanding of the other party's requirements and to expand or broaden the range of possible solutions. After these introductory steps, the delegates can then define the parameters for the bargaining that is about to take place. In this phase, the arguments are established in general terms.

To achieve a favorable solution, both parties should agree that the discussion will be open and constructive. The purpose of the argumentation phase is to locate the NegoEconomic value in the transaction. This is found by identifying alternative solutions, which will allow you to increase the size of the pie to be shared by both parties.

Take the Initiative

The party who can take and hold the initiative in the negotiation is more likely to define the patterns of the interpersonal dynamic. The initiative can be taken in many ways:

- By tabling an opening offer on which you intend to base the continuing negotiations. The buyer takes the initiative to establish a new price agreement and does not wait for the supplier to demand a price increase. Around the New Year, he says: *We would like to extend the agreement another six months if you'll accept a 4 percent price reduction.*
- By presenting your own agenda.
- By being silent and letting the other party speak.
- By asking questions and offering summaries. (Only rarely does the party who speaks have the initiative.)
- By asking for a break, you can reclaim the initiative, if you have lost it.
- By shifting the focus. You can jump from one issue to another when your opponent has placed you under stress. In combination with a break, this causes the other party to lose impetus, direction, and, in the end, the initiative.

Very often your preparations will determine your ability to take and keep the initiative. Preparations create security and allow you to chart alternatives that will provide an overview of alternative solutions. If you have familiarized yourself with the other party's situation and the questions that might conceivably be brought up, the risk of your losing the initiative because of a surprise will become negligible.

Get the Details

Obtain more information. Arguments are not the same as demands. A statement that something is too expensive need not be the equivalent of a demand for a price reduction. It might just as well mean: *Please, show me what it is that I will be getting for my money.* You must obtain more information about what the other party wants. Ask questions: *Could you please explain or go into more detail about your ideas?*

Before you decide how to accommodate the other party, think through the following questions:

- What are the consequences of the other party's demands on you?
- What are the possible solutions you could accept?
- What should you demand in return?
- Why is the other party making these demands?
- What are the demands worth to the other party?
- What are his alternatives?
- Are the demands of the other party within the boundaries you have to maintain?
- What will he gain from his suggested alternative?

Documentation

Forward appropriate documentation that will support your arguments and positions prior to the negotiation. The other party will be more receptive to your message, better prepared, and more equipped to ask meaningful questions. You will waste time and lose trust if you take the other party by surprise at the negotiating table. He will be unable to answer your questions and will become flustered. He can't benefit from the information when it is given to him all at once, and this information overload may cause him to feel overwhelmed, insecure, and unable to act.

Analyze the Other Party's Requirements

When you have obtained the answers you need, take a break before deciding on your next step. The demands the other party made may have been unexpected. Knowing which way to move calls for a detailed analysis. After you have thoroughly reviewed the situation, develop your own list of alternatives.

The argumentation phase is a testing ground for prospective solutions. Do not concede any important points during this phase. Make your decisions following this absolute rule: NEVER GIVE ANYTHING AWAY WITHOUT GETTING SOMETHING BACK.

Don't make up your mind about the other party's requirements one by one. Allowing this to happen will likely result in a negotiation in which the other party plucks you like a chicken, feather by feather, and you risk being left with nothing. You must have a full picture before you can determine what is best. Know all the objections and demands before you make your decision. Get all the requirements out in the open. Lock down the bargain and get confirmation that you are in agreement. Ask: *Provided I can meet your demands, do we have a deal?*

It may be necessary to repeat and clarify your arguments. When you present and develop your own proposal, you must make sure that the other party receives it in a way that he or she will easily understand. If possible, try to illustrate your arguments visually and be ready to substantiate them. Illustrate what the consequences of your approach would be. If the other party can save a lot of money, it's not enough to claim: *If you accept our proposal, you will earn a lot of money.* In cases like this, actions speak far louder than words. You need to be more specific and show them how much and how you reached the figures you are illustrating. Use the whiteboard to show a simple example of what the savings could be.

Ensure that you get concrete counterproposals, so that you can determine how far apart you really are, and what you have agreed upon. Never try to guess what the other party wants or would be willing to accept. Summarize the point of departure again, and be sure to emphasize the things on which you agree and the common ground you have found. Then itemize the problems and needs you hope to resolve. This enhances credibility and makes your counterclaims and conditions more palatable.

Fish for the NegoEconomic Value

> *Buyer*: We have taken several bids to compare them with yours. There are other suppliers who can meet our requirements in a satisfactory manner. What surprises us is your high price. Could there possibly be a miscalculation in your quotation?

What is it that the buyer wants to achieve by this approach? More than likely, he is testing to see whether you will offer a lower price. He does not know whether your quotation is your best offer, or whether it is a negotiable opening offer. The buyer doesn't want to pay more than he has to. He refers to the other suppliers whom he claims are on an equal footing and who can offer much lower prices. By mentioning the possibility of a miscalculation, he offers you an opportunity to adjust the price without making it obvious that you have tried to sell to him at an inflated price, thus offering you an opportunity to save face. In reality, there may be other suppliers who can offer better prices. Often it is hard to tell what is genuine and what is bluff.

The Value of Silence

Don't forget the effectiveness of silence. You may want to listen for a while without providing direct answers to the questions put to you. If you counter everything you hear directly, you run the risk of allowing the negotiation to deteriorate into verbal combat. Pressure results in counter pressure.

Silence is an underutilized but very effective tool. Many negotiations have failed because someone spoke too much, but few negotiations have failed because of silence.

Not everything that is said in the course of a negotiation requires a response or comment. The objective of a negotiation is not to be right on each and every point, or to persuade the other party to abandon his views. The objective of the cooperative negotiator is to find a solution that meets the requirements of both parties. Learn to master silence, and seek to understand why the other party is silent when he has chosen this approach. Is it because he does not want to answer your question and he has run out of arguments, or is it because he hopes that you will break the silence and start negotiating with yourself?

Silence, or the absence of a reaction, creates insecurity and stress. The supplier who introduces his offer with the words: *I think it will be possible for us to come down 3 to 4 percent*, and is met with silence, will be more likely to say: *We can probably give you 4 percent. The payment conditions can also be changed. . . .*

Example: A Moment of Silence

Rupert decided to sell his house. After six months, the real estate agent had not found a serious buyer willing to make an offer at his asking price. The agent made it clear that if Rupert wanted to sell the house, he had to reduce his asking price by $10,000. Once Rupert agreed to the reduction, the realtor produced a buyer almost immediately.

Rupert made his calculations and found that there was enough of a margin to go through with the deal at the lower price. He played out in his head several alternative arrangements for the financing that would leave him with the cash he needed. His threshold of pain was a reduction of $13,000. Rupert considered himself prepared for the negotiations, which were to be held the next day.

Later in the evening, it struck him that he knew nothing about the buyers and their situation. What were their objectives, and what must happen for them to be comfortable moving forward with the purchase? He tried to put himself in the role of the buyer. "If I were the buyer, what would be my concerns?" The following points occurred to him:

- Cash for the down payment
- Monthly mortgage costs
- Selling their old house
- Move-in date
- Possible renovation or improvements
- Schools, child-care facilities
- Public transportation and distance to work

Rupert realized that he didn't know enough about the buyers to be able to properly prepare for the negotiation. He didn't know their names, how many children they had, what they did for work, and where they were currently living. He realized that he had to get more information before the price discussions began. He decided to remain silent—a classic tactic to get the other party talking.

It worked. The buyers told him that they had a house they had not yet been able to sell. The wife was worried about the time it might take to get it sold. She was also worried about their ability to make both mortgage payments in the interim. She said that Rupert's house was perfect when it came to style, location, and size. When she was speaking, Rupert could see that mentally she had already moved into the house and had arranged her furniture in the rooms. The only problem was affording the double mortgage payments. The buyers intended to solve this problem by bargaining on the purchase price.

Rupert saw a different solution and decided to put it on the table. If the buyers would accept his original asking price, he would continue to be responsible for the mortgage payments on the house until they were able to sell their old house. On hearing his offer, the wife turned to her husband and said: *That would solve all our problems.* Her husband replied: *Will we agree to his original asking price then? We really cannot afford to pay both mortgages.*

Rupert left the room, so the husband and wife could negotiate between themselves. Since he had given them a direct solution to their problem, they accepted the offer. Completing the transaction was more important to them than squeezing Rupert down on the price.

Taking a minute to think about the circumstances of the other party, plus a moment of silence, turned out to be worth $10,000 to Rupert. At the same time, the buyers got a satisfactory solution to their problem. When their house sold, the parties made the final settlement, and Rupert was reimbursed for the payments he had made, plus interest.

This example illustrates the usefulness of being silent and biding your time. After a few seconds of silence, most people will start talking. Let them! Question, listen, work with hypotheses, prompt them to suggest solutions, and draw your conclusions on the basis of what you've learned! Take your time, and do not make up your mind right away.

As the expression goes, sometimes silence truly is golden. There is no danger in listening to the other party. Knowledge and information will provide you with a stronger bargaining position. Listening does not mean that you have to agree with the other party and abandon your own point of view. It is essential, however, to avoid misinterpreting silence for agreement. Do not make the mistake of believing that you have reached an agreement just because the other party listens to you without stating any objections. Silence in a negotiation does not automatically equal consent.

Do not become threatened when your opponent is using silence as a tactic. Question, summarize, or take a break. If you want to provoke the other party into breaking his silence, you only have to summarize incorrectly, and he will correct you.

Don't Drift into Verbal Combat

If the negotiation slips into verbal combat, it morphs into a test of strength and will between the parties. In some cases, the most skillful debater may win the initiative and reach a conclusion without having to make any concessions. Other times, however, the dynamic of the negotiation becomes a zero-sum game in which everything is won at the expense of the other party. As a result of this combat, the prevailing party will come away from the table with a smaller share of the value of the transaction than he could have had, and he will bear more of the costs and risks.

Phase 5: Charting the Negotiation Options

Learn to view the negotiation from a broad perspective. The following questions will prepare you for bargaining:

- What is your offer?
- What is the room for negotiation?
- Can we divide the value instead of lowering the price?

- What is there to offer the opponent other than money? What can be added to the offer by way of extra services and products? One benefit of providing extra services or products is that the costs to you may be considerably lower than the value to the other party. In other words, you are getting leverage. The effect might even be high enough for you to raise your price.
- Can the scope of the package be reduced? Sometimes the key to accessing the added value lies in simplifying your package. Ask yourself the following questions:
  - Which services and products can be taken out of the deal?
  - What are the elements that the other party can do for himself?
  - Is there a simpler solution?
- What is the way out if the other party is not interested in bargaining?

In the heat of battle, sometimes the banner is swung too high. You must make sure that you have a safe route of retreat, in the event that that reality is different from what you expected. Objective arguments based on facts become necessary if it appears that the other party can't or won't appreciate the advantages of your offer. When you are perceived as credible and you have substantiating arguments, you may influence the other party to change his or her mind. However, this presupposes that the other party can view reality in the same way you do. Ingemar Stenmark, the champion skier, is reported to have once said to a journalist: *You can only talk to someone who understands what you are saying!*

Arguments versus Signals

Negotiators can send signals that show that other solutions are possible and that there is room for additional compromise. The difference between arguments and signals is that a signal contains a specific message, whereas an argument is often hard to assess. Arguments establish and test positions of strength, whereas signals are there to identify opportunity for further discussion. Negotiators tend to respond more positively to signals than arguments, as arguments can sometimes be misconstrued.

ARGUMENTS

- *It's too expensive.*
- *This is our lowest price.*
- *We need better payment terms.*
- *You charge too much for the installation.*

SIGNALS

Buyer: We can't pay more than $8.75 / lb. (The buyer signals a new level for the continuing negotiation.)

Supplier: This is our lowest price for the quantity in question. (The supplier is signaling that a different quantity may lead to a different price.)

Buyer: We are short of liquidity and must have better payment terms (A signal indicating that this is a genuine need.)

Supplier: We can lend you a couple of workers, provided that this will lead to a hefty reduction in the installation price. (The signal is very clear here. In this instance an actual concession is promised.)

Unfortunately, many negotiators, especially on the purchasing side, are reluctant to send very clear signals indicating that they are ready to come to terms. They prefer to sit tight, hoping that the other party will open up. Some buyers think it's wrong to send signals, as they feel that this will make things too easy for the other party. The result of this reluctance is a return to the previous argumentation phase. Negotiations are deadlocked rather than taken forward toward completion.

Missing Each Other's Signals

By sending signals, you open doors that allow the negotiations to move forward. What happens if you miss the signals sent by the other party? Missing or misreading signals is caused by the following:

- You receive unclear signals.
- You have not listened well.
- You are locked into your own proposal, and you cannot see the openings offered by the other party.
- You never leave the argumentation phase, and ego-driven competitiveness takes over and you sink into verbal combat. You become defensive, rather than attempting to leverage the opening proposals of the other party.

It is important that *you* pay attention to whether or not the other party has read and understood *your* signals. Ask the other party to summarize your proposals. It is a good idea to write them on the whiteboard, so that the other party has a visual guideline. Put pressure on the other party and demand that he adopt a position one way or the other: *What do you think about my proposal?*

Get All the Demands on the Table

When all the demands of other party are on the table, be sure you know the reasons behind all of his demands:

- Ask questions.
- Find out why these demands are made and what are the needs behind them.
- Keep your own viewpoints and arguments to yourself.
- Obtain more information before you start working with the demands and viewpoints concerning a future agreement.
- Pin down the other party: *If I manage to meet all your requirements in the course of this negotiation, will we then have a deal?*

A break might be appropriate so that you can review the other party's demands: where is the asymmetric value located? What can be removed? What can you accept? Test the boundaries. You will rarely have to meet all the other party's requirements.

Before making any concessions, try to establish how, through alternative solutions and a restructuring of your offer, you can create asymmetric value. If you can create asymmetric value, you are more likely to give the other party what he wants.

Ask Your Counterpart to Summarize

You have presented an alternative solution, and the other side expresses interest and asks for a short break so they can discuss your proposal. They leave the room, and you begin to wonder: what if they have missed the point of your proposal and don't really understand it? To avoid this risk, always ask the other party to summarize your proposal before they leave to consider it: *Before you leave, could you please give me a short summary of the new solution we have under consideration so that I can see if I've expressed myself clearly enough?*

Asking questions like these is dangerous: *Do we agree? Do you understand the essence of our proposal? Do you think this will work?* Avoid presenting alternatives in a way that calls for a yes or no response. If the other party says yes, do you really know what it is they're saying yes to? Instead you should ask, *How do you think this will work? Do we agree? Can we summarize where we are?*

Make it a hard-and-fast rule to summarize before finalizing a point in the discussion in order to move on to the next topic on the agenda. Have the other party do the summary, and listen carefully to his interpretation.

His choice of words can tell you a lot about his assessments, and how much ground you have covered. Many people spontaneously summarize when they are satisfied. The summary serves to assure them that they have managed to include all the important points of their perceived deal.

When You Should Summarize

Summarize the message of the other party: *What you're telling me is that you can't make a decision today.* In this way, you avoid misunderstandings, and you force the other party to send clear signals. You give the other party an opportunity to explain himself. You can also subtly provoke the other party in your summary in order to test boundaries by summarizing "incorrectly." You add things, you subtract things, and you modify.

Example: Testing the Boundaries through Summary

The supplier has said that, provided the buyer purchases his entire annual requirements at one time, he can reduce his price by 3 to 4 percent. After 20 minutes of negotiating, the buyer comes back and says: *Let me summarize—If we place an order for our entire annual requirements all at the same time, you'll reduce your price by 5 to 6 percent.* This comment is made to test the supplier's boundaries. If he has any room for negotiation left, or a poor memory, he may become uncertain of whether he really promised a price reduction of 5 to 6 percent.

When Your Opponent Refuses to Bargain

What do you do when the other party has no interest in bargaining with you? Aim for a compromise. If your opening price is $118,000, and the threshold of pain is $103,000, then the room for negotiation is $15,000. You define your objective as: to make the deal, but give away as little as possible of the $15,000. If you form your objective this way, you risk finding yourself in a zero-sum game.

Do not give away money in return for making the deal. If you reduce your price by $5,000, you reduce your profits by $5,000, and the other party's gains are increased by $5,000 more than the original deal.

Consider these steps:

- Get a counteroffer. You want $118,000. The buyer is offering $88,000.

- Split the difference, you will land on $103,000. This is the buyer's likely objective.
- Split the difference once again, and you will land on $110,500. This is the buyer's likely threshold of pain.
- Place your offer at $107,500 and see how the other party reacts.
- If you do not follow this model, but start with cautious one-sided concessions moving down to $115,000, there is a serious risk that you will have to go on making concessions until you reach the bottom.

Example: Action Explores Alternatives to Add Value

Jena receives an offer for ten computers with the software included. The software is to be installed and the computers are to be delivered to Jena's office. The asking price of the supplier, Action Computing, is $118,000 for this package. Jena has obtained an alternative offer for similar computers, and she demands that Action reduce its price to under $100,000. Action's threshold of pain is $103,000. Instead of attempting to accommodate Jena's demands through a unilateral price reduction to see if the difference can be split around $110,000, Action asks itself: *What services and products can we add to the package? If we offer Jena software training for five of her staff, what would that mean for us? We hold courses every week, and the standard price for these courses is $4,500 per person. However, usually one or two places are vacant in any one course. If we offer these surplus places to Jena, it will not cost us anything.*

Action tells Jena that if there are free places in a course, she can send two of her employees to the course each week. The offer is good for five people. These five participants will get a discount of 50 percent on the course fee. If Jena does not accept this offer, the number of people who can participate on these terms can be raised, or the discount can be increased. As an alternative, Action can offer to supply bigger screens or another type of hardware upgrade at discount prices.

If Jena does not feel that Action's offer provides any added value, she is not likely to be interested in increasing the package. If Jena would rather buy at the lowest possible price, Action will have to see if it can reduce the package. If Jena installs the programs and picks up the computers at Action's warehouse, the company can save $4,000 in operating costs. If Jena assumes these responsibilities, she will receive a reduction of $3,000. Action attempts to hold on to $1,000 to bolster its net profit on the transaction. If Jena does not bite, Action can suggest that if she pays cash in advance, instead of getting 30 days' credit, she will get a price reduction. The price reduction is somewhat lower than the interest gain achieved by Action. If this does not work, all that is left is haggling.

Take a Break

After your respective positions have been articulated, it often makes sense to call for a break so that the other party can consider your proposal in peace and quiet. The other party will consider your proposal with his own group or by himself. During the quiet time, the parties will talk among themselves and lower their original expectations.

Take aways

- Identify when you need to negotiate.
- Be able to identify the phase you are in.
- Be analytical and evaluate motives and alternatives constantly.
- Preparation is vital to a successful outcome.
- Memorize the six steps for a strong opening.
- Be careful of to much argumentation.
- Identify all the potential variables.

CHAPTER 6

Creating a Culture of Trust and Openness

An arrangement that is exclusively based on one party's victory over the other is barbaric and can never be humanized. It can only be maintained as long as the party with superior bargaining equity can force the opponent into submission, and sooner or later it will collapse. The alternative is cooperation and SMARTnership. However, the negotiator who does not understand the theoretical reasoning behind the ideas of SMARTnership and NegoEconomics is not motivated to be open and assume the risks inherent in an open negotiation climate. In order to cooperate, both parties must buy into the underlying theory of cooperation.

Negotiations carried out in a spirit of cooperation and trust are more efficient and achieve better results for the parties. Unnecessary conflict can be avoided by creating a positive negotiation climate built on a foundation of open, honest communication. This is best achieved if the negotiators make an investment in the interpersonal dynamic before getting down to business. When the personal chemistry clicks, delegates often make decisions based on their feelings rather than logic and rationality. Their perception of the situation becomes so positive that their decision-making may become skewed in favor of the opponent's solutions.

Build Rapport with Your Counterpart:
First, Talk about the Weather or Sports

Take an interest in the other party. Tell her about yourself and ask questions about who she is. Discuss the news headlines or sports.

Share a meal, or have a drink and enjoy each other's company. In some countries, no one would think of beginning serious negotiations without sharing a meal first, or a least a drink. Though these tactics may sound simple, many people find this approach incredibly difficult. Others feel it is a total waste of time.

According to ancient Chinese wisdom, negotiations should never be pursued on an empty stomach. Only when good food and drink have been served should negotiations begin. This rule is not based on etiquette; rather, it is based on hard science. When people eat and drink together, the brain produces a drug called oxytocin, which promotes likeability and trust. The chances of creating a good relationship are improved when dining! Within the first 15 minutes of interplay with a counterpart, I can predict with reasonable precision whether a negotiation will be successful or not.

How Long Should You Talk about the Weather?

When negotiators meet, they often have limited information about each other. The negotiator rarely has answers to these questions:

- How does my counterpart look at things?
- How interested is he or she in the outcome?
- What decisions have been made previously?
- What priorities have been set?
- What does he or she want to achieve?
- Does he or she have an alternative?

If the negotiators do not spend time building rapport, then the first few minutes of the negotiation often are characterized by combat over who gets the floor and who takes the initiative. This combat will likely lead to early deadlock. Instead of a constructive dialogue, the parties will be speaking at cross-purposes and find themselves in destructive verbal combat.

Your emotions and the mood you are in will affect your ability to communicate and develop rapport. In order to be a successful negotiator, it is essential to keep your cool. In some cases, the negotiation situation may even require you to hide your feelings altogether.

When parties are very anxious and expectations are high, the exchange of information is reduced. You are inclined to push forward your own proposals, and not listen to the other party. Only when the other party has been able to say what is on his mind, and understands that you are listening, will he listen to you. You do not have to be the first to present a solution.

When you are negotiating with delegates whom you know well, the deal can be made in a few minutes. In other circumstances, it may take weeks. In some cultures, attempts to skip the opening phase and quickly get into hard-core bargaining can constitute a serious breach of etiquette. Breaches of protocol can render further negotiations impossible.

People who come from a technical background and those who do not regularly deal with new contacts in their day-to-day work environment sometimes have difficulty establishing rapport with strangers. This reluctance can cause problems, especially in international negotiations, where socializing between the parties is far more common than in North America. Irrespective of nationality, we tend to do business with people whom we know and like. Personal relations can mean more to the transaction than technical matters, presentation style, or financial terms.

Example: The Importance of Good Personal Relations

One of the big commercial banks investigated why some loans were granted and others were refused. The banker responsible was asked the following:

Which factor was the most important in your decision whether or not to comply with a request for a loan?

A: The borrower presented good collateral.
B: The borrower presented a financial calculation proving that he could service the loan.
C: The borrower is trustworthy.

Most respondents answered C. A follow-up question was then asked: *Why did you chose C?*

The response: *I need to see that I can trust the borrower as a person. You can always reach an agreement on the technical details, such as collateral and servicing of the loan.*

Two-way Communication

One-way communication leads to misunderstandings and protracted negotiation with poor results. The hallmark of good communication is that it is two-way. Effective negotiators listen to each other, ask questions, answer questions, make use of these answers, and discuss alternatives. The parties avoid trouble by steering clear of combat and instead consider the demands and requirements that need to be met.

Delegates should attempt to put themselves in the shoes of the other party.

If communication does not work satisfactorily from the beginning, the parties will not be able to find common ground or opportunities for cooperation. It will be difficult to assess the intentions of the other party. You will be inclined to hold back information or become entrenched in your own positions. The other party will show no interest in listening and no willingness to bargain. The negotiation will become deadlocked, and any possibility of building NegoEconomic value will vaporize, not because the parties do not share the same interests, but because they are speaking at cross-purposes.

Communication does not work well when parties are in conflict. In that case, both parties become defensive, and neither is perceived as credible. The possibilities of an open exchange are minimized. Both parties try to get the other to assume the responsibility for the conflict. Frustration mounts, and misunderstanding between the parties grows. Find the common ground, if you are interested in resolving the conflict and continuing to cooperate. If both parties are willing to work together, you can find solutions to the problems, and you will be able to let go of the conflict and move on. If you focus on identifying the guilty party, however, you will not be able to move ahead.

Both parties must exchange credible information for the negotiation to be effective. Whether the information you offer is credible or not will be determined by your counterpart. A statement like: *It does not seem as if he believes me. That is his fault,* shows that the message has not been correctly interpreted. The recipient should not be blamed for the miscommunication. The transmitter is responsible for accurately sending his message to the opponent.

Constructive Dialogue

Two-way communication means that, instead of listening passively, you involve yourself by asking questions and summarizing what you hear. Be sure that your understanding agrees with the message that the transmitter intended to send. Never hesitate to ask a question when you do not understand, are uncertain, want to have more details, or want to test alternative solutions.

Openness should not be total. A negotiator who puts all her cards on the table is naive and exposes herself to the risk of being taken advantage of. When preparing to negotiate, decide in advance what information is required to expand the room for negotiation and what does not contribute to the process of identifying the potential asymmetric value.

Listen Actively

To listen actively, you must be well prepared; if not, you will be distracted, making mental checklists while the other party is talking. If you take an active role in what the other party is saying, you tune out competing signals. Do not listen only with your ears. Establish eye contact and concentrate on the other party. Ask questions to demonstrate your interest, to get more information on the table, and to clarify.

According to University of Missouri faculty members Dick Lee and Delmar Hatesohl, research suggests that we remember between 25 percent and 50 percent of what we hear. "Numerous tests confirm that we are inefficient listeners. Studies have shown that immediately after listening to a 10-minute oral presentation, the average listener has heard, understood and retained 50% of what was said. Within 48 hours, that drops off another 50% to a final level of 25% efficiency. In other words, we often comprehend and retain only one fourth of what we hear."[1]

In an article titled, "Secrets of Successful Business Negotiation," former FBI hostage negotiator Chris Voss explains that active listening is the first step to getting what you want. "I thought maybe (business negotiating) would be a more refined and gentlemanly endeavor (than hostage negotiating)...but I realized that it was all the same thing. It was just that the stakes were different."[2]

A separate study by Special Agent Gary Noesner and Dr. Mike Webster of the FBI concluded, "Despite the popular notion that listening is a passive behavior, abundant clinical evidence and research suggest that active listening is an effective way to induce behavioral change in others."[3]

Do not overestimate your ability to remember factual details after the negotiation, such as what was said, by whom, and when it was said. You should record your perceptions of the other party's reaction to your signals, or your own emotional responses to the other party's signals. Always use a pen and paper when you listen.

Active listening and notation of the interpersonal dynamic will mean that your conscious sensing and filtration of the other party's signals will be intensified. You will have much better control over the signals that are leaked and those stored in your long-term memory. You will not be distracted by competing signals, and your learning curve will improve.

How to Send a Negative Message

It is important to speak plainly and be open. Your message can easily be misunderstood. If your message is negative, there is a danger that your opponent will perceive you as threatening, or as someone who is difficult to negotiate with. A natural reaction, then, will be an attempt at self-protection. Your opponent will not want to listen to you, and, subconsciously, he will respond by preparing for combat. It would be better first to give a thorough background description of the message you wish to transmit. Make sure that you both have the same perception of reality before you transmit your negative message.

Procurement officers will sometimes open the meeting by saying to the counterpart: *You are not competitive. Your price is far above the alternative proposals we have received.* A very negative opening. **The better approach would be for the procurement officer to say:** *We have made a detailed analysis of the market, comparing apples and apples, and we have concluded that your total proposal is less competitive than the market average.*

State What You Want

If you do not have a clear purpose for your communication, there is a serious risk that you will say anything that springs to mind. What do you need to say to accomplish your objective? If you have a structure to your presentation and your ideas are presented logically, it will be easier for the other party to follow your thought process and continue to pay attention. The other party can only assimilate three or four facts at a time. Express yourself in simple terms and be concise. Too much information or too many details can sometimes do more harm than good.

Ask yourself what the other party truly wants to know. The other party is most receptive to new information that jives with his needs and solves his problems. Put yourself in the other party's position. What questions might he have?

Inexperienced negotiators will sometimes not speak plainly because they do not know what they want. They are afraid to be met with rejection, so they say something shallow or nothing at all. Then the more experienced negotiator must guess what the novice wants to accomplish.

Instead of saying what they want, some delegates say what they do not want. This takes the dynamic into the realm of guessing games. Do not assume that the other party can guess your needs, or that he intuitively knows what it is you are looking for. It is up to you and no one else to make sure your opponent understand your needs and wishes.

What are the results you wish to achieve? Do you want to influence the other party and change his attitudes or get him to reframe what he tells you he needs? Do you want to provide information and background information? Do you want to create awareness of an important issue? Do you want information from the other party? Your primary purpose is to capture the attention of the other party. You have no more than 20 or 30 seconds before her interest declines, and she returns to her own thoughts.

Support Your Message with Visuals

If you transmit using several modalities simultaneously, your listener will be more engaged and attentive to your content. People remember visual messages better than verbal content. An extensive and complex message will be better received if words and images are combined. If there is no blackboard or whiteboard, you can always use paper and pen. Virtually everything can be expressed and summarized in images: columns of figures, pie charts, timetables, graphics, and so on. You can use stories, examples, and references to create an image that the other party can see. By appealing to their sense of sight, you activate information and experiences stored deep in their long-term memory. By using pictures, you will facilitate understanding and illustrate connections.

If you demonstrate your message, you activate several senses in the other party. A product can be demonstrated by having the other party try it out or experience it. But how do you demonstrate an idea?

Link your message to well-known situations that people can easily relate to. Describe the concept using an example that is simple and down-to-earth. When people listen to you, they will be able to see the chain of events. When you have presented the idea and your listener understand the principles, ask a question like: *What happens if you switch to . . . ?* This forces people to apply your ideas and think about what it means to them. You receive feedback as to whether they have understood the message, and get a reaction concerning their assessment of it. You will know based on these factors whether the message was received as you intended it. This creates "aha" moments, reduces uncertainty, and builds trust.

Be Clear and Direct, Then Confirm

A person's being very direct when communicating can seem threatening to some people. It may provoke conflict. Avoid saying anything that the other party might perceive as accusatory. Avoid creating situations in which the other party must defend himself. Describe the situation as you see it. Do not say: *You're wrong, you know this won't work.* Instead say: *I don't understand what you are saying. Could you show me how this would work?*

Example: Vagueness Leads to Disaster

The following negotiation takes place in the beginning of the year between Kim, the manager, and Frederick, an employee of the company. For the last 20 years, the company has closed for the month of July. Frederick comes into Kim's office and asks:

> *Frederick:* How do you feel about my taking some time off in September this year?
> *Kim:* I really don't know what to say to that. We usually close the whole place in July.
> *Frederick:* I know, that's why I wanted to check with you. By the way, have you heard whether we've received the order from Bulgaria yet?

Quickly, the conversation is directed toward other subjects. In mid-August, Frederick and Kim meet in the corridor, and the conversation continues:

> *Frederick:* I will not be seeing you for quite some time, so—take care.
> *Kim:* Really, what are you doing?
> *Frederick:* I'm going to Greece.
> *Kim:* To Greece? Have we got any business going there?
> *Frederick:* No, I'm going on vacation for three weeks.
> *Kim:* For three weeks, what do you mean? Here in September, when we are so busy? Why didn't you go in July? You can't leave now!
> *Frederick:* We talked about it early in the year, and you said it was okay!
> *Kim:* I never approved that. You can't just leave the company in the lurch and run out on us.
> *Frederick:* You can't simply break our agreement!
> *Kim:* We haven't made any agreement.

The conflict develops. Both parties are equally uncomprehending and astonished. Both feel they are in the right, and are outraged. Emotions enter the picture, rational thinking is blocked, and it becomes difficult for them to handle the conflict. Who is right and who is wrong? They both must bear an equal share of the responsibility. What happened?

Frederick chose a vague form of wording because he was afraid of being turned down. He should have introduced the topic by saying: *How do you feel about my taking some time off for a vacation in September?* Frederick lacks the courage to explain that the duration of his vacation is in fact three weeks. Kim hears him, but makes an unclear reply. He doesn't want to be negative and chooses to avoid a possible conflict. Kim replies: *I really don't know what to say.* That answer is certainly blowing in the wind. What does it mean?

Here Frederick should have stopped to ask: *What does that mean in plain words? Is it a yes or a no to my taking a bit of vacation in September?* Always make sure you get an answer you can understand. Immediately thereafter, summarize to check that you have not been speaking at cross-purposes: *Then we agree that I will ___.*

Kim should not have allowed Frederick to change the subject to the order from Bulgaria. He should have stopped to summarize:

Kim: This vacation question, did we reach an agreement about that?
Frederick: Yes.
Kim: Really, so what did we agree on?

Kim forces Frederick to summarize, but since there is no agreement, the parties discover that they have misunderstood each other. Instead of avoiding this awkward moment, provoking a more serious conflict, they can at an early stage uncover their respective positions. By using less emotion and more rationality, they can find a solution acceptable to both.

Summarizing

Summarizing, or asking the other party to summarize, is a simple tactic to avoid misunderstandings and uncertainty. It should be used:

- At the conclusion of the negotiation
- Before a break
- After a lengthy discussion
- When the negotiations are resumed after a long interruption

Put Yourself in the Other Party's Shoes

Negotiators rarely put themselves in the other party's shoes. Your own needs, problems, and interests are at the center of your attention. If you want to be successful, the solution you work toward will have to take into account the interests of the other party. If you are unable or unwilling to see things from the point of view of the other party, you may find yourself in an unfortunate situation in the long run.

If you try to dictate conditions on the basis of your perspective, you risk backing the other party into a corner and forcing her into an agreement that is not workable. In that case, the benefits to you may be short-lived. As soon as chance allows or conditions change to the advantage of the other party, she will most likely abandon the agreement or, even worse, try to retaliate. At a minimum, she will not live up to her commitments, which may leave you with very serious difficulties. Failing to see the negotiation from the perspective of the other party exposes you to the risk of giving too much away or of missing signals.

Example: Flow of Information and Perspective Enhance the Asymmetric Value

A factory owner in Pittsburgh is about to sell his company because he wants to stop working and enjoy his retirement. He works with the management and the bank, and the value of the company is determined. They agreed that a satisfactory bid would lie between $500,000 and $1 million. He is pleased when the three bids received are all above $1 million.

Allen bid $1.4 million, Bailey bid $1.6 million, and Cohen bid $2.1 million. The factory owner is ready to accept Cohen's bid. It is so much higher than the other two bids that any further negotiation with Allen and Bailey seemed unnecessary. Many negotiators would react in the same way as the factory owner, but after thinking it over, he does not accept Cohen's offer. He realizes that he does not know enough about why Allen, Bailey, and Cohen wanted to purchase his company. What are the needs they want to meet by purchasing the factory? If he does not know what the buyers need, he will not know what the business is worth to them. How, then, can he determine which bid is reasonable and negotiable?

Allen, Bailey, and Cohen are brought together, not to discuss the terms and conditions in connection with the transaction, but in order to explain how they intend to run the factory in the future. Allen is interested in the premises and machinery, intending to run a type of business that is completely different from the existing one. He has a relatively tight budget that he must stick to, and under no circumstances can he raise his bid of $1.4 million. Bailey is interested in the industrial property for investment purposes. He intends to sell the machinery and rent the premises. Cohen is interested in the production run by the factory owner, his products, and well-established brand name. The buyers do not need to compete, and this explains the disparity among the amounts of the bids. Cooperation is possible.

The deal is managed in the following manner: Cohen buys the existing products, the sales rights in the production, and decides to manufacture abroad. Cohen does not have to bother with the effort of selling the rest of the enterprise. Bailey buys the property and rents it to Allen, who buys the machinery needed for his new business.

The owner receives over $3 million for his factory and feels like a winner. In the worst-case scenario he would have sold his factory for half a million dollars, the value the bank had arrived at in the course of its assessment. Allen, Bailey, and Cohen also feel like winners. They have met their requirements, but at a lower cost than originally envisioned. This turned out to be a cooperative negotiation in which it was possible to create considerable added value.

Rapport Can Be Facilitated by a Third Party

The participation of a third party can facilitate communication and open the way for good rapport. The most important task of this person is to listen and to determine whether the parties have been speaking at cross-purposes. She should point out the common denominators, clear up misunderstandings, and, through informal contacts with both sides, point out opportunities for exploration of mutual gains. She should suggest solutions that could lead to further opportunities.

An expert, a lawyer, or an accountant can step into a role—a tough one, a nice one, or an impartial one—and try to pave the way, mediate, or finalize the bargain. An external group who stands to be impacted by the outcome of the negotiation can also play a role in finding creative solutions. A third party can, more or less neutrally, attempt to mediate between the parties. Bargaining continues to be possible, and the decisions can be based on sound commercial interests.

The mediating role can be played by someone whom both parties have agreed upon, or by someone representing one of the parties. The mediator can persuade both parties to assess the situation more realistically, allowing each one to understand the other better.

Use Informal Contacts

Use informal contacts to move the negotiations forward, to obtain and provide information, to make threats, to anchor offers, and to avoid deadlock. Informal contacts deliver results, because the parties tend to be more open and understanding toward each other than is the case in formal negotiations. The problem of dual loyalty disappears. There are no witnesses, and the external pressure on the negotiation is absent. If you discuss principles rather than opening up to specific alternatives, the general openness will increase. You may discover that, while fundamentally you are in agreement about important principles, the other party has in fact misunderstood some key concepts.

Informal preliminary contacts can improve mutual understanding prior to the negotiation. The parties can meet on a casual basis and are not bound by the discussion or monitored by the rest of their team.

Backdoor Selling

Contact with the people who do not directly participate in the negotiations may be informative. The end user, the maintenance staff, administrators, and so forth have a lot of knowledge about how different products and systems work and about their shortcomings and strong points. Sometimes they have very strong wishes to see a product blacklisted. Warehousing and maintenance staff and people in production are well informed and have the potential to leak information. They are not tactical negotiators, and are open and honest.

Example: A Tour of the Plant

In connection with a tour of the supplier's manufacturing plant, a potential buyer asks the factory workers and supervisors: *Do you have a lot of overtime?* They respond: *We get no overtime at all.* From this information, the buyer infers that no more than 70 percent of the production capacity of the plant is being utilized.

Next, the buyer visits the service technicians: *How did things go with the new system you installed in the spring?* They tell him: *Oh, the installation was a mess. There was a lot of work involved and too much downtime. Companies that buy this system ought to be given more training. The workers need more instruction in how to handle the machines. Plus, the manual is a problem, because it is has not been translated into Spanish.*

The buyer is an experienced negotiator and has learned how to obtain a lot of information, which he uses to create alternative solutions or expand the range of variables that can enhance the NegoEconomic value in the deal.

However, the supplier's technician may be used as a pawn. One technician pulls the other to the side and says, *Your competitors have promised us that we'll be sent to a special training course in the UK.*

The perks are directed to the factory workers who will be using the product. The workers are provided with all sorts of service assistance, and the buyer feels that the supplier will solve his problems. User seminars and factory visits, coffee and doughnuts, or holiday gifts all contribute to the strengthening of ties between the supplier and the end user of the product.

Open Calculations

Showing how you arrived at your calculations might foster a spirit of cooperation. If you are sure that the intentions of the other party are honorable, you need not fear revealing the mathematical assumptions behind your offer, or why you find an approach unworkable. There may be situations in which you choose to show the other party your calculations in order to be able to argue for a higher price or to facilitate future negotiations. However, always keep in mind that the price you are offering is just a price, not your cost, and that nothing is set in stone until a formal agreement has been reached.

When the buyer demands to know the supplier's calculations, his reasoning may be:

- He wants to know what he is paying for.
- He wants more information about the asymmetric value that can be generated and about how it can be distributed.
- He wants to line up arguments prior to the upcoming negotiation.
- He wants to know how future prices will be affected by changes in the cost situation and other variables.
- He wants to see whether you have a sound calculation, and that you are not earning too much or too little.
- He wants to break the contract into small pieces that can be bid separately to minimize his costs.

Use Alternatives to Create a Competitive Environment

The party who has no alternative buyers, suppliers, or solutions is at the mercy of the opposite party. Dependence constitutes a major handicap. Alternatives provide equilibrium and a better basis for decisions, making it easier to determine what is threatening and what is useful.

Alternatives generate competition, and are probably the best tactic a buyer can employ to put pressure on the suppliers. Generally, the more offers/alternatives you have, the wider the gap between the highest and the lowest offer/bid. The buyer who only obtains offers from two or three suppliers runs the risk of having to pay considerably more than the buyer who obtains offers from five or six suppliers. The risk of paying too much is especially high if you turn to the same group of suppliers every time.

Even when you know in advance from whom you plan to buy, you should still make sure you have alternatives. Make it clear to the supplier that purchases are made in competition. He can never know for sure what his competitors are offering and at what prices and conditions. Competing offers can provide you with new impulses for alternative solutions that strengthen your position and generate asymmetric value. You may receive offers that will make you reconsider your choice of supplier. Therefore, you should keep the negotiation with alternative suppliers running until the very day the agreement is signed.

Use an Alternative as a Trial Balloon

If you wish to gain insight into the other party's evaluation of different options, their limitations, and their potential, you can introduce alternatives at the negotiating table—a trial balloon. A trial balloon diverts the attention of the other party. He forms an opinion about the suggestion, and subsequently accepts or rejects it. He may then provide you with information about his assessments, knowledge, resources, options, and restraints.

For instance, if technical discussions are taking place with the technicians of the other party, you might leak information through your own staff or "accidentally" leave documents behind. The negotiators on the other side will receive this information, and you can read and utilize their reaction. This tactic is typical in politics. A minister sends up a trial balloon to get the reaction to a political move he is planning. Newspaper editors and other politicians make statements about it, and the minister is able to take the political temperature of the country.

If you are the receiver of a trial balloon, remember that it is unwise to react immediately to everything that is being said. Use questions to investigate: *How do you see that alternative playing out?* Find out whether the alternative is realistic and what intentions the party who sent up the trial balloon had in mind. Try to determine how likely it is that the trial balloon could actually come to fruition.

Don't Allow the Negotiations to Become Deadlocked

Sometimes a negotiation grinds to a halt or ends in a stalemate, and the process yields no result. Instead of finding new cooperative solutions, the parties dwell on old arguments and the negotiations deteriorate into verbal combat. The arguments are along these lines:

- *It's too expensive.*
- *We can't manage it in such a short time.*
- *You must give us better guarantees.*

When a negotiation is deadlocked you have the following options:

1. **Feed more and new information into the negotiations.** Verify and develop your demands. If your argument is to be perceived as credible, it must be verifiable. You must have the courage to specify what you mean by *better guarantees* and then support your demand so it can be verified. By feeding new information into the negotiations, you can avoid deadlock. Present and test alternative solutions.

2. **Ash for more information.** Do not view all requests for more information as threats. If you manage to get all the requirements on the table at one time stated in a way that contemplates the other party's needs and issues, this is likely to open up new perspectives on problem solving.

3. **Realize that it is not possible to cooperate with everyone.** Some people will interpret your openness as weakness and be tempted to adopt very aggressive behavior, trying to put you at a disadvantage. In this case, you have the choice of either forgoing to negotiate with this party or playing the zero-sum game.

4. **Convince the other party to accept your demand by offering alternatives that are realistic and will yield acceptable solutions.**

5. **Do not give in to break the deadlock; you may risk sending the wrong signals.** Make it plain that you are only giving in concerning a point to allow the negotiation to proceed. Never concede more than the other party demands.

6. **Consider interrupting the negotiation.** If you have equally good alternatives, and if you are short on time, you might consider interrupting the negotiation.

7. **Stall.** Give both sides a chance to sleep on it. However, keep in mind that stalling may aggravate the problems. It may also put the parties under time pressure, creating difficulties in maintaining cooperation.

Example: Caving In Too Soon

Chang-Su, the supplier, can guarantee the buyer 97 percent accessibility on a service agreement. Antonia, the buyer, says that she must have a minimum of 99 percent accessibility. Chang-Su wants to demonstrate the good will of his company. What would he get in return for giving in? What advantages could be offered instead of 99 percent? Antonia suggests a two-month earlier delivery. Chang-Su gives in without inquiring as to the advantage of the earlier delivery, thinking he has no associated costs. He made a unilateral concession ceasing negotiations.

When bargaining has become deadlocked, one party will have to give way on an issue in order to break the stalemate and move the negotiation forward. In order to move forward, the negotiators must either reopen the discussion of the available options or become more specific in their demands.

Example: Moving Past Deadlock

Instead of saying, *$10/lb. is too expensive,* Trevor, the buyer, can make a counteroffer: *We will not pay more than $8.75/lb. pound.* Inez, the supplier, now has a baseline from which she can assess her options.

Suppose that Trevor's offer for $8.75/lb. is $1.25 below the price Inez planned to suggest. The opening price of $10.00/lb. was calculated on the basis of a quantity of ten thousand pounds. Inez's absolute bottom line is $9.00/lb. for the quality required; otherwise, she will not make a profit. Three options are available to her.

Option A: Inez Makes a Unilateral Concession

Inez reduces her price without asking for anything in return, aiming for a compromise. The transaction becomes reminiscent of a Turkish bazaar.

> *Inez:* We can go down to $9.75/lb.
> *Trevor:* That's not enough; you can do better than that.
> *Inez:* If I get the order today, I can go down another 25 cents.
> *Trevor:* My demand is $8.75/lb., and you're offering $9.50/lb., that means that the difference is 75 cents. If we split the difference, we end up at $9.10/lb. That's the best I can do.
> *Inez:* OK, we have a deal!

In the course of a few minutes, the supplier has given away $9,000 without first having looked for other solutions. The negotiation turns into a zero-sum game. Trevor plucks $9,000 off the back of the supplier without having to give anything in return. Inez accepts any solution that is within her negotiation limit.

As a result of this sloppy technique, revenue is lost for no good reason. Inez is not setting up a genuine compromise. She unilaterally lowers her price by $9,000. A genuine compromise would require both parties to give up something. In a situation like this, the counterbid is often designed to get the other party to make concessions.

Option B: Inez Offers a Larger Quantity

Inez is searching for the added value. A larger quantity increases her margin, and she is willing to let Trevor have a share of this.

Inez: If you were to take a larger quantity, we might have another look at the price.
Trevor: How big a reduction do you think you might let me have?
Inez: Can we increase the order to fifteen thousand pounds?
Trevor: I shall look into that.
Inez: While you do, I'll take a further look at my calculation.

Neither of the parties is making a concession, but they agree in principle that a larger quantity may lead to a lower price. If the supplier had been incautious, the following scenario might have ensued:

Inez: We can go down to $9.00/lb., if you take fifteen thousand pounds.
Trevor: I've taken note of your price of $9.00/lb. We shall come back to the quantity. I want you to absorb the cost of delivery. We will not pay the $150.00/ton. Your competitors always include the cost of delivery in their pricing.
Inez: Then you'll take fifteen thousand pounds?
Trevor: I shall take a look at the quantity and come back to you, but what do you have to say about the freight charges?
Inez: Perhaps we can deliver everything at one time.
Trevor: We are flexible as far as the delivery date is concerned. We want it before the end of the month. You'll have ample time to plan a single delivery so that we can exclude freight. And we can accept the price of $9.00/lb. I will get back to you this afternoon to let you know how much we require.
Inez: OK, I will wait for your call.

Inez, in this scenario, is too quick to grant concessions. The result of her opening signals is that she is the only one to make any concessions. She is in danger of losing all of the NegoEconomic value she has created. All Trevor needs to do is to stand tough and refuse to grant the counter concession required of him. Inez must learn to demand something in return before she signals what she is ready to concede. Here, the important word **provided** enters the picture.

*Inez: **Provided** you take fifteen thousand pounds, I'll see if I can do something about the price.*

She should wait for Trevor's reply. If he does not agree to the increased quantity, then she should postpone her concession. Inez should demand another concession: *Would you be willing to accept packages of 500 pounds rather than 50 pounds?* In this way, she sends a signal indicating that give and take is a precondition for changing the offer.

Option C: Inez Looks for Other Counter-benefits.

Inez might say:

- *Provided we are given the responsibility for supplying your total requirements, we can.*
- *Against cash payment, we can always do that.*
- *Provided you can accept the quality specified, we can.*
- *What can you do to make it possible for us to___?*

Breaking the Stalemate

If the negotiation grinds to a halt, it may be due to the fact that both parties have become locked into their positions and are issuing demands rather than asking questions. Do not fall into the trap of viewing debate as a threat rather than an opportunity. You can take control by adding new data that further specifies your needs and requirements. Or, in contrast, you can ask the other party to provide specifics and give you more details on her needs and requirements. Use this technique to get past the deadlock and move the negotiation forward. Your argument will have to be further developed before constructive negotiation will again become possible.

Look behind the arguments the other party is making in an effort to gain insight into her needs. Your objective is to accommodate her needs, if possible. If you encourage her to explain her arguments and requirements, you may find that the need lying behind the demand differs from what you originally thought. If she insists: *Reduce your price*, this does not necessarily mean that her need is a price reduction. Instead her need might be:

1. **To receive affirmation of her ability to perform.** In this case, your opponent wants to showcase her skills. Let her propose her own solution, but do not reduce the price without having obtained something in return.

2. **To have an offer within her quarterly budgetary limit.** Offer her an easy solution: propose to subdivide the invoice into several budgetary periods.
3. **To make your quotation appear to be the lowest one.** According to her own internal rules, she may be under an obligation to choose the lowest offer, but she prefers having you as the supplier. She can go along with the price you are asking, but she has to play within her boundaries. If this is the case, your costs can be redistributed on a service agreement, or as spare parts, or as some other variable that places it outside the quote for the principle part of the order.
4. **To test the supplier.** She doesn't know whether your offer is in fact your best one, and she wants to test your limits in order to reach her decision.
5. **To gain time.** Find out why she wants to drag things out without applying unnecessary pressure. Anticipate her next step by understanding why she feels that she needs more time.
6. **To convince you that you are making too much on the deal.** Ask her to relate the price to the benefit she will reap from your offer. Forcing her to consider the benefits can be useful in getting your opponent to see your side of the negotiation as fair.

As long as your objections are factual, you have a good chance of steering the negotiation into a safe harbor.

> ***When the argument is:*** We thought we'd get more for our money.
> ***Do reply:*** What is it that you're missing?
> ***Don't reply:*** This is our standard offer. Anything extra will involve additional fees.

When the arguments put forth are obvious or trivial, they rarely form a good basis for negotiation. If you become defensive and try to justify your price, you will be speaking at cross-purposes. You will not perceive the buyer's objections as credible, and you will be more inclined to view them as a pretext to cause you to reduce your price.

> ***When the argument is:*** The operating costs for your plant are too high.
> ***Do reply:*** What did you expect them to be? How had you arrived at that figure?
> ***Don't reply:*** Our documented productivity ratio is as high as 92 percent. We are more efficient than any of our competitors.

What does the customer mean by saying that the operating costs are too high? Is he saying that the energy consumption is too high? Is he suggesting the aggregated costs for energy, supervision, and maintenance are excessive? When you ask how he reached his calculation, you will most likely discover the true reason behind his argument. You may find that to him operating costs mean something different from what they mean to you. He might have included maintenance, which you did not, and the amount he arrived at will be too high. If you obtain more information, it will provide you with new opportunities.

A possible opportunity would be to offer him a service contract at a reduced cost, sparing him the trouble of maintenance. You put forward additional value that will benefit both parties.

If your offer is too expensive, look for solutions that will reduce the costs of the other party and risks that will increase his profits. Give him more value for his money, but don't reduce the price. Look for solutions that will mean the costs are lower than the benefit the customer will reap from the services you are offering. By doing so, you will appease the customer and create asymmetric value.

Information Flow Imbalance

Some negotiations become deadlocked because there is an imbalance in the information flow. When only one party is receiving information, and one party giving information, the party giving information will, after a while, feel that something is wrong. After a time, the negotiation will become deadlocked, and eventually the parties will consider abandoning the process. The grounds given will often be: *We're not getting anywhere; they are simply pumping us for information without answering our questions in return.* The information giver feels manipulated and used. The fact that the other side might need the answers to a number of questions in order to be able to find good solutions is something he has not considered. The one-sidedness of the information flow is perceived as threatening.

The negotiators can avoid situations like this if, from the outset, they define the Rules of the Game, use an agenda, and agree to a Code of Conduct. By employing this method, each party will see how the imbalance in the information flow fits into a broader context, and the delegate will be better able to accept the imbalance because he understands the context.

Don't Let Your Counterpart Define Your Range of Options

Avoid limiting yourself to the alternatives presented by the other party. Your counterpart should not be allowed to set the framework for your negotiation. Gather additional information by asking questions, and present your own alternatives on which the other party can take a position.

The buyer tells the supplier: *If we are going to make this deal, you must reduce your price by somewhere between 3.5 and 5 percent; otherwise, I can't do business with you.*

If the buyer's range is below the supplier's negotiation limit, most suppliers will agree to a reduction of 3.5 percent. The buyer acquiesces by saying: *I have the authority to accept this offer.* The concession is unilateral, and the only result that has been achieved is that the price has been lowered for the balance of the bargaining.

Example: Quoting Range Pricing Verbally to Test Intentions

A consultant is preparing an offer for a major project. He and the client are in agreement about the project specifications, but he finds it difficult to determine how much the client is willing to pay. Pricing will be decided by the existing competition, by whether or not the client can execute the project himself, whether or not similar projects already exist, and so on. Instead of quoting a fixed price, the consultant quotes a range of pricing. He says he wants $275,000 to $365,000 in professional fees. The prices are quoted by word of mouth so that he can read the spontaneous reaction of the client. Possible reactions might be:

- *We don't have more than $300,000 in our budget for this. Will it be possible for you to stay below that limit?* The consultant can say yes or no depending on whether the client will execute part of the work himself. He tries to find out whether the project can be increased, or whether some of the costs can be invoiced to another account, or whether part of the work can be invoiced during the next budgetary year.
- If the client answers: *We don't have more than $250,000 in the budget,* the same method is employed.
- If the client replies: *We need a firm price,* the consultant can explain why it is difficult to quote a fixed fee. He can only do so if he carries out a feasibility study that will cost $15,000. It is much easier for the client to make a $15,000 decision than a $365,000 one. The feasibility study provides the consultant with a good opportunity to assess what it is possible for the client to pay.
- If the client replies: *That's too much. None of your competitors have asked for more than $250,000,* the consultant can present a proposal for $250,000 that differs from the original proposal.

He should demonstrate what the advantages are compared to the competitors' proposals. Perhaps he can make a proposal based on a technical level that is less advanced, in order to be able to reduce his price. When the assignment is well under way, he can suggest the necessary complements to the study, allowing him to increase the fee accordingly.

Using Questions as a Negotiation Technique

The best way to gain a proper understanding of the other side is by asking questions. Many negotiators have a poorly developed questioning technique. In the course of half an hour's negotiation, they ask only three or four questions, many of which, they answer themselves: *What do you do when you're short of raw materials? Stop production, I assume.* They don't allow the other party to provide a complete answer. They interrupt, and immediately counter his assertions to defend their own intentions.

Questions allow for give and take, and open up the opportunities for exchange with the other side. The negotiators gain an insight into each other's situations, and they can engage in solving problems together. When preparing to negotiate, draft questions in the same way you draft arguments. You can use questions for different purposes:

To obtain information: How many? Who's responsible for this? When will production start? Note that all these questions begin with an interrogatory word: who, what, where, why, when, and how. Avoid questions that can be answered by a yes or no, for instance, *Do you have long delivery times?* The answer you get will often be of no value, perhaps even dangerous. It is ambiguous. What is a long delivery time? To the buyer it may be anything above two to three weeks, but for the supplier a long delivery time might mean two to three months.

To provide information or draw attention to information: *Are you aware that costs have risen by 24 percent? Do you know what the result of this was?*

In order to reach a decision: *What does that mean in plain language? Yes or no?*

Follow these rules when asking questions:

- Avoid asking a question that will provoke the other party if you don't want unnecessary tension.
- Write down all the important questions when you prepare. If you don't, you will forget them.

- Ask constructive questions, instead of questions that will make the other party lose face or lose his credibility vis-a-vis other parties.
- Limit the number of questions you ask. A negotiation is not the same as an interrogation of a witness, but is instead a give-and-take situation when it comes to information.
- Questions must be asked at the appropriate times. Plan to ask important questions at a time that suits both parties equally.
- Be disciplined. Refrain from asking questions that will spoil your colleagues' plans and tactics.
- In order to get the other party going and to soften him up, it may sometimes be a good idea to ask questions to which you already know the answer.
- Pay attention to the answer you are given. Repeat the question if the answer doesn't provide you with the information you are looking for. Don't be afraid to say: *Sorry, but I don't understand what you mean.*
- Be quiet when you or one of your colleagues has asked a question. The answer should come from the other party, not from you.
- Avoid leading questions of the following type: *I take it you know what you're going to do since you've sold the company?*
- If you want to know what the other party is planning, it's better to ask: *What are you going to do now that the company has been sold?*
- Often it's easier to obtain the information before sitting down at the negotiating table. Informal contacts may provide more information.

Hypothetical Questions

Hypothetical questions can be very useful when you're looking for an opening:

- *What happens if we double the order?*
- *What can you give us if we commit ourselves to buying all of our annual requirements?*
- *What will you offer us in return for not demanding a warranty?*

Be cautious in answering hypothetical questions. Find out what the other party is truly looking for. Do not state the price for double the quantity until you know whether this is a realistic alternative for the other party. You might find yourself in a situation where your answers are interpreted as concessions. The other party may reply: *I've taken note of this new, low price. I'll revert to the matter of the quantity we're going to take.*

This is a tactic whereby, in the form of questions, you table a number of alternatives to try to find an opening in the negotiations:

- *If it turns out to be possible for us to purchase another 25 percent, how would that affect your prices?*
- *If we place the shipment two months earlier, what advantages would that give you?*
- *Let's assume that we can accept your demands, what would that give me?*

The interesting thing about hypothetical questions is that, more often than not, they are answered, binding the negotiator and providing the questioner with important information. However, the person asking the question makes no promises: *I said if we can, not that we can.*

Be wary if the other party makes use of hypotheses in the course of the negotiation. Use counter questions to explore what he is after:

- *How can you increase your purchases by 25 percent?*
- *Does that mean that we can reach a decision here today?*

Take aways

- Listen to the value in a sentence and not the words.
- Be visual—use audio-visual aids to support your message.
- Be aware of different tactics you can use.
- Be aware of unilateral concessions.

CHAPTER 7

Where the "Bigger" Comes from: Expanding the Range of NegoEconomic Potential

Expanding the Room for Negotiation

The room for negotiation can be defined as the difference between the highest price that a buyer is willing to pay and the lowest price to which a supplier will come down. For a deal to be struck, there must be positive room for negotiation. The buyer must be willing to pay a price above the supplier's threshold of pain.

> Maximum price buyer will pay
> −Supplier's threshold of pain
> _____
> Traditional Room for Negotiation
> +Asymmetric Value Uncovered
> _____
> NegoEconomic Room for Negotiating

If the maximum price that a buyer can pay is $120,500, and the lowest price the supplier will come down to is $90,500, the difference of $30,000 constitutes the room for negotiation within which a deal can be struck. However, the actual room for negotiation is normally larger. It consists of the sum of the room for negotiation plus the NegoEconomic value that may be created. This allows the parties to reach an agreement even if the highest price that the buyer is willing pay is below the lowest price the supplier will come down to.

Example: Single Variable Negotiation versus Expanding the Room for Negotiation

Johnson wants Davis to join him in a project. Johnson has a second choice in Chandler. Davis is interested in being part of Johnson's project, but he also has an alternative in Simmons.

Johnson knows the following: the second choice, Chandler, wants $100,000 for his participation. If Davis does not agree to the terms, he will choose Chandler. The project can be executed more or less equally well with Chandler or Davis. But he prefers Davis because he has higher likability and seems more trustworthy. Johnson has estimated that he is willing to pay $10,000 more to get Davis. Johnson is tough and decides to put Davis to the test. He makes an initial low offer of $75,000.

Davis knows the following: if he works with Simmons, he will get $80,000. He would prefer working with Johnson for the same amount. Davis decides to make a high demand, asking for $115,000.

Both parties are still uncertain about how far the other one is willing to go and uncertain about how much to concede in order to achieve agreement.

Johnson has offered $75,000; Davis has offered $115,000. Both parties have made an offer, and the boundaries for the transaction have been set. Boundaries make negotiations easier. The situation would have been more difficult for Davis, if Johnson had made no offer at all, but had simply stated that Davis's demand was too expensive.

SMARTner Tip™ for the Advanced Practitioner:

Make sure you get responses to your suggestions other than general arguments of this type:

- *I'm sure you can do better than that.*
- *That's too much.*
- *That doesn't sound like a very good proposal.*

Insist that the other party specify in further detail:

- *What do you mean by reasonable costs?*
- *How do you want the agreement to be worded?*

Davis has asked for $115,000.
Johnson can accept $110,000.
The stake = the room for negotiation = $30,000

Davis can accept $80,000.
Johnson has offered $75,000.

This is a typical buying and selling negotiation. For a supplier attempting to optimize his profits, it is acceptable to achieve $110,000. To a buyer attempting to minimize his costs, it is acceptable to squeeze the price down to $80,000.

A surprisingly small number of negotiators will accept the first bid. A strikingly high number of them choose to accept an offer that is an improvement on any alternative that is within their budgetary limit. Most likely, these negotiators perceive negotiation as something unpleasant, and they want to get it over with as quickly as possible. Others attempt to bargain for higher profits, and their efforts are rewarded.

The above case is a single-issue negotiation. The only thing the parties are negotiating about is price. In real life, many negotiators attempt to make very complex negotiations into single-issue negotiations. They prefer comparing price to looking at costs. This makes it easier to compare bids without alternatives. However, price fixation makes it difficult for them to locate the asymmetric value. Price fixation leads to mistaken choices when the negotiators do not weigh short-term and long-term effects or tangible and non-tangible effects against each other. Reducing the negotiation to the single issue of price leads to conflict between the buyer and the supplier.

The supplier demands that the buyer look at more than just the price and suggests that the buyer should look at what he gets for his money. The buyer claims that he has already taken into account the differences that exist and that he has netted out the alternatives. The buyer does not want to have to explain his rationale and insists that the supplier come down in order to keep the conversation going.

The supplier, on the other hand, does not want to discuss price. He wants to take up other issues that allow him to take the temperature of the buyer and receive new information to determine whether he might make another offer. This information is required in order for him to arrive at a more certain decision and for the supplier to be able to submit the offer that gives the buyer the best value for his money.

The supplier wants to utilize any room for negotiation he might have in order to make concessions where they have the highest effect. The buyer does not want to open up to the questions of the supplier because, in a zero-sum game, his success depends on the supplier remaining uncertain and making unilateral concessions.

The parties disagree about the next step. One party wants to start with the price, whereas the other wants to look at alternatives. As a result of their failure to see eye to eye, a struggle ensues that might complicate the openness and trust required for cooperation.

Question the division of responsibility between the delegations. Find out if unnecessary duplication of effort is taking place. Ask yourself the following questions:

- Where are the risks located? Who is best suited to handle and take the risks?
- What is the time parameter and how can it be reduced?
- Are there superfluous intermediaries? Might e-commerce be an option?
- Where are the gains generated—money, experience, and goodwill? Who will benefit most from these gains?
- Where are costs generated? Which party has the best cost efficiency?

Avenues Where Potential Value May Be Found

Virtually every commercial transaction has a wealth of untapped resources that have NegoEconomic potential. To fully realize the opportunities buried in the deal that is in front of him, the SMARTnership negotiator should ask:

- Why does the project look the way it does?
- Why are we doing things the way we are?
- What could be managed differently?
- Who is better suited to handle specific tasks over the long term?
- Where are the opportunities and risks?
- Can responsibilities, costs, and rewards be shared differently?
- What are the alternative solutions?
- Will the alternative solutions make things better or worse?
- Can we discover something new or innovative?

The answers to these questions allow the delegates to expand the range of variables under consideration in the bargaining.

Identifying Variables That Reveal the Non-visible Asymmetric Value

SMARTnership negotiators work to identify as many variables as possible that offer the potential for NegoEconomic leveraging. Virtually

Figure 7.1 Negotiators can unlock up to 42 percent more value by abandoning distrust and a zero-sum mindset. Source: MarketWatch Centre for Negotiation.

every negotiator is aware of the basic set of variables that come into play in course of commercial bargaining: price, quantity, delivery time, guarantee, storage, and financing terms. The delegate using the SMARTnership strategy will look beyond these basics in an effort to creatively bargain on a much larger playing field.

In a negotiation, there is the traditional negotiation space that represents the value of the deal using only the basic variables. This approach leaves completely untapped the potential for asymmetric value that comes into play when the range of variables is expanded. Only by leveraging the traditional negotiation space and the asymmetric value can the NegoEconomic value of the negotiation be found. By finding the NegoEconomic value, two things take place:

1. Negotiation becomes easier, as there is more opportunity for identifying common ground
2. Because additional space has been utilized, negotiations give rise to improved results

Below is a list of variables that frequently have the potential be to create asymmetric value:

- Terms of payment
- Conversion
- Price

- Production volume
- Platemaking
- INCO terms
- Technical specification
- Penalty
- Legal issues
- Volume
- Preform (weight)
- Extended shelf life
- Contract length
- Transportation
- Insurance
- Marketing contribution
- Guarantees
- Specification
- Production location
- Stock size
- Batch size
- Service
- Documentation
- Incentive
- Procurement performed by owner
- Test certification
- Balance of Plant
- Site parameters
- Time
- Effective date
- Commencement date
- Time for completion
- Inventory on site
- Time of taking over
- Liability
- Availability warranty
- Power curve warranty
- Escalation
- Staff
- Performance bond
- Risk and reward in general
- Currency
- Training
- Contracting
- Service and warranty period

- Exclusivity
- Royalty
- Termination

The exploration of additional variables is not rocket science. It requires creativity, a new way of perceiving things, and openness to change. It is often useful to assemble a creative team who undertakes a brainstorming session that produces a list of every possible variable that could impact the outcome of the transaction.

How Many Variables Are There When Purchasing a Car? Or Does Red Have a Value?

Purchasing a car is a major investment for the vast majority of people. Car buying generally happens 10 to 15 times during your life. How many variables are there at issue when purchasing a car? Most people assume two or three. The answer is closer to 40:

1. Price
2. Time of delivery
3. Warranty
4. Service plans/options
5. Size/power of engine
6. Insurance costs
7. Sound system
8. Weather-related issues
9. Miles-per-gallon
10. Financing terms
11. Sunroof or convertible
12. Color
13. Metallic paint
14. Interior design
15. Leather seats
16. Floor mats
17. Style/status factors related to brand or design
18. TV/DVD
19. Model
20. Tires / winter tires
21. Navigation system
22. Alternative fuel or electronic power
23. Trunk space
24. Extra equipment

These variables should be divided into several categories:

Commercial and Technical Variables

These are factors that have a contract or are of financial consequence. Though technical variables do indeed have financial consequences, they also lead to improvements or changes to whatever the car has to offer.

Objective or Subjective Variables

Metallic paint usually costs at least $1,000 more than standard paint. Delivery in one week is more expensive than delivery in two months. Subjective variables are more difficult to price. Why would some people prefer to have an Audi rather than a Chevrolet? Why is it that some people prefer to have five doors rather than three doors? Why do some people prefer to have a red car rather than a black car? At first glance, there is no appreciation in value either way!

Variables That Generate Asymmetric Value

Let us assume that the dealer offers you an extended warranty on a new car that will cost approximately $1,200. Using the extended warranty as an additional variable subject to bargaining, will you be better off trying to negotiate a reduction in the purchase price of $1,200? Or asking the dealer to throw in the warranty at no extra cost to you? In all likelihood, it is much easier to get the dealer to throw in the extended warranty since his actual cost will be less than $1,200.

A combination of an objective variable and a subjective variable could be choice of color. Perhaps you would like your new car to be red. To get a red car might mean the negotiator has to order a car from the factory, which takes time to arrive and which also means extra work and financing for him. In his warehouse, he has the model that you wanted, but in white, not red. Perhaps he would like to sell off his stock and is therefore contemplating another price if you choose the color he has in stock! (It is always possible to debate the second-hand value of a used car in different colors).

Evaluate how much room you have to bargain on these variables. This assessment provides you with a picture of the flexibility you have and the alternatives you can utilize. Figure out what the consequences will be if you give more or less on any one of the variables at issue. This analysis will provide you with an awareness of your own bargaining equity, a measure of the other party's bargaining equity, and the parameters within which both of you can maneuver. NegoEconomics exposes alternative solutions that will enhance the overall value of the transaction.

NegoEconomics provides delegates with the means to identify the asymmetric value in the transaction at the outset and the skills to access that value at the bargaining table. If more value is to be realized, you must leverage your bargaining equity so that your counterpart assumes the higher costs, the greater risks, and more exposure to future liabilities. When delegates are motivated, have an open mind, and have been given the freedom to look for new paths, considerable asymmetric value can be created—if you know where to look.

Develop a Holistic View of the Transaction

A broad view of the transaction from 50,000 feet enables you to consider every angle before committing yourself to a solution. It enables you to analyze all of the bargaining options, to capitalize on the evident and hidden opportunities, and arrive at the most profitable arrangement.

Shifting your perspective to the arms-length viewpoint starts with getting an overview of the situation. The overview is necessary for the pieces to fall into place and for you to be able to see the whole picture. This picture is your baseline—the point of departure with which all conceivable modifications should be compared. It is often necessary to track events step by step to see what is happening. Take notes on the variables at issue and outline the details of the potential working arrangement. For each step, the well-prepared negotiator should ask questions like these:

- Why are things done this way? Never accept these answers: That's how we've always done it. That's normal practice in the industry. We just follow our routines because they have been successful in the past.
- What will happen when the need that is the focus of this transaction no longer exists and the production or the service is abandoned? Will the machine be scrapped? Can its life be prolonged? Can it be sold off? Is the system flexible enough so that it can be extended or modernized?
- How does the situation work currently? What are the individual elements? How do these elements affect costs, risks, and profits? How do they affect time, reliability, and useful life?
- What are the factors that have a negative impact on time, costs, reliability, and useful life?

- What could be done instead? What would happen in that case? Will it be a positive or negative change? Where are the opportunities, risks, and problems? Compare these to the baseline.
- Who will do the work that has to be done? Will it be the more cost-effective party that will benefit most from the experience or the more risk-oriented party that can sustain adversity? How do we solve the problem if it becomes necessary to transfer the responsibility? Do we need to redesign the product, or will anyone require extra training?
- What advantages can new technology provide? How is the innovation created? How do the parties share the value of the innovation that has resulted from the collaboration?

The process of discovering the NegoEconomic potential of the transaction will increase the room for negotiation and the size of the pie to be divided.

The Importance of Good Information

Using the SMARTnership approach that enables NegoEconomics to function, the delegates will be required to exchange pertinent information rather than withhold it. The SMARTnership negotiator demonstrates a willingness and sincerity to share information if they expect to receive valuable data from the other side. Openness at the bargaining table generates trust. Not only does trust add value to the ongoing negotiation but it also engenders long-standing relationships even after the deal is closed. Do not be afraid to initiate openness; the move will demonstrate that you have the courage to take the first step.

Analyze the information you have been able to compile to determine all of your strategic options. Every option comes with more variables, opportunities, and consequences. These need to be unpacked and assessed as components of the big picture. Thorough and accurate evaluation of all the information at your disposal will help to build a practical view of the negotiation. Bargaining options and their correlating variables should be viewed as tools to create additional value.

The SMARTnership negotiator should next determine the proportion of the asymmetric value that might be bargained away and what value would be gained in return. With a holistic view of the information, the negotiator will be able to determine the level of detail he should reveal when it comes time to present alternatives to the other party. More importantly, the well-prepared negotiator is able to negotiate past the traditional sticking points because the process becomes focused on creating benefits for all the delegations involved.

> **SMARTner Tip for the Advanced Practitioner: Anticipate the room for negotiation**
> In order to analyze the situation effectively, you can either engage in bargaining, so that additional information comes to light quickly, or rely on your personal network to gain more information through informal channels.

If you negotiate based on your initial assumptions, without revealing what a change in conditions would mean to you, you are in a better position for the final zero-sum negotiation that will come later when you are ready to divide—or share—the asymmetric value that has been created during the bargaining process. Working from your initial assumptions enables you to indicate interest, options, and direction without compromising your bargaining equity: *We'll see what we can do about the delivery time. We should be able to shorten it. It's possible that certain extra efforts will have to be made, but I believe it'll still be worth your while.*

This dialogue signals a willingness to bargain, and it indicates an opening for discussion. Try to obtain as much information as possible, while maintaining an eagerness to answer questions and share facts. If the other party indicates that there is room to maneuver, the effective negotiator will gain a flexible advantage.

> **SMARTner Tip for the Advanced Practitioner:**
> From the supplier's perspective, it is usually best to obtain an overall solution and information on the costs acceptable to the buyer. For the buyer, it is normally best to squeeze the total amount first, locate the potential asymmetric value, and then combine everything into the new package, the total price of which will be squeezed in a final negotiation round.

Variables Likely to Yield NegoEconomic Potential

1. Leveraging Differences

Fundamental differences between delegations can result in NegoEconomic potential. Negotiating parties will always have inherent differences—physical assets, experience, industry reputation, brand equity, number of products, total employees. When particular differences become relevant to the negotiation, then the bargaining equity of one delegate increases, and he or she has the opportunity to offer NegoEconomic potential as a bargaining incentive.

SMARTner Tip for the Advanced Practitioner:

In some situations, effective use of bargaining equity can level the playing field, because a well-established company can leverage their market share to offer a smaller start-up asymmetric value in a deal. The start-up can accept the proposal, where they give and receive value relative to the difference in the parties' market share. Even when the parties bring broad differences, NegoEconomics will generate win-win scenarios because neither party has to relinquish their original needs. Projects that seemed impossible to achieve between two parties become possible.

Example: NegoEconomics Done with Storage Costs

Taunton Manufacturing is Fimco's widget supplier. In order for Fimco's production line to run without disruption and for Fimco to be able to vary the production rate on a daily basis, 10,000 widgets always need to be in stock. The inventory of widgets has historically been kept at Fimco's facility, but recently the CFO of Fimco has learned about the Japanese model of just-in-time delivery.

Fimco's cost for storage is $250,000. Taunton can store at a cost of $150,000. If instead of storing the widgets at Fimco, Taunton provides the storage, Fimco's costs are reduced significantly. By storing the widgets on the premises of the party that has the lowest storage costs, the SMARTNERship negotiators have generated asymmetric value that they can share—$100,000 is now in play.

If *all the costs* incurred in a project were examined without any bias, what would be the impact on the transaction? What would happen if a third party were put in charge of some aspect of the work? SMARTnership negotiators should examine all possible alternative solutions in an effort to identify the NegoEconomic potential in the deal. However, the parties should also be alert to potential risks and ancillary cost increases that might arise as a result of the alternative arrangement.

When it comes to dividing the asymmetric value, the supplier should confront the buyer, warning him that he should not attempt to keep the entire NegoEconomic outcome for himself. He must share it. Why would he choose to do so? Inform him that he will be running the risk of losing everything if he tries to keep too much for himself—the personal relationship will suffer and trust will be compromised. The difficulty of this task lies in creating an appropriate degree of pressure and uncertainty without making the other party wish to retaliate.

How do you get the other party to concede a point?

- Appeal to her emotions: *It would be easier for me to win support for a solution that gives us.... As things look now, you put me in a very difficult position.*
- Try to gain his compassion. Get the other party to make your problems his problem: *You're asking me to run a big risk. That's OK, but in that case, we must have reasonable profits, so that I can afford to run that risk. We have to survive, you know. On these conditions, I can't keep my people on the payroll.*
- Refer to objective facts: *I must recover my direct costs. We agreed that this would take at least 50 hours, and my programmers cost $300 per hour. I must earn $15,000.*
- Exploit alternatives or market forces: *Actually, I think your demands are quite reasonable, but you must realize that my alternatives are.... That's why I can't give you more than...*
- Do not appear too eager. Consider testing the other party with the gambit: *You can do better than that, I'm afraid it's a little too costly. Leave the table and see if the other party changes her offer.*
- Make an offer and make it clear to the other party that he has to choose between accepting your offer or losing the entire deal. If he does choose to walk away from the deal, it is necessary for you to be able to do without him. Make sure that you have a fallback position in place, and refrain from bluffing.
- Make a counteroffer and signal that it is negotiable. The other party might be looking for a solution where you meet halfway. You must send a clear signal that your offer is negotiable, so that he realizes the possibility of reaching a compromise: *if we are to reach an agreement, I think we must be able to meet somewhere around $400,000.*

2. Economies of Scale

Example: The Banker Spots the Synergy

Karl and Diane are doing business in the same town developing and manufacturing electronics. While they have a vague idea of each other's businesses, they have not met. They use the same bank. One day their banker introduces them to each other. The personal chemistry clicks, and they agree to the following:

- Let's share an office. We'll get bigger, better, and more up-to-date space at a lower cost.
- We can share a secretary and administrative staff.
- We can employ one salesman who will work for both of us.
- Our respective experience seems to complement each other's, yielding substantial synergies.

Instead of having two suppliers manufacturing the same product, the entire production process could be assigned to one of them. In the example above, Karl could aggregate all the costs of production over double the number of production units, allowing him to squeeze his own purchasing costs as he doubles the number of orders. Stock could be kept in only one place, and the size of the inventory could be reduced. Transport costs could also be reduced, as could the administrative costs. The parties have eliminated duplication of development, tools, and management. Diane is free to focus on sales and marketing, which are her greatest strengths.

SMARTner Tip for the Advanced Practitioner:

The motivation behind many mergers is the economy of scale that the parties can achieve by spreading development costs, overhead, and distribution over a higher number of units produced. However, these gains must be viewed in relation to the changes that will be a consequence of the larger-scale operation.

The asymmetric value generated must also be looked at in light of the increased risks and the intensified future dependence. The new combined supplier organization also requires a different relationship between the buyer and the supplier. The buyer can no longer flaunt his bargaining equity over the suppliers as he could in price negotiations of previous years, when he could play the suppliers against each other. The buyer has to be more inclined to find and develop the NegoEconomic potential, instead of holding onto the old solutions by trying to squeeze the price as much as possible. The supplier must participate in the uncertainties and risk facing the buyer in the marketplace. The supplier will undergo tough scrutiny before the cooperation can begin.

The choice of supplier must be made with precision because the interdependence between buyer and supplier will be intensified. Short-term profit orientation, in which the horizon is one budgetary period, will have to be replaced by a longer-term strategy. The buyer must accept a higher degree of dependence on suppliers. The buyer must also accept that the supplier will get a share of the asymmetric value generated in the bargaining process. Financial realities will eventually force them to accept SMARTnership as a basis for business. If not, they will disappear from the market.

The list of advantages associated with economies of scale is long. However, there are limits to these advantages. Combining several enterprises under one umbrella does not always work. NegoEconomics can sometimes result in increased costs, more red tape, and inefficiency. In some cases, searching for the asymmetric value through a collaborative process may need to take a backseat to protecting your individual business interests.

Example: Piggybacking on Someone Else's Marketing Power

Angel, a seminar provider, hopes to postal mail his catalogue to 10,000 potential attendees. The costs involved are: developing or acquiring a database, printing the catalogue, and postage. The campaign will cost between $9,000 and $12,500. If he joins forces with a colleague who provides another training seminar that is not in competition with his, the two providers can share the expenses of the mailing.

Alternatively, if Angel cooperates with a large-scale seminar provider who markets several hundred programs, has her own mailing list, has volume pricing from a direct mail service, and can send out information for five or six seminars in the same envelope, Angel could reduce the costs to one-tenth of the originally anticipated expense.

What are the disadvantages of working in cooperation with the large-scale seminar provider? First and foremost, Angel's message may be lost among the other marketing materials. If the recipient does not think that the first one or two programs sound interesting, he may be inclined to dump all the material into the wastepaper basket. If the recipient dislikes one of the courses offered, there is a chance that she will dislike all of them.

Angel might also be required to present his offering in a format that is uniform with the others, so that his brand identity disappears. He might have to accept that he must modify his offering so that it fits the model of the large-scale seminar provider. Economies of scale can be attained at a price, but the price should be balanced against the concomitant benefits.

3. Cooperating with Your Counterpart

Negotiators can leverage SMARTnership strategies to create collaboration, rather than competition, and to encourage mutually beneficial deal-making. Cooperation provides delegates opportunities to reduce costs by reallocating the obligations and merging resources. Two or three parties might pool financial resources in order to obtain a lower cost on a particular raw material needed to manufacture their various products. Negotiating partners could also share mutually exclusive expertise. If a company with years of experience designing hardware devices manages to strike a deal with an innovative software start-up, then the alliance could yield a finished product that might be superior to others on the market or even an altogether revolutionary device. A strong business alliance can help fulfill mutual needs and reduce costs. The SMARTnership strategy is an ideal way to increase incentives for all parties involved.

Being SMART with Time

Many commercial collaborations are based on the principle of time sharing. While it may seem glaringly obvious to an outsider, negotiators often overlook the true value of time.

Example: The Night Shift Provides the Solution

Cody Tool & Dye and Ryan Products are located in the same industrial park. They discover at a networking breakfast sponsored by the park management that they both need an expensive piece of equipment—a metal stamping machine—to streamline their manufacturing process. Ryan needs metal stamping capability every day between 8 a.m. and 4 p.m. Cody requires eleven hours' use of the machine anytime, day or night. They arrange to share the cost of acquisition of the machine, with Ryan using it during the day, and Cody using it only on the night shift. Ryan and Cody have taken advantage of their differences in needs and distributed the economies of scale. Now, they must determine whether the benefit to one exceeds the costs to the other.

4. Clarifying Communication

NegoEconomics requires consistent and clear communication. Global negotiators bring different languages, cultures, experiences, and expectations to the bargaining table, and each party will perceive threats, dangers, and opportunities differently. To avoid misunderstandings between delegates, SMARTnership negotiators should speak and correspond using professional business language, stating concise terms and conditions in written documents and avoiding vague, regional, or colloquial expressions.

Example: Alternative Scenarios

BeBe asks her counterpart: *Daniel, would you consider letting us have an advance?*

Daniel says *no*, without knowing what he is turning down, because he is not used to giving advances and sees it as risky.

If instead, BeBe asks: *If we were to reduce the price a little, would you consider letting us have an advance?* then in this scenario, BeBe would reduce the risk of getting an automatic rejection because maybe Daniel would want to hear how much she is willing to come down.

If BeBe says: *Let us have a 30 percent advance, and we'll reduce the price by 3.4 percent,* there is even less risk of getting an automatic rejection.

5. Use Alternatives to Increase the Room for Negotiation

In most negotiation situations, you will be able to think of a number of alternatives that will open up the bargaining. Think through the variables on which you can be flexible and where you should provide information sparingly, so as not to expose your weak points. This prevents the other party from taking unfair advantage. Suggesting alternatives is a way to locate the asymmetric value.

Example: Haggling Over the Price of a Piece of Property

Two parties are seeking to reach an agreement on the purchase of real estate. The seller is asking $5 million for his property. The buyer has made an offer of $4 million. As long as the price remains at the center of the discussion and they fail to discuss alternatives, the negotiation will be characterized by one of the following scenarios:

• Total deadlock: The parties are entrenched in their positions because each perceives the offer of the other party as phony;

therefore, neither party is interested in initiating compromise. The negotiation is derailed, and the parties leave the table empty-handed.

- An imbalance in power: If the buyer knows that the seller desperately needs the money and he has no other offers, the buyer's position is so strong that he can dictate terms.
- Horse trading: Both parties argue their case, and counteroffers are made, but always on the basis of the original terms. They both are trying to advance their own position. In the end, they meet halfway.
- Manipulation: Each party attempts to make the other party change his offer by means of an open discussion: *Where did you get that number?* Each tries to influence the other party's judgment and locate a calculation error.

The parties should discuss variables other than price and find alternatives to the asking price of $5 million and the bid of $4 million in order to locate a solution yielding asymmetric value:

- Does the buyer need to take over all the tenants, or can the seller move some of them out of their current leasing arrangements?
- Is the buyer interested in some other form of financing?
- Can the seller keep an empty flat for her own use?
- Can part of the payment be the exchange of a commercial / industrial property owned by the buyer?

6. Financial Terms and Conditions

The financial variables that can be leveraged to access asymmetric value include:

- Terms of Payment
- Purchasing, Leasing, Renting, Shared Ownership, or Outsourcing
- Pricing
- Mode of Payment
- Advance Payments and Royalties

Self-limiting Practices

Frequently, companies follow routines and practices of the industry without questioning whether changing the conditions might yield asymmetric value. The company policy has never been questioned.

It has been in place for many years, and no one remembers what the reasons for establishing it were.

Frequently, corporate negotiators are not authorized to discuss conditions other than the standard provisions. The people who have determined these standard provisions are rarely present at the negotiating table, and therefore have little knowledge of what could be achieved by letting the negotiator have a free hand.

Other negotiators selfishly represent their own internal department and focus only on their own interests and needs. Competition and territorial turf battles between departments are normal, but lead to suboptimization when decisions are to be made. These negotiators are not motivated to look for and exploit asymmetric value that will benefit other departments. For example, they say: *Why should I offer various financing options when the gains we make will only be entered into the books as an interest gain for which the finance department will get the credit? This won't benefit our position.*

A. Terms of Payment

Some negotiators are hesitant to discuss modifying the terms of payment. They believe that the gains accruing from this would end up credited somewhere else in the organization's accounting so that they would not be recognized for creating the benefit from the gain.

Efforts to create asymmetric value by modifying terms of payment can also fail because of insufficient communication and poor negotiation skills. The parties are looking straight ahead; their own limitations prevent them from seeing new ideas or thinking along unconventional lines. Sometimes they are disempowered and have not been given the freedom to bargain by their superiors in the organization. Thinking along the lines of "suppliers should not receive an advance" and "who do they think they are, anyway, messing with our internal policies?" dominate the mindset of the unsophisticated negotiator. These individuals are not able to negotiate creatively, and the result is that the NegoEconomic potential is not exploited.

Organizations wishing to survive and grow must make certain to take advantage of NegoEconomic opportunities: staff competencies should be developed and supported on a continuing basis, and individuals must be given the authority to freely discuss issues and ask questions about different solutions. However, it is not always necessary to delegate the decision-making authority concerning which new routes are acceptable. Management should provide concrete guidelines for determining terms of payment while keeping in mind the potential asymmetric value to be created.

Example: Expanding the Conversation

Most suppliers will adjust the terms of payment—net cash 10, 20, or 30 days. They never discuss any other terms or conditions.

The following dialogue is not unusual:

Errol, the supplier asks: *Would you be willing to consider paying an advance?*

Jaime, the buyer replies: *No, that's out of the question.*

This is a knee-jerk reaction on the part of many buyers. They do not think that the supplier should be given an advance. Granting an advance can only be done if the supplier can document that he will have considerable expenses accruing over the course of the project. In that case, the advance would have to be correlated to these expenses.

No is the wrong answer in this case. Jaime has slammed the door without knowing what he is declining. He does not have enough information to make an appropriate judgment call. How big an advance is Errol asking for, and if he gets the advance, what is he willing to give in return? It is only when Jaime can see both elements that he will be able to determine whether any asymmetric value can be created by changing the terms of payment. Continuing dialogue, openness, and a clear proposal are missing. There is no give and take.

A fundamental rule of negotiation is: if you want something, you must be prepared to show what you are willing to give in return. One-sided demands will be met with rejection. An offer will usually lead to constructive dialogue. Example: *Provided we can get an advance of $300,000, we can accommodate your needs and take on a considerable share of the costs in adapting the system to your requirements.*

Jaime should be proactive in charting the potential options. Why does Errol need an advance? What is it worth to him? Can Jaime exchange it for something that is more valuable to him? Both parties should be proactive in the way they negotiate.

Jaime should create a dialogue by asking the following questions:

- *So you would like an advance? How much?*
- *Why do you want the advance?*
- *What is your collateral?*
- *If we let you have this advance, what will you give us in return?*

Errol must learn to express himself by making a concrete offer that makes clear what he wants and what he is willing to give:

- *If you let us have 30 percent in advance, we can lower the price by $12,000.*
- *If you let us have 30 percent in advance, we can guarantee that you will take delivery of the shipment before summer.*
- *If you let us have 30 percent in advance, we can offer you free service for the entire warranty period.*

When No Does Not Necessarily Mean No

You must realize that *no* in a negotiation does not necessarily mean: *No, under no circumstances. No* is a knee-jerk reaction for some people. The supplier should make sure he gets an explanation for the buyer's negative response.

Example: How to Ask for an Advance

Raquel: I see that you don't take kindly to the idea of letting us have an advance. Why is that?

Samuel: We don't grant advances on principle.

Raquel: Why is that?

Samuel: It's a risk as well as a cost.

Raquel: If our bank guarantees the advance, would there be any risk involved as far as you can see?

Samuel: No, but it would cost us money.

Raquel: How much would it cost you to grant us an advance of $100,000?

Samuel: Approximately $10,000.

Raquel: If, in return, we were to offer you free service—this is something that normally costs about $12,000 a year—would you then be willing to let us have an advance?

Samuel: Let me think about it.

This constructive dialogue requires openness. If Samuel does not reply by indicating a specific amount, it will be difficult for Raquel to determine whether an advance is a way to move forward. When faced with silence from the buyer, many suppliers give up.

A better alternative is to send up a trial balloon by making an offer just to see what the reaction is going to be: *If we can have an advance of $100,000, we can let you have a full year's service in return. Normally, that would cost you $12,000. Why don't you think about it?* In making this clear opening, Raquel provides Samuel with an opportunity to evaluate and assess the suggestion.

A result of such openness could also be that the parties see opportunities for creating asymmetric value in ways other than granting an advance.

> *Samuel*: Our liquidity situation doesn't allow us to grant you an advance. We are being charged a relatively high interest rate, for which we would have to be compensated if we were to let you have an advance.
> *Raquel*: What is the interest rate you'd have to pay?
> *Samuel*: Between 12 and 13 percent.
> *Raquel*: Then I see another option: We can offer you 90 days' credit instead of 30 days if you can handle the installation of the equipment. I'm sure the credit will be worth more to you than your installation costs.

If you cannot create asymmetric value by changing conditions in one respect, you may wish to turn 180 degrees to see what will happen if you move in the opposite direction. Offer longer credit terms instead of the advance originally asked for.

SMARTner Tip for the Advanced Practitioner: Currency, Money, Goods, or Services?

In which currency should the price be paid—euros, US dollars, or British pounds (GBP)? The answer to this question entails risks and opportunities. Hedging the exchange rates involves risks, but if you are knowledgeable and willing to take a risk, manipulating currency exchange can create asymmetric value.

Some negotiators from large corporations do not take interest losses or gains into consideration. In these companies, annual investment needs are counted in billions of dollars. Managers are free to spend the money they have allocated for their project anywhere they want over the course of the project period. The implication is that with investments of that magnitude, their companies risk losing a realizable asymmetric value of several millions every year.

B. Purchasing, Leasing, Renting, Shared Ownership, and Outsourcing

Purchasing, leasing, renting, shared ownership, and outsourcing are familiar alternatives to most business persons. Negotiators want to locate the solution that best meets their requirements at the lowest cost and risk. What are the questions delegates need to consider before deciding how to acquire resources required for a new project?

- Is it ownership or use that matters? What is it you really need?
- Should the equipment be viewed as an investment that must be profitable so that you will get your money back when you sell it?
- Is there any benefit of actual ownership?
- Is the need permanent or temporary?
- Is the requirement spread evenly over the year, or is it cyclical?
- What are the financial opportunities or tax benefits that should be factored into the considerations?
- Do you have the internal or external resources to maintain the equipment?
- How could you benefit from deploying the financial and human resources elsewhere?
- Are the requirements today the same as they were five years ago?

C. Pricing

Price is of central importance in most business transactions. A negotiator's success is often measured by the price he or she achieves in the deal. Price is reflected on the bottom line and can be easily measured. Often price will constitute the point in a negotiation where the interests of the parties are on a collision course. It is possible to create asymmetric value from this conflict. More information is needed about the way the other party views price to test whether accessing the asymmetric value is achievable. The word price means different things to different people, such as:

- price equals cost
- price as related to budget
- price indicating the usefulness of something as relates to the alternatives available
- price as relates to the cost or effort that the other party must provide to create the product
- price as a strategic statement, such as the asking price is an opening offer and is consequently inflated
- price that provides cash in hand, which can be used for other requirement
- price as a confirmation of worth or as a reflection of perception of value, such as indicating status associated with high-cost luxury items, such as Louis Vuitton or Chanel, or discount pricing associated with Sam's Club or Walmart

You do not always have to go to battle over the price. It may be possible to create a positive NegoEconomic outcome by first having a discussion and then agreeing on a method for establishing the price. Pricing can be determined based on many different factors. It can be fixed or variable. It can be a maximum price, defined by performance variables, or an incentive through which the parties share extra costs and profits. A price can be adjusted by means of indexes. American and European negotiators tend to live by a culture of fixed prices. Why? Fear of conflict, reluctance to haggle, and poor bargaining skills are among the most common explanations.

There are a variety of ways to determine price that may open the door to create asymmetric value:

Fixed price: With a fixed price, there is an incentive for the supplier to be exact in her calculation to ensure that she yields a profit. Without this incentive, many buyers know that the price can be random or subjective.

It can be difficult to make a correct assessment of contribution in terms of effort, costs, problems, and risks. It is more difficult for the buyer than for the supplier to carry out this calculation. The buyer who needs a fixed price is not willing to take risks. He may have had an unpleasant experience with open account terms; perhaps he must stay within a specified budget; or maybe he needs to be able to compare the costs associated with different alternatives. The buyer might be willing to pay a risk premium in order to achieve the fixed price. The risk premium might exceed what the supplier needs in order to cover his costs.

Flexible price: In situations where uncertainty is a major component of the project, fixed prices are impossible. The risk premium can become excessive. Risks may be underestimated, leading to future disputes over unforeseen costs. It can be difficult to ascertain whether invoices are unfairly inflated. Disclosure agreements and provisions entitling a party to scrutinize accounting records may be a solution. The supplier will be reimbursed for documented costs, plus an agreed-upon additional amount that will allow him to make a profit. Don't overlook the opportunities to combine price with the factors of time and quantity.

The negotiator may need to sell the deal internally. If the negotiator can show that she has been able to keep the pricing of the previous year in effect through the first quarter of the current year, she might be able to get in-house support by agreeing to let the supplier get the increase he is looking for, beginning with the second quarter of the current year.

Example: Publishing Royalties

If your publisher can persuade you to let them pay you a reduced royalty of 10 percent for the first 3,000 copies of your book sold, they may be able to get the publishing committee to approve publication. For copies sold above the first 3,000, they will gladly pay a royalty of 20 percent.

Price defined by performance variables: In connection with incentives and a division of extra costs and profits, the parties have a shared responsibility for assessing the costs of the project in a concrete manner if they are to bear a share of any unforeseen costs. The parties' common interest in operating in a cost-efficient manner will increase if they can share in the profits.

Fixed price linked to an index: Instead of sitting at the negotiating table arguing about who is the most skillful forecaster and who is best at guesstimating price developments, it is possible retroactively to regulate price deviations by means of an index or a follow-up calculation. It is important to agree on the index, the basis value, and whether the index is to apply to all or only some of the costs.

Price on the basis of results: The price will be calculated retroactively, and the buyer will pay in relation to the results achieved. This is a nontraditional method that is often met with suspicion.

Example: Paid Based on Success

A consultant is planning a direct advertising campaign and wants to know what it will cost. The consultant is looking for an overall price or a specified statement of the cost of the individual components of the campaign. The marketing firm comes back with a proposal that is highly unusual: *For every response leading to an order being placed within six months, we want $44.* The consultant objects, saying he wants a "normal" price.

Instead of looking to see what he can gain from the transaction and relating the costs at $44 for each new order to what this is worth, the consultant is fixated on how much the marketing firm will make. The consultant does not get the point, which is that the more money the marketing firm makes, the more he will make as well!

Do not object to this method. Is there any method that can measure results with more certainty? It is the effort and skill of the supplier that affects the result. Try to make a realistic assessment of the result that could be achieved and negotiate a payment option that provides the other party with an incentive so that he will give his best effort.

Splitting up the cost: The price paid can be split up on different accounts, or by types of costs, budgetary years, or by taking tax regulations into account. A problem can be addressed through the technicalities of bookkeeping. Redistribution of costs over time or between different accounts can provide a solution. Some costs can be written off right away, while others must be written off over a number of years. What are the tax implications of redistributing costs?

Some buyers focus their interest on the purchase price and ignore the psychological impact. The amount charged to the buyer's budget might be of greater psychological importance to the supplier than to the buyer. By allowing the supplier to win the price discussion, the buyer may receive a quid pro quo that offsets the additional costs.

Example: Enhancing the Trade-in, Reducing the Discount

Auto dealers frequently use this sales technique—when the customer wants to buy a new car and trade in her old car as part of the deal, she is told that her old car is in good shape and that its trade-in value is high. Instead of squeezing down the value of the old car by pointing out all its defects, flaws, and signs of age, the dealer offers the customer a good trade-in price and, in return, he gives her a low discount on the new car.

Barter: The price does not necessarily have to be expressed only in monetary terms. What are the opportunities and risks involved in accepting payment in goods or services?

Three Examples:

1. A firm working in direct advertising has provided shoddy work in connection with a campaign. Nathan complains, and the firm offers him a refund of $1,500—a ludicrously low amount. Nathan speaks to a lawyer, who tries to dissuade him from bringing legal action. Experience shows that the burden of proof is difficult, and the court prefers settlements to judgments. An alternative might be to go for compensation in services rather than in money. Nathan asks the firm to give him contact details for 5,000 prospects from their mailing list database free of charge.
2. Airlines try to gain the loyalty of travelers by being generous with frequent-flyer miles and special offers on airfares. It does not cost them extra to put a premium customer in an empty seat.
3. Henri is in the business of selling machinery for producing food packaging. FoodPro owes him money, and is short of cash.

FoodPro produces high-quality food and has excess production capacity. Accepting payment in the form of finished food products will probably be more profitable for Henri than insisting on payment in cash. He can then sell the food himself to a supermarket chain.

D. Mode of Payment

Learn to see the opportunities in different modes of payment. Handling small transactions, invoices, payments, and cash is expensive. Generating invoices in amounts smaller than the cost to create them is not profitable. Mobile phone companies have experienced this problem with low-use customers. To solve this problem, they created service plans that allow the customer to pay in advance and make phone calls until the credit runs out. Other monthly membership-type businesses have reduced their administrative costs by encouraging their customers to agree to automatic billing from a credit or debit card.

Example: Customer Loyalty and Credit

A European discount department store created asymmetric value for its customers by launching a unique card system. Under this system, the customer deposited an amount of money with the retailer that she could draw from as she purchased merchandise in the store. The customer received a better rate of interest on her money than what the bank was willing to pay, and she received a monthly statement detailing her purchases. The retailer also got to use the funds on deposit, and customer loyalty grew because the card tied the customer to the store. Useful statistical information on how well different items sell was also obtained for use in advertising campaigns.

E. Advance Payments and Royalties

Advance payments, lump sum payments, and royalties are the usual types of payment for writers and inventors. Why don't more businesses explore this financial model? The principle of a guaranteed flat fee plus a result-orientated remuneration is gaining ground.

Example: Negotiating for Broader Distribution

A publishing house wants to publish certain books. No one can predict in advance how many copies will be sold. In the course of talking with the publishing house, the author receives signals that she is dealing with cautious people and that risky new projects are not being taken on.

Though they are forecasting that the book will sell well, the publisher wants to minimize their up-front investment. They are reluctantly drawn into a discussion about a high guaranteed minimum royalty (lump sum) upon the signature of the publishing contract.

The author has great confidence in her book, and she anticipates that the satisfaction of seeing it on display in bookstores in many countries will be even greater. If the publishing house can establish contacts with their colleagues in several countries, the author will adjust the content of the book to an international market. If the publishing house can help the author reach a wider market, she can drop her demand for the large advance. Gradually backing down from this demand, she hopes to be able to increase the percentage royalty payment, thus achieving a much higher return in the long run.

Example: Internet Sales of Cheap Cosmetics

Your company is competing for the contract to develop an e-commerce system for CheapCosmetics.com. Do you intend to charge the company by:

1. A fixed price for the entire project?
2. A flexible price based on the actual number of hours required to develop the system?
3. A low, fixed price plus a flexible payment on each transaction made by CheapCosmetics?
4. A flexible payment on the basis of each sale?

Decisions must be made on a case-by-case basis: How do you view the project and its potential? How costly will it be to develop? Does your financial position permit a postponement of payment until CheapCosmetics' system is up and running? If not, will you be able to get a third party to finance the development on the strength of the contract? What does the bank say?

Why not choose compensation on the basis of each transaction when your system is used? This is appropriate if CheapCosmetics is concerned about development costs and if CheapCosmetics can charge their end user for transaction costs. Will the end user accept a processing fee of $1 each time she uses her debit card to pay for purchases made while using the e-commerce system? The amount is negligible to the end user, but it will make you a multimillionaire as the developer of the system.

What will your competitors do? What signals has CheapCosmetics sent? Are they sensitive to the size of development costs? Will they be able to charge the end user the processing fee on a transaction-by-transaction basis? Every time the end user uses her debit card that is linked to her bank account to pay for purchases made over the Internet, her bank account is debited a negligible amount. This bank charge is in addition to the $1 processing fee you have proposed as the developer.

Can you close the deal by making an arrangement that allows you to sell the e-commerce system to other customers? If so, should CheapCosmetics be entitled to a percentage payment on these sales? If they are indeed entitled to this, would CheapCosmetics be willing to modify their technical specification requirements in such a way as to facilitate future resale? Much asymmetric value can be found in organizing transactions in an unconventional manner such as this. The other consideration is the ownership of the intellectual property of the e-commerce system, which has now become a collaborative effort between you and CheapCosmetics. Look for opportunities to discuss payment today or payment tomorrow.

7. Design, Development, and Innovation

The design and technical specifications of a project not only determine the quality and performance of a product or a system, but they also influence costs, scheduling, allocation of risk, and application. How should a specification of requirements be perceived? Are they non-negotiable demands or are they preferences? What knowledge of existing alternatives does the person who has written the specification of requirements have? How have the priorities been set? What has been intentionally left out? What needs have governed the wording of the specifications?

There are many questions that need to be answered before you can understand the thoughts and wishes behind a company's specification of requirements. After these questions have been adequately answered, you can attempt an unbiased discussion about what the optimal specification of requirements will look like, how much room you have to maneuver, and what types of opportunities you have to create asymmetric value.

Set Out a Systematic Analysis of All Requirements

In order to fully understand the requirements made, they have to be evaluated one at a time. Quality and performance will affect costs during the different phases of a project. The technical specification of requirements is made up of a mixture of possible benefits and requirements that have to be met for the project to work. There might be technical requirements of lesser importance that you can use as bargaining chips in the course of the negotiation.

It is important to keep in mind that the specification of requirements should not be left entirely to operators and technicians. Their reasons for including or deleting certain functions may be of an operational nature and may not always be made in the best interest of the company.

Costs, risks, time consumption, and physical effort must always be related to the useful effect that can be achieved during the different phases of new product development:

- Design and development
- Production
- Service and maintenance
- Winding up

The specification of requirements will influence:

- Flexibility, extensibility, and compatibility
- Possibility of selling to several users
- Possibility of extending the useful life of the product
- Reliability and environmental impact
- Useful life
- User friendliness and working environment

8. Time

Time is one of the most critical factors in any agreement. The issue of time that is most frequently discussed in a negotiation is the delivery date. How much would earlier delivery cost? What could be gained by getting started ahead of schedule? What is the cost involved in a delay? What can be gained if we do not have to accelerate the project? However, there are some aspects of time that may require you to follow the established practice rather than seeking alternatives, such as:

- Duration of the agreement
- Start date / end date
- Period of notice

- Winding-up period
- Period of suborders

Many agreements tend to run for a year. Why is this? Companies report their results every year, and budgets look ahead for a year. Why would you choose another period? Companies generally structure their business and financial planning in 12-month increments. Many cooperative ventures entail risks, costs, and advantages in concluding an agreement for standard terms. Generally, either the duration of an agreement is not sufficiently discussed or the options are not thoroughly considered.

Cancellation: It matters a great deal to the party who has to replan his activities whether an agreement is terminated at 6 or 12 months' notice. Short cancellation times can be extremely valuable to another party.

Service Agreements: What is the use of a service agreement for a computer system in which the supplier promises to be on-site within six hours? Will the system be up and running within six hours? The crucial factor is not how quickly the technician arrives. What truly matters is how quickly the problem can be remedied.

Time effects negotiations in unexpected ways. Often, the importance of time in a negotiation is not realized until it is in short supply and the other party is losing something as a result. Consider these examples:

- How much does the stockbroker lose if his customers cannot complete their deals for a whole day because his Internet server is down?
- How important is it to a traveler to have a guaranteed seat on a plane if he confirms the booking just six hours before departure?
- How much can my wholesaler earn if all orders are confirmed no less than one week in advance? Could he perhaps take on the expenses involved in carrying emergency stocks so that he never risks being left without raw materials?

9. Rights—Intellectual Property, Distribution, and Derivative Products

In many contracts there are rights that need to be discussed, allocated, and, sometimes, regulated. Rights such as the ownership of intellectual property, foreign distribution, derivative products, options, and transfers or assignments all can open doors to creative opportunities for accessing hidden value.

Example: New Product Development

Zeno Company retains a vendor to develop a new product. Zeno pays for the development and receives a product with which he is satisfied. Consider the following questions:

- Will the vendor be entitled to sell this or similar products to other customers?
- Will this right be unrestricted, or will it be restricted to certain markets and specific periods?
- Should only some customers be prevented from purchasing this product, or should it be a full year before anyone else can buy the same product?
- Is Zeno, who funded the development, entitled to some kind of royalty? Is Zeno subsequently entitled to a status of most favored customer, that is, will Zeno always be entitled to a free upgrading of the system, and that nobody else can buy at lower costs than he?

CASE STUDY: Bargaining in the Real World— United / Continental Airlines Corporate Merger

Corporate mergers and acquisitions provide executives with the opportunity to generate growth within a particular sector or expand operations into new markets. Negotiating firms will combine organizational authority into a single entity through a joint venture or via acquisition, where one company essentially buys up and absorbs the other firm. In an increasingly uncertain and demanding corporate environment, effective negotiators typically pursue alternative approaches to business transactions in order to maximize gains. Innovative deals have begun to blur the division between mergers and acquisitions, resulting in hybrid strategies intended to appease stakeholders with asymmetric value incentives. Regardless of the particular approach, a newly merged corporate entity should benefit from an improvement in position relative to other firms in the market.

Negotiating through a merger presents a wealth of opportunities for executives to generate mutually beneficial value for their companies. The airline sector witnessed a significant corporate negotiation in May 2010 when United Airlines (UAL) and Continental Airlines combined forces. Both corporations benefited from the deal with increased access to pooled resources and, more importantly, the new corporate entity was able to immediately lower operational costs by eliminating redundant systems and departments. Capitalizing on these opportunities was crucial for negotiating executives, because both corporations had suffered substantial losses the previous year. Prior to the deal, UAL reported losses of $1.1 billion, while Continental had reported a net loss of more than $280 million. The airlines attributed the deficits to a decline in leisure traffic and premium, first-class fares resulting from the economic downturn, which their low-cost competitors had actually benefited from. The deal between the two airlines not only provided opportunities to reduce deficit spending, but the agreement has also established the world's largest airline in terms of fiscal competitiveness with an estimated $29 billion in combined revenues.

In addition to generating immediate benefits for the new airline, executives were able to address stakeholder concerns by leveraging bargaining equity to create asymmetric value. The deal was financed through an all-share transaction—shares in the separate companies are transferred to shares in the new company—worth an estimated $3 billion. Since United's parent company, UAL Corporation, was responsible for the bulk of the purchase, the deal could be considered an acquisition of Continental Airlines.

In an oversimplified evaluation, shareholders often perceive acquisitions as a large, successful company leveraging market share or fiscal power over a smaller, less successful organization. Shareholders in both companies assume that the firm being purchased is floundering toward collapse and that the deal will eventually devalue the stock of the consolidated firm. In order to address these concerns, Continental and Untied executives were able to promote the deal as a merger between equals by adding mutual value to the deal. The newly formed airline will operate with the United name using the Continental logo as its marketing banner. Continental's former chief executive will provide corporate leadership of United Continental Holdings, headquartered in the United offices in Chicago. Both companies were able to realize the additional benefit of merging individual components of each airline into a single entity. Whether those strategies were just for show or not, the fact is that the merger was considered a success, and shareholders unanimously approved the merger.

In mutually beneficial negotiations, asymmetric value is generated and shared using NegoEconomics, but the benefits may not be apparent on the surface. Executives approach deals with needs to fulfill, demands to be met, or expectations to contend with. These preconceived notions encumber negotiating executives with a type of tunnel vision, where they are focused solely on one-sided gains. When executives enter into a SMARTnership approach, the blinders are removed and asymmetric value emerges in the peripheral view. In the case of the United / Continental merger, both companies sought mutually exclusive means to reduce operational deficits, and they shared the burden of shareholder perception. Rather than forcing a hostile takeover or some other one-sided action, the airlines were able to generate the asymmetric value of a joint corporate identity to appease shareholder perceptions, and the revamped airline was able to expand operations while consolidating operating costs.

In the final phases of negotiations, the negotiators must find a fair, but not necessarily equal, division of the deal's asymmetric value. This approach will engender trust among negotiating parties, as well as the confidence of stakeholders. In the airline deal, United and Continental could not generate asymmetric value without a deal aimed at mutual benefit, nor could they have divided any additional value without establishing the fact that United Airlines had superior bargaining equity over Continental based on client traffic, fleet size, and revenue figures. By agreeing on the relative power positions through open negotiations, United was able to acquire Continental. The airlines were able to promote the deal as a merger of equals, benefiting shareholders, and ultimately creating the world's most powerful airline.

Incentive Agreements

In connection with incentive agreements there are certain critical questions to consider:

- Where should you set the number on which the incentive is based—what is normal?
- What should the remuneration be for normal performance?

- How large a share of the profits do you have to give away in order to interest the other party?
- Should you set aside part of the profits for a reserve to be used in future lean years?
- Are losses to be divided in the same way as gains?
- What should be the duration of the agreement? Should the number be raised in the forthcoming agreement period?

SMARTner Tip for the Advanced Practitioner: NegoEconomics with Competitive Bidders

In a competitive bidding situation, all competitors should be given the same conditions. The buyer must make it clear to all interested parties that this is a competition. The buyer must also use constructive dialogue to generate NegoEconomic potential. Give the competing suppliers a free hand, invite suggestions, and insist that they explain what the consequences of the suggestions will be. If the suggestion entails advantages to the buyer, he should reap the asymmetric value, but test the boundaries to see whether the supplier has more to give. Compare this to what the other competitors have to offer, assuming they are working from the same terms and conditions.

This approach to bargaining introduces an important and difficult problem: should you inform the other suppliers of the solutions and asymmetric value that was generated by the individual bargaining? If you do share, most suppliers will be reluctant to disclose their creativity and knowledge. They do not want to run the risk of having their know-how conveyed to their competitors. They will not want to become involved in the project only to end up in a bidding war with their competitors.

The buyer runs the risk that the competent suppliers will refuse to participate. Buyers who, unknown to their suppliers, secretly pass on information and know-how, are pursuing a short-term and risky gambit. The ethics of their actions are questionable and reflect poorly on their delegation.

Take aways

- Ask your counterpart the following question: "I am here to help you reduce your cost, liabilities, and risks and at the same time help you improve your profits...do you want me to do that?"

- Try to value all variables. If you can't, they are either not important or are a subjective variable.
- Questions and openness are the key to the creation of NegoEconomics.
- The potentials for NegoEconomics are everywhere.

PART C

*Dividing the Bigger Pie, Making the Deal,
and Defining the Future*

CHAPTER 8

Style Choices

The Function of Style Choices

Negotiators have style choices that reflect their attitude and govern their behavior during a negotiation. These style choices can be used with any of the strategic choices, although some are less compatible, such as combat (the style choice) in conjunction with SMARTnership (the strategic choice). Cooperation is generally more compatible with SMARTnership, while combat is more compatible with zero-sum.

Style choices define the manner in which the delegate conducts him- or herself at the negotiating table. Understanding these style choices, the impact they have on the negotiation climate, and the tactics associated with each choice are essential skills in the negotiator's toolbox. These role options define the negotiation climate and influence the rapport between the parties and the interpersonal dynamic among the delegates.

Your choice of style is often affected by your emotions or expectations regarding the bargaining process, and this will influence the signals you send and receive from the other party. For instance, if you believe that the other party is looking for a zero-sum solution, you might be more inclined to be combative without first examining whether another style would be better suited to your purpose. If you register aggressive signals from the other party, you are more likely to spontaneously respond aggressively. However, if the other party appears to be willing to cooperate, you might tend to be more cooperative.

Negotiations tend to have a life of their own, and they often develop quite differently from what was anticipated when emotions take over and determine the style choice. A delegate may become emotional during the negotiation, for example, and find herself unintentionally slipping into combat. Or the loyal opposition may suddenly become manipulative and adversarial. When this happens, the inexperienced negotiator will adjust his behavior to the moment and shift his role in a poorly planned manner. Consequently, he will be provoked into making decisions that he subsequently regrets.

The culture of your company and your worldview also affect your choice. The behavior that you demonstrate in a business negotiation often parallels your behavior vis-a-vis your family members, your friends, and colleagues. The effective negotiator will adjust his or her behavior to accommodate the goals and expectations of the party he or she represents.

Style Switching—The Adaptable Negotiator

The negotiator's style choice reveals the delegate's personality, attitude, and level of professionalism. It also dictates bargaining strategies and tactics, and permeates the entire negotiation process, ultimately determining how deals are made. The negotiator's style choice develops from an initial strategic decision, befitting the bargaining equity inherent in that transaction. Effective negotiators constantly adjust their choice—or style switch—in response to the situation before them. The effective negotiator will employ several styles.

A thorough understanding of negotiation styles equips business leaders with the skills to design and implement a personal negotiation style. Although individual style options can seem incompatible—combat versus cooperation, for example—effective negotiators are able to select the most relevant and constructive functionality of each style, moving fluidly between the options. Choosing thoughtfully among the various style options allows the delegate to remain flexible throughout the process.

Negotiation is an art and a science that requires you to work with probabilities while still expecting the improbable. You cannot predict with complete certainty how the other party is going to perceive the negotiation you are about to begin, and you cannot assume that she will perceive your signals as you intended. You cannot be sure how she is going to react, because you do not know her needs, her subconscious drives, or the feelings that govern her decision-making. As a result of so much uncertainty, you cannot plan your entire negotiation strategy in advance or structure it around any single approach or style choice.

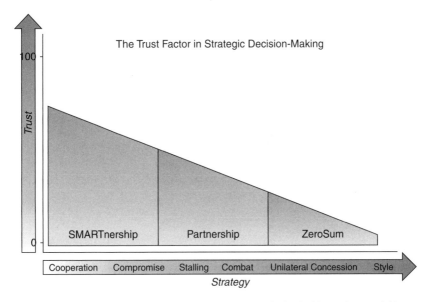

Figure 8.1 A high level of trust is required to unlock the hidden value available in SMARTnership.

Some negotiators select a single negotiation method and stick with it throughout the entire proceeding. Other negotiators are inflexible and try to adjust the negotiation to the situation that they originally imagined rather than shifting their strategy or their style choice to reflect the dynamic at the table. Yet you as the negotiator must be responsive and adaptable so that you can quickly adjust, or style switch, to the reality that you are facing in the moment. Whenever you find that the negotiation is slipping from your grip: TAKE A BREAK. Analyze what is happening and decide whether you need to switch your style or make use of a different tactic in order to get the negotiation back on track and moving in the direction you want it to go.

Style Choices

There is no single negotiation style that is better than the others.

The different style choices of the negotiator can be categorized as follows:

- Unilateral Concession
- Stalling
- Compromise
- Cooperation
- Combat

CONCESSIONS: UNILATERAL OR TACTICAL

The Tactical Concession

There are circumstances in which the delegate may choose to make a concession as a tactic in the negotiation. You determine the room for negotiation in advance and build NegoEconomic currency when you present your first offer. NegoEconomic currency may be money, time, warranties, extras, or any variable that brings value to the other party. This currency is to be spent in the course of the bargaining, and is exchanged for various gains. It is not a matter of relinquishing your own needs or profitability, nor does it entail taking unplanned risks.

The Purpose of the Tactical Concession

- To speed up the negotiation if it has become deadlocked. However, you must attempt to get something in return before you make a unilateral concession. You must be firm and make it clear to the other party that you are only giving in on this particular point in order to keep the negotiation going. You must not make another concession—even if they pressure you—without getting something more in return.
- To demonstrate good will by letting the other party succeed. In doing so, you satisfy his personal performance need.
- To keep the other party at the table by giving her an early win in the negotiation. This lowers her guard because she expects to be able to make an easy conclusion. You lure her into investing time, resources, and her personal status in the bargaining. The more she invests, the more difficult it will be for her to break off the negotiation in the event that you raise your demands later on. She may reason: *We can't quit now. We've spent over $100,000 on the project already.*
- To reduce the insecurity of the other party if there is an imbalance in bargaining equity between the delegates, which might provoke defensive tactics, combat, or deadlock.
- To provide the other party with the necessary arguments to sell the agreement within the organization he represents. If you do not assist him in this way, problems may arise because people other than those who were at the negotiating table will implement the agreement.
- To allow the other party to grandstand. You fulfill her personal need to determine and dictate conditions. The negotiation becomes a play to the gallery.

- To achieve a conclusion. This presupposes that you have tied down the negotiation, won all your demands, and received confirmation that the deal will be concluded if you will only give in concerning some particular areas. If you have not tied down the negotiation, it could easily turn into an auction in which your competitors outbid you and force you to make further concessions.

Unilateral Concessions

Unilateral concessions are perceived as a sign of weakness. If you are the party making the concession, it is a sign that you have lowered your expectation of the outcome or you have considerable room to maneuver. The pressure on you will increase and start a chain reaction of more concessions. You will be forced to keep giving until you have nothing left. The party that starts making unilateral concessions is most frequently the party that ends up with the least favorable result.

Example: Gabrielle Waffles and Compromises Her Bargaining Equity

Anis: I'm sorry, but we can't use you as our supplier. You're too expensive.

Gabrielle: There isn't a lot I can do about price. Are you looking for a discount?

Anis: Yes, that's a good place to start, what can you give me?

Gabrielle: I can let you have...maybe 3 percent.

Anis: I'm afraid that's not enough.

Gabrielle: I'm not authorized to go beyond 5 percent.

Gabrielle is trying to wiggle out of an unpleasant situation by means of a dangerous strategy: making a unilateral concession. She is making this concession without demanding something in return. She does not defend her demands and caves in to get out of a negotiation that she perceives as mentally strenuous.

Gabrielle states that there is not much she can do about the price. However, through her choice of words, she signals that she is uncertain and that there is probably a small margin that she can give away. The unilateral concession that she makes raises the buyer's level of expectation—if it is that easy to achieve a price reduction, there is probably more to be gained. Unilateral concessions usually lead to a chain reaction. The delegate who gives in unilaterally will have to keep giving until he has given everything away.

Gabrielle committed the following mistakes:

1. She made no effort to find out what Anis meant by saying that the price was too expensive. Too expensive compared to what? How much should it be? Has Anis produced a cost calculation?
2. She negotiated the price instead of discussing total costs and factoring in other variables. She made up her mind about the price without knowing what Anis thought about the delivery time, volume, quality, warranties, performances, or other conditions.
3. By emphasizing that she *isn't authorized to go beyond 5 percent*, she signaled that there was a greater discount that her boss could approve.

If Gabrielle had replied: *If you let us have an advance of 20 percent, I can give you a discount,* the negotiations would have developed completely differently. Asking for something in return does not affect her position negatively, nor does it signal insecurity; rather, it would have displayed openness and a willingness to discuss various demands.

Let the other party take an initiative before you make a unilateral concession. Concessions at the beginning of the negotiation often bear no fruit. No progress is made, and the other party is only testing your limits. It is important, for psychological reasons, that your opponent must work hard to get you to agree to a unilateral concession. If not, he does not get to demonstrate his negotiating skills, and he feels no satisfaction in the process.

A unilateral concession can sneak up on you when:

- Pressure becomes excessive and you attempt to flee the negotiation. You are insecure, stressed, and wary of conflict.
- You attempt to gain the acceptance of the other party by being accommodating and compliant. This, however, is a futile attempt to purchase a good relationship.

Do not relinquish your own needs or limit yourself to less than you had originally intended. If you choose to flee, you run the risk of the transaction generating a loss by drifting into a number of unplanned concessions.

When pressure becomes excessive, there is normally only one way out: ask for a break. Whether you have been negotiating for five minutes or five hours, you do not have to give any reason for the break. Simply say: *Excuse me, I need to stretch my legs for a few minutes.* In the course of the break, you can calm down in order to think of an alternative for the unilateral concession.

SMARTner Tip For the Advanced Practitioner: Strategic Use of a Unilateral Concession

A unilateral concession may be made with great caution at the end of the negotiation and should be employed either to finalize the deal or to unblock a negotiation that has become stuck. It must not be followed by further concessions until the other party gives you something in return or makes a counteroffer. A unilateral concession must be linked to a demand for something in return or else the bargaining equity will shift adversely for you.

When Your Opponent Is Requesting a Unilateral Concession, Ask Why

A manufacturer's plant supervisor demands that a vendor reduce his delivery time. The vendor can do this without incurring additional costs or risks. He tells the plant supervisor: *If it would suit you, we can have the equipment in place in three months.* This unilateral concession does not involve any additional costs for the vendor. While he asks for nothing in return, he does not look at the demand from the point of view of the plant supervisor. What is the shorter delivery time worth to the supervisor? Behind the supervisor's demand, there is a need. The shorter delivery time will probably yield a return on the investment at an earlier date, which results in added value to the manufacturer. If the vendor fails to see this, he gets no share in the increased benefit to the manufacturer. If the vendor can anticipate the benefit, he is then in a position to negotiate and reap some of the benefit. Make it a habit always to ask the other party: *Why do you want things to be the way that you are asking for them to be?*

When you are considering making a unilateral concession with a corresponding financial trade-off, think first of the price you are paying and then of the unilateral concession you will make. If you do not, the following can happen:

Aron: We might reduce our price by 5 percent, but then you must buy 20 percent of your annual requirements from us.

Liang: Five percent, you say...what's the new price going to be then?

Aron: $20.67 per unit.

Liang: I'll round off the figure to $20.50 in your quotation. I suppose we can agree to a small adjustment. We want current month plus 30 days net.

Aron: Yes, well, what do you have to say about the increase in quantity?

Liang: I'll come back to that. Do we agree about the payment conditions?

Aron: Yes.
Liang: Can you let us have this ___? That's what your competitors are offering.

Aron does not succeed in pinning down the buyer. He loses his grip on the negotiation. He shows his hand and has to make one concession after the other.

A supplier who is familiar with this trap works in a different way:

Klaus: If you buy another 20 percent of your annual requirements from us, I can do something about the price.
Martina: What price are you offering me, then?
Klaus: Do we have an agreement that you will buy another 20 percent?
Martina: That will depend on the price you can let me have.
Klaus: Can we deliver 20 percent during the first quarter?
Martina: That's okay, but what's the price?
Klaus: Are we agreed about all the other matters? Only the price is still outstanding?
Martina: Yes.
Klaus: Can you make a decision now?
Martina: Yes.
Klaus: What's a good price for you?
Martina: Around $20.
Klaus: It would be difficult for me to go down so low. The highest I can give you is 3 or 4 percent.

Do the Math!

Example: Bring your Calculator

A corporate fleet manager wanted to lease 120 cars for three years. In the very last minute of the negotiation, which has been taking place over three rounds, he demands that the car-leasing company must, free of charge, put iPad docks in the cars if the users ask for them. If the company agrees, the contract will be ready for signature. He tells the leasing agent: *You only charge $85/month for the iPad dock anyway. If we are in agreement, I'll sign the contract.* The leasing agent thinks about it for a few moments and says: *Okay.*

He never calculated how much that unilateral concession would cost. All 120 car users want the docking station. The charge per month is $85, and the cars are going to be leased for 36 months. Complex multiplication is difficult at the negotiating table. The end result can be more expensive than you expect, especially if you are not using a calculator. In the present case it was $367,200.

When preparing to negotiate, you must anticipate all the alternative claims you might make and receive from the other party. When the negotiation is under way and the other party makes his demands, you will rarely have the time to think about what counteroffer would be reasonable. Know what you are spending and what you are getting in terms of money. Know the value of your concession to the other party. Make unilateral concessions that cost you nothing, but that have considerable value for the other party.

Be Clear and Direct in Your Responses

If you cannot accept the other party's demands, say no. Do not say:

I don't think we can manage that.
I don't have the authority.
I'll think about it.
Probably there isn't anything we can do about the price.
By and large, we've gone as far as we can.

In these cases, the other party intends to have his way. When you use vague expressions, he discerns that there is some uncertainty that he can exploit. Instead, learn to say *no* and stick to your no.

Do not make unnecessary concessions if you can gain acceptance of your conditions in any other way. Make it clear to the other party that if he wants the deal, the offer he has received is the one that applies. It is his choice. Be tough on substance, but mild in manner.

Deliberate

You do not have to make a decision about the other party's demands right away. A break provides you with an opportunity to find new solutions. The break will make the other party uncertain as to whether or not he has gone too far.

If you do not know what to do, you can always try to pin down the other party and take his offer home so you can think about it. Ask the other party for options. When you ask for an option, you are not bound by any sort of obligation; rather, you are free to pick and choose. He, by contrast, is bound by his offer: *I can't decide about your offer here and now. If you'll let me look into it for a couple of days, I'll let you know. If we can accept your offer, the agreement will be ready for signature.*

You can:

- Accept the offer.
- Accept parts of it and negotiate about other elements in it.
- Propose an alternative.
- Reject the offer.

When You Are on the Receiving End of a Unilateral Concession

Say *thank you* and accept the concession, but avoid agreements that conclude with an obvious winner or loser. The agreement will be of no value to you—in fact, it might even be dangerous to you if the other party feels she has been taken advantage of, or if she has insufficient resources to fulfill her end of the bargain. It may be necessary for you to assist a weak negotiator by being generous to her in order to avoid future problems. You must ensure that the other party understands what she's agreeing to and that she has sufficient resources to execute the deal. It would be helpful for you to restate the terms of the agreement and ask for the other party's confirmation.

When the Concession Is Really an Admission of a Mistake

The third type of concession is the most difficult one. It shows personal strength to be able to concede to having made mistakes in substance. This is obviously important because you know that your arguments are frail. The concession may evoke the sympathy of the other party and increase his confidence in you.

STALLING

Stalling is a delaying tactic that allows the conclusion of certain issues under dispute to be postponed until later. Sometimes it is important to draw out the negotiations and stall. By stalling, you can gain extra time that you need. Stalling a negotiation is effective if the other party is running out of time or if prolonged negotiations will diminish his bargaining equity or increase his costs. Some tactics used for stalling are:

- Presenting new alternatives that were previously not on the table.
- Demanding more documentation.

- Requesting missing permits from public authorities.
- Taking a break with your delegation for an internal review.
- Claiming that you do not have the necessary authority, competence, or access to technical information or production plans.
- Taking up irrelevant questions for discussion.
- Leaving the negotiations to new members of your delegation. They can come back and start anew.

Example: Avoiding Pamela's Trap

Pamela, the buyer, invites Watson, the supplier, to a meeting to finalize a deal. Pamela asks Watson to explain his offer. She listens, but does not say anything about his arguments. When Watson has finished Pamela asks: *Is this your best offer?*

> *Watson*: Yes.
>
> *Pamela*: In that case, continuing these negotiations doesn't make sense. Your proposal is much too high compared to other alternatives. There's no point in wasting our time. You should check with your colleagues and reevaluate your offer. It looks to me as if you've made a miscalculation. We can resume our negotiations next Friday, at which point I will be expecting a different offer from you.

Watson, who has traveled a long way for this meeting, reluctantly returns to his company headquarters. He sees this as a failure on his part and becomes insecure. If he has other contacts in Pamela's organization, he can try to obtain more information. Watson starts negotiating within his own organization. He is looking for better conditions that will increase his chances of winning the order the next week. He cannot see that he is playing into Pamela's hands.

Why does Pamela structure the negotiation in this way? Hasn't she got anything better to do? Why has she not put forward a single factual argument? Why has she not made any opening bids? The answer is that she will probably employ the strategy of "offense is the best defense." Watson needs to keep his cool, and view this as a purchasing signal. He must take it easy and try to make the most of the situation.

Watson should stall and put Pamela under time pressure. Maybe he will show his hand by opening the negotiation. He must be wary of his bargaining equity and not push Pamela into a corner. A loss of bargaining equity can be perceived as a threat, which may ruin the dynamic of the entire negotiation. If stalling does not do the trick, he should present alternative solutions, rearrange what he has offered, or make an entirely new offer.

> **SMARTner Tip for the Advanced Practitioner: Suppliers Like to Stall**
>
> Suppliers tend to rely on stalling far more frequently than buyers do. The buyer will find it easier to take a new initiative for negotiation. If this particular tactic fails, the supplier may use the stalling tactic to lower the buyer's level of expectation. The buyer, who early in the negotiation is told that his demands are unreasonable, and that the supplier has no choice but to discontinue the negotiation, may be affected by the stalling.

Many suppliers are weak. They do not want to lose the deal, as they perceive this as failure. However, if they never have the courage to test the buyer, they may end up giving away too much. A transaction that never happens does not have to be a failure. You should not expect to complete ten out of ten transactions. If you do, it is a certainty that you are selling yourself short.

Example: Elena Puts Fernand in a Jam

At the end of a lengthy negotiation, Elena, the buyer says: *That's it. I'll call you Tuesday to let you know whether we have a deal or not.*

This way of ending the meeting is surprising as well as disappointing to Fernand, the supplier. He wants to know if a deal is forthcoming, and it is frustrating to leave the negotiation table with such uncertainty. Fernand will reevaluate his position.

Let us assume that Fernand has not gone down to his very lowest price. He asks himself if his chances would be improved if he were to lower his price. However, if he has already gone down to his very lowest price, he asks himself if he could look at his own profit margin, or if there is any other way of arriving at a lower price.

In this situation, many suppliers will offer a lower price. Fernand does not want to run the risk of waiting, for fear the job will slip through his fingers. Since Elena interrupted the negotiation, Fernand is forced to negotiate with himself and his superiors.

The classic error that Fernand might make is to call Elena before the following Tuesday to ask: *How does it look?* This is all that is needed for Fernand to have to quote a new price. At the same time, he has to explain why he can quote a new and lower price. He must, of course, save his credibility. While Fernand should protect his own interests and keep in touch with Elena, he should not phone her to ask: *How does it look?* By using this approach, he appears weak, and his bargaining equity is threatened.

Example: Is This Your Best Offer?

In the final phase of negotiating a contract following a long day of bargaining, all questions seem to have been settled. The results of the negotiation have been summarized on the flip chart. Lisel, the buyer asks: *Is this your best offer?* Gerard, the supplier, is uncertain about what Lisel means. Gerard feels like he has met all of his requirements and demands. Gerard asks: *What do you mean?*

> *Lisel*: Is this your best offer—the offer you want me to base my decision on?
> *Gerard*: Yes. *(He can't answer no. That would be tantamount to outbidding himself.)*
> *Lisel*: I guess that means today's negotiations are concluded. I'll be back next Friday at 3:00 p.m. to let you know whether we can accept your offer.

Gerard is surprised. Before the negotiation began, he had confirmed that Lisel was authorized to make the decision and that he had presented all of his demands. Gerard now feels nervous and does not want to postpone the deal.

> *Gerard*: Why don't we settle this matter here and now? What is it that you're uncertain about?

Despite his questions, he receives no answer. Gerard leaves the building without knowing the reason why Lisel is stalling. He attempts to analyze the negotiation. He discusses it internally with his colleagues. His uncertainty grows. Are there competing offers that are better than his? Should he remain passive and wait for Lisel's answer, or should he contact her before next Friday in order to make a better offer?

Gerard calls Lisel and asks her the classic question: *How are things?*

> *Lisel*: Not good.
> *Gerard*: I'm sorry to hear that. I'm calling because I assume that you've been discussing my offer internally during the week, and perhaps a question has come up...
> *Lisel*: If there were a question, I would have called you.
> *Gerard*: Oh, I see. I have been thinking about the offer I submitted, and I can come down by another...

Gerard has allowed himself to slip into the hands of Lisel, and is now outbidding himself. This was the reason for her stalling. He cannot handle the uncertainty, and in the course of the discussion with his colleagues, they decided to improve the offer.

If Gerard had not called, Lisel could have continued the negotiation the following Friday by saying: *I'm sorry, but I'm afraid that we haven't been able to get our executive group to accept the offer you and I negotiated last week. We have to meet once more to look at a few details.*

In this situation, Gerard must remain ice cold. If Lisel wants to conclude an agreement with Gerard, she will be forced to find an opening to get the conversation going again.

Tactical Stalling

When stalling is used as an intentional strategy that has been planned in advance, the objective is often to strengthen your own bargaining equity. This can be achieved by:

- Sweeping the problems under the carpet when you do not want the conflict to be concluded. You hope that the other party will be interested in continuing the negotiation and that she will lower her expectations.
- Putting your opponent and any competitors under time pressure. Someone who is pressed for time will often lower his expectations. Therefore, if there is no special reason to do so, you should never inform the other party of your deadlines: when your plane is leaving, how many nights you have booked your hotel room, and so forth.
- Asking for time to check references, collect more information, and examine other solutions.
- Making the other party feel uncertain in order to elicit a better offer. The other party should believe that there are other alternatives.
- Getting to know the other party and building trust.

How to Recognize Planned Stalling

- The negotiator keeps speaking about unimportant technical details in order to avoid reaching a conclusion and continuing the negotiations.
- The other party wants more information and asks you to write a memo, look at a drawing, or test samples, even though ample basis for making a decision is already available.

- The decision is postponed to a later time, such as the next budget year, or until the boss has returned home.
- A promise is made of a better offer and a more generous attitude to be dealt with next week.
- The same old arguments are put forward again and again. The stalling is due to uncertainty, poor preparation, and insufficient experience.

Risks Involved in Tactical Stalling

- The other party perceives you as being unwilling to negotiate and unprofessional. They may terminate the negotiations.
- Decisions are not made in time. Risk, costs, and harmful effects may increase.
- Others may get the deal ahead of you. You should never leave the negotiation without trying to tie down the other party by demanding a binding option or by concluding an agreement that binds the other party to you without limiting the options of your party.
- Sending the wrong signals. The other party perceives you as cowardly, afraid of conflict, and insecure. She continues to follow her strategy, hoping you will cave in if she intensifies the pressure.

How to Avoid Tactical Stalling

- Put the other party under pressure.
- Wait out the other party if it is to your advantage. This can be an efficient strategy if you can block his activities. The effect is to intensify the pressure exerted by third parties, economic conditions, the media, and public opinion on the negotiators. A disadvantage can be that the pie to be shared is shrinking while you wait.
- Make sure you get all possible alternatives on the table at the beginning of the negotiation. Consider pursuing parallel negotiations with the available alternatives if the negotiations entail a threat to you.
- Use informal contacts and paths to pursue the negotiations.
- Start by getting an agreement on the timetable and the deadline for conclusion. If the other party cannot accept these parameters, find out why. Is the obstacle genuine? If so, can it be removed? Otherwise, consider waiting until the opposing delegation is ready to make a decision.

When Stalling Is Unplanned and Used Unintentionally

Sometimes, when the negotiator is unskilled in managing conflict, insecure, or indecisive, he or she may wish to put off an unsatisfactory agreement or a conflict, but stalling will not always ensure an improvement of the negotiating position. It is a tactic of escape that might be a better strategy than an unplanned concession.

Risks Involved in Unplanned Stalling

- You avoid making up your mind and expressing yourself clearly. You miss finding out where the parties stand. Misunderstandings arise, and you begin to mistrust the other party.
- It becomes a comfortable escape route away from the negotiation and the decision. This is used all too often when the negotiation gets tough or when conflicts arise.
- The supplier loses the deal to a competitor.

How to Recognize Unplanned Stalling

- The negotiator says she will come back later with a decision. If you ask her to explain why she cannot make a decision, you will see that this question puts her under pressure and makes her ill at ease.
- The negotiator hides behind formalities and procedural issues.
- The negotiator rephrases the purpose of the negotiation to avoid having to decide: *Well, the purpose of this meeting was simply for us to meet in order to . . .*

How to Counteract Unplanned Stalling

- Make an agreement with the other party about the objective of the negotiation. If the objective was agreed on earlier, restate it and seek confirmation from all parties.
- Inform the other party in advance of the questions you wish to discuss so that he can prepare. Do not expose him to unnecessary surprises or tough gambits that create uncertainty if you have not intentionally planned for combative negotiations.
- Insist that you meet with negotiators who are authorized to conclude an agreement.
- Ensure that you have alternatives so that you can flee the negotiation if you must and close the deal with another party.

COMPROMISE

A genuine compromise is characterized by a type of bargaining in which both parties give and take: *If you'll let me have an advance of 20 percent, I can let you have a 3 percent discount.* This type of bargaining is often a component of cooperation.

In a genuine compromise, the negotiators:

- Employ tactical gambits in a friendly negotiation climate without the threats or harsh styles associated with combative strategies.
- Create two-way communication by asking and answering questions.
- Chart the needs of the opponent before presenting their own offer or forming an opinion about the other party's proposal. Avoid fighting over which solution is the better one until they have fully grasped the opponent's requirements.

If the other party does not pursue a constructive course or inform you of the background for his requirements, you are facing a compromise negotiation that, in many respects, looks like combat. In this situation, you will often choose the same approach as you would for combat. If you want the other party to abandon her demands, you can try to say *yes*, but at the same time demand something in return that you know the other party cannot let you have.

A better method is to offer alternatives. Try to accommodate the other party on the points where negotiation is possible, but always demand something in return: this is the nature of genuine compromise. Be mild in manner, but firm in substance.

A Compromise Does Not Mean You Have to Meet Halfway

Many compromises result in the parties meeting halfway—splitting the difference. Proceed with caution, when your opponent suggests that you share an expense of $100,000. It is not certain by any means that you need go so far as to cover $50,000. When the other party suggests this compromise, he has given up. He is anxious to reach a conclusion and is prepared to cover at least $50,000 himself to make the problem go away. Perhaps he also says: *Let's split it 50/50.*

Determining the Threshold of Pain

Experience shows that you can often interpret the other party's offer in the following way: If he suggests a compromise, the purpose is to make a 50/50 split. He aims to land at $50,000. But where is his threshold of pain? Divide by two again! The likely threshold of pain is $75,000 as against $25,000. Suggest an amount just below his threshold of pain, testing how he reacts: *I can afford $50,000. I could accept $20,000.*

If the other party is stubborn and sticks to the $50,000, he might be one of those people who does not adhere to the rule. If his answer is: *That's not enough. I can't go further than $25,000*, then to avoid being the loser, you should handle this with caution.

How to Recognize a Compromise:

- One-way communication and arguments emerge. The negotiators work with allegations instead of with questions. No attempt is made to investigate what the other party needs
- The parties do not have the courage to be open and honest.
- A negotiator claims to be aiming for a "spurious compromise" and demands something that belongs to the other party, but later argues about what proportion of his original demand he might relinquish. This type of compromise is unilateral because the relinquishing party gets nothing in return.

Tactics commonly employed to get the other party to abandon his position include orchestrated facts, bluffing, competition, time pressure, promises of future compensation, old friendship, and direct threats: *If you don't accommodate us, we're forced to...* Negotiators invest a great deal of energy in arguing and orchestrating facts.

Communication becomes one-way because both parties prefer arguing instead of asking and answering questions. Neither listens to the other, but they try to sway the other by means of arguments, which are often biased and untruthful. When negotiators use untruthful arguments, the opposition will quickly lose confidence.

Example: An Inadequate Solution That Costs Too Much

Laura, the buyer, opens the negotiation by saying: *There's a point in your quotation, Vikram, that we must straighten out before we can discuss it. We requested 90-day terms of credit, but you've only offered 30 days.*

> *Vikram*: Thirty days is the longest credit we offer our customers.
> *Laura*: In that case, we can't accept the quotation. Our demand for 90 days is non-negotiable.

Vikram: I don't have the authority to offer you more than 30 days. Thirty days is our international maximum credit period.

Laura: Phone your home office, then!

Vikram: That would be a waste of time. Our financing terms are structured around 10, 20, or 30 days credit, and I've already offered you the best credit terms available.

Laura: In that case, Vikram, I will put aside your offer. It's no longer of interest to us.

Vikram: What I can do is offer you 45 days credit, which is my last and final offer. No one else has been granted better credit terms.

Laura: Is this a compromise offer on your part?

Vikram: Yes, Laura.

Laura: What you're proposing is an insult. Where is the justice in our giving 45 days, when you're only giving 15? If you'd said 60 days, we'd each have gone halfway.

Vikram: Are you going to accept if we give you 60 days?

If neither party wants to give in, one party usually resorts to threats in order to force the other party to abandon their position or to test whether the threat is genuine. The solution is usually in-between the original positions. No one wishes to lose by the division, and give or get more than the other. In our example, Vikram has suddenly been authorized to negotiate about payment conditions. He first offered 45 days credit, then 60 days credit, despite the fact that he had previously said that his organization only offers 10-, 20-, or 30-day terms of credit. Vikram delivers his absolute best offer after only a few minutes of haggling. Laura accepts 60 days despite the fact that she previously stated 90 days was non-negotiable.

Did the parties arrive at a good solution? Vikram had to give another month's credit, which costs money. But what did he get in return? Laura gave him nothing. This compromise is one-sided because only one party is giving anything.

Suppose that Laura genuinely needs 90 days credit. Have her needs been met? No, she will be short of money when the invoice comes due. Once they have agreed on a solution of 60 days credit, it is clear to both parties that the other party had been untruthful in their arguments. Continuing negotiations are likely to be marred by mistrust.

If you ask Vikram why he gave in, his answer will be: *I'd rather do that than lose the deal altogether. That's why I'm happy to take on the cost for the extended credit. That will cost me $85,000, but I have room for negotiation of $120,000. I can afford that.*

If you ask Laura why she insisted so strenuously on longer credit terms, she will say: *We make a lot of money on supplier credit. In this case, the extended credit was worth $60,000 to us.*

It costs Vikram $85,000, but it is only worth $60,000 to the buyer! What happens to the difference of $25,000? This $25,000 is the price the negotiators have paid for using the wrong strategy.

Through their compromise, the parties have agreed on a partial solution that is far too expensive. Vikram's concessions do not give Laura an optimal solution. Instead of searching for the added value, they managed to reduce the stakes for both!

Laura committed the classic mistake of looking only at what the changing conditions will mean to her. If she does not know whether Vikram's costs are more or less than her gain of $60,000, she cannot make a correct decision. Laura should have asked Vikram: *What will it cost for you to extend the credit terms?*

If Vikram is open and speaks the truth, Laura will receive the answer: *Approximately $85,000.* Then, she can offer the supplier 30 days credit and lower the price by $80,000 in return. In that case, Vikram will win $5,000 (the difference between the $85,000 he would have lost by extending the payment terms and reducing the price by $80,000 with the original 30-day payment term), and Laura will gain $20,000 (the difference between the $80,000 price reduction and the $60,000 she would have gained from the 90-day payment term). It would be better to offer Vikram an advance and get a price reduction ($80,000) that would exceed Laura's interest costs ($60,000) in return.

> *Spurious compromises, threats and combat often lead to a solution with two losers.*

Do not think that the negotiation has been concluded just because the parties have reached an agreement on the conditions of payment. Vikram knows that Laura has more demands. He does not know whether he has sufficient room left for negotiation to meet her demands or if he has accommodated her enough for his concession to yield the best results.

Laura achieved better conditions of payment without having to give anything in return. Because it was easy to get a concession, her expectations will rise.

What Should Vikram Have Done?

Vikram should have asked Laura: *Why do you need 90 days credit?* If she answered: *We have a liquidity issue this quarter,* Vikram would have understood that the demand was not plucked out of thin air.

Vikram's next question should have been: *How much are you willing to pay for this credit?*

Laura might have answered: *Nothing. Since you're so expensive, I can't accept any further price increases. We will discuss your demands, but as you'll understand, it will cost us money to let you have longer credit terms. The one who can borrow at the lowest rate of interest should be responsible for the financing. How much do you have to pay for credit?*

By establishing two-way communication and asking about the background for the demands raised by the other party, the parties can get closer and initiate an open and trusting cooperative agreement.

An alternative strategy would be to begin bargaining immediately by insisting on being given something in return: *If you can increase your order by 20–30 percent, I'll see what I can do about the conditions of payment.*

Before Vikram submits a concrete offer, he must examine all of Laura's demands. It is better and safer to reach an agreement concerning the entire package rather than trying to meet the demands one by one.

The supplier should also insist on having an answer to the question: *If we can meet these requirements, do we have a deal?*

When to Use Compromise Intentionally:

- You have to choose between two evils. You must be pragmatic. No matter how convinced you are that your ideas are right, you will only be successful if you persuade other people to support them. If you cannot succeed in doing so, you may be forced to use compromise as your strategy.
- Your needs compete for the available resources when more resources cannot be generated between parties.
- You have not learned to cooperate, or you have not recognized the advantages of trying to examine what needs are behind the other party's demands.
- The other party is not willing to cooperate and open up. Compromise is a far better alternative than combat.
- You need to reach a conclusion under time pressure. Note that the compromise should be kept for the end of the negotiation, after you have received confirmation that the agreement is ready for signature and provided that only minor points remain to be cleared up.
- You want to get out of a fight that you feel you are about to lose.

- You think you can outsmart the other party and achieve better results by bargaining instead of using any of the other strategies.
- You know that the other party will try to resolve the negotiation by proposing a compromise, so you begin the negotiation with ample room for bargaining. Despite the compromise, you will still reach your objective.
- You can accept a temporary solution and wait for better conditions.
- You can agree to revise the agreement and follow up on it later.
- You want to let the other party win by agreeing to let him have more than half the pie.

When Compromise Is Used Unintentionally:

- You resist conflict and feel insecure. You do not have the courage to speak in a clear-cut manner, send direct messages, or clarify the existing differences between you and your opponent. You attempt to hide your insecurity by accommodating her in every respect.
- You have inferior bargaining equity.
- You see the negotiation as a game you can win. You avoid combat and direct confrontation, but cannot handle the openness and trust required for cooperation.
- It becomes a matter of status. You will not give in. You have to go along with the other party's solution. However, if you can force the other party to retreat, you may have enhanced your own bargaining equity.

Risks Involved in Compromise:

- You do not achieve a result that is optimal for both parties because you do not utilize the joint resources in the best possible way. The potential for asymmetric value remains unexploited, and the party in the lesser bargaining equity is forced to accept solutions that may be harmful to the project and make it more costly.
- You create an atmosphere and develop a business philosophy in which playacting and status become important factors.
- You manipulate others by means of bluffing, and consequently they find it difficult to determine which information is truthful and which is orchestrated to be a power play. Any previous trust that might have been present is ruined.

- You avoid looking for new solutions or alternatives, and negotiations become deadlocked.
- Your needs will not be met, but you will postpone the conflict.
- You stop negotiating as soon as you reach a result below your budgetary limit.

COOPERATION

Cooperation is based on the highest level of trust, and open and honest communication between the parties that is driven by a willingness to listen and understand the other party's needs and requirements. Cooperation does not mean shirking the issues or relinquishing your own needs or bargaining equity. The purpose is to make the stake as large as possible for the benefit of both parties.

You Must Lay the Groundwork for Cooperation Ahead of Time

Cooperation is neither simple nor obvious. It makes serious demands on you and on the other party. When preparing and analyzing the negotiations, you must attune yourself mentally toward cooperation. This means that you must demonstrate a certain degree of generosity, be open and constructive, and not let your emotions take over. Insecurity, the desire to fight, and deadlocks can best be avoided by asking for a break.

When to Use Cooperation Intentionally:

- To achieve long-term agreements in which the needs of both parties are respected and met.
- To find optimal solutions.
- To create synergy.
- To avoid having to compete.
- When you have an innate feeling for fair play.
- When you are convinced that cooperation leads to the best and most sustainable result.
- To form a long-term relationship, particularly if you are or might become dependent on the other party.
- To take advantage of the resources of both parties—not for combat, but to meet the needs and the mutual interests of both parties in the best possible manner.
- To avoid competing. (Avoid forming a monopoly or a cartel.)

- To apply the golden rule: "what you demand from the other party, you must also demand from yourself."
- To offer the other party a deal she cannot refuse. This deal is better than all the other deals, and is one that she can sell internally.
- When your needs are not in competition with the requirements of the opposing delegation.

When Cooperation Is Used Unintentionally:

- You feel that the personal chemistry is working well. Many experts think good deal-making is more likely the result of good personal relations than of resolution of issues of price and performance. Be careful, however, not to be naive or too eager to speed up the pace of the negotiations as soon as you feel that the personal chemistry is working.
- You wish to avoid a conflict. No conflict will arise if you are willing to share, but there is a serious risk that you will be leaning toward concessions.

Risks Involved in Cooperation:

- Your openness could be exploited, and the other party might interpret the signals you send as signs of weakness. He will respond with combat because you have opened up prematurely before assessing your bargaining equity as it relates to his. You are not aware that your openness has been unilateral.
- The time it takes to build up the requisite personal chemistry and trust may not be available to you. You are under time pressure and fearful that you cannot land the deal.
- You are up against a typical combative negotiator. Cooperation may be difficult.

Beware of Wolves in Sheep's Clothing:
The Art of Achieving Cooperation

Cooperation is not something that happens all by itself. The path to it can be long and arduous, and sometimes one who seeks cooperation is actually a wolf in sheep's clothing. He sees cooperation as a sign of weakness and takes advantage of the willingness to cooperate by outmaneuvering the other party.

Many negotiators are tense during the first few minutes of the negotiation. They are so focused on what they are going to say that they completely overlook valuable information provided by the other party in the negotiation's opening phase.

When the other party has said what he wants to say, he can relax and listen to you. Only then does it make sense to get your own message across. By listening to him, you have gained his trust, and by extension, his attention. Negotiators often use the other party as a mirror emulating the behavior of the other.

How to Recognize Cooperation:

- Communication is two-way. You listen, question, and answer questions in an open and honest manner.
- Clever gambits are avoided. Instead, you go for openness and trust.
- The negotiators treat each other as equal partners.
- Negotiations do not focus exclusively on the result and the combat surrounding it. Needs, problems, and opportunities are charted before alternative solutions are launched.

Cooperation does not mean that gains and risks are divided evenly between the parties. Your proposal must meet the needs of the other party better than all the other alternatives. The other party is to be treated as an equal, the information you release must be true, and you must openly explain the purpose behind the agreement you wish to conclude. Your most serious problem is to obtain information about the alternatives available. You need to have this information in order to know how far to go in order to meet the needs of the other party. Cooperation does not exclude a tough stance on the issues under negotiation.

If you are willing to live according to the golden rule, "do unto others as you wish others to do unto you," you should respond with cooperation and take advantage of the existing opportunities to find a better solution. Build up and utilize trust. Make sure the stream of information is kept flowing. Chart the needs of the loyal opposition. Accept that different parties have different values. Seek solutions that meet the needs of your opponent and do not start conflicts about whose life philosophy is the right one.

Cooperation in Action

When two companies enter into a cooperation agreement, there will always be redundancy of some functions. One finance department will generally suffice, and the function is transferred to the party that can perform the job at the lowest cost. Whether the added value can be realized is determined by the extent to which the savings are managed and by the company's ability to make use of the freed resources in a productive way.

When the experience, the knowledge, and the creativity existing between the two parties starts to work together, synergy arises. The sum of two plus two equals significantly more than four. The added value comes about when the parties begin experiencing personal chemistry in the new constellation.

But what about all the small daily negotiations that are necessary for the company to function effectively while seeking added value and while dealing with the plans dictated by management? How is this added value being used? Many companies face problems and failure. The reality of commercial bargaining shows how hard it is to put the theories of added value into practice at the negotiation table.

Cooperation is far from unproblematic. In fact, many configurations are not possible. There is no patent solution that automatically solves the problems and streamlines the activities. When cooperation works, we get more effective solutions. The cooperating parties act on a safer, more exhaustive, and better basis for decision-making. The quality of the decision is often proportional to the amount of information the parties have when they make their decisions. The increased information enables them to see new alternatives. This also means that the parties more easily discover which changes will lead to accessing the added value and which will make the project more expensive. The risk of making the wrong decisions is reduced.

Parties that cooperate tend to work more constructively. They do not spend their energy on fighting about whose solution is the right one. They do not need to waste their time on flexing their muscles and running the risk of destroying the negotiation climate. Instead, they often act on a joint analysis of the situation. They spend their energy on finding the best solution together. The parties may find that they have far more uniting needs than competitive needs. The parties complement each other and concentrate their resources in their individual areas.

COMBAT

The Combative Negotiator

Since 2007, I have seen more examples of combat in negotiations than ever before. The reason is obvious. When people are under pressure, afraid, or desperate, they act desperately. Combative behavior comes from the primitive instincts that saved us thousand of years ago in the wild. But today, we should have grown into something more advanced, where we capitalize on the differences instead of fighting.

Combat has to do with the attitude the negotiator adopts at the table. There are individuals, companies, and entire cultures that use combat as their preferred negotiation strategy. Human beings have evolved to survive in a tough world. Aggression is a precondition for survival and, according to the process of natural selection, only the strong survive. Combative behavior is the natural and generally appropriate response to aggression, and only rarely is this response challenged.

The combative negotiator is condescending, provocative, manipulative, and dishonest. He takes advantage of people. These opponents will create a negative negotiation climate using tactical moves such as threats, bluffs, humiliations, personal attacks, ultimatums, time pressure, silence, pretend offers, the assertion that the negotiator does not have the authority to conclude the deal, and other psychological ploys intended to disarm you and cause you to lose your effectiveness. Through attacks and provocations, they hope to create enough stress to paralyze you. The combat-prone delegate's behavior destroys trust, ruins relationships, and makes you want to seek revenge. For these combatants, cooperation is a signal of weakness.

How to Recognize Combat

The behaviors that most typically signify combat are:

One-way communication: Arguments, demands, and threats, which are difficult to verify or validate. Questions are met with silence, and argumentation is based on orchestrated facts or lies. The mode of communication is usually aggressive, and the messages are terse. A typical combative negotiator makes expensive demands without verifying or explaining the demands. If you are on the receiving end of this style, you will find it difficult to determine what is right and what is wrong. You are short of information, but nevertheless forced to make a decision because you are put under time pressure.

Provocations: Personal attacks and disparaging remarks are used.

Hidden intentions: The intentions behind the negotiation are kept secret. The combative negotiator may initially be very pleasant; however, he is often a wolf in sheep's clothing. As a ploy, he will listen carefully and give the impression that he wants to understand your position. The noncombatant is duped in order to gain trust, to obtain information, and to lower his guard. Before he shows his true colors, the combative delegate will have made sure that you have already revealed too much.

Combative gambits: Demonstrative gambits are used to show negotiation strength, and they usually aim to make you feel inferior and insecure because the other party knows that a stressed counterpart will be more likely to flee the tension by giving in. Flight is the beginning of a concessionary strategy. You have several escape routes to choose from—compromise will usually provide you with a better result.

Differentiate Combativeness from Conciseness

Do not confuse combat with a tough, uncompromising stance. Some negotiators perceive the party that sends clear, honest, and direct messages as a combative negotiator, especially if the message presented is negative and contains demands and criticism.

A negotiator who is direct, clear, and tough on substantive issues, but who also tries to be open and assertive in his attitude is not a combative negotiator. She aims to establish two-way communication because she does not want to create uncertainty, confusion, or misunderstandings. She wants good personal relations, and endeavors to create trust in herself, her cause, and her organization.

Risks Involved in Combat

If you are contemplating combative behavior yourself, you should be conscious of the risks and consider whether it is the most appropriate style choice. Combat may result in:

- **An Unsatisfactory Result:** Unfair methods are shortsighted and rarely yield favorable outcomes. The trust and openness required for the formation of a SMARTnership will be missing. Many people follow the rule: *Don't do business with somebody you don't trust.*
- **Harmed Relations:** You harm the good relationship you have established and destroy the trust you have built with the other party. The credibility gap and the wish for revenge that might arise will not only hurt you personally, but it will also damage the reputation of the organization you represent.
- **Retaliation:** If you hoodwink the other party, you are going to pay for it down the road. The other party will want to get even. If he can't take revenge on you, he'll take revenge on your

organization. Sooner or later, a situation will arise in which you will be dependent on him and need a favor.

• **Deadlock:** When your opponent responds with combat, the negotiation often becomes deadlocked. You find yourself at an impasse.

When to Use Combat Intentionally

Combat can be used strategically when:

• You are moving toward difficult market conditions, profitability is declining, margins are shrinking, and everyone must justify their demands. Few negotiators are capable of being tough on the substantive issues without sliding into combat.

• You work for a company that has a combative culture. You want to be perceived as a member of the team and accepted by your peers and the boss. A combative culture is often predominant in industries with many suppliers selling identical products and in connection with one-off transactions.

• The other party wants to win by pressuring you into making unilateral concessions. All gains are made at your expense. You are expected to give in when it comes to gains, and you must also assume the risks and costs.

• You are working to reach a quick agreement by exploiting a bargaining equity advantage over your opponent. You give the opposition no time to prepare, consider alternatives, or reorient herself following a surprise gambit.

• Your non-negotiable demands must prevail.

• The other side attempts to exploit your willingness to cooperate and be open. They see a chance to grab the whole pie and you must respond.

• You must overcompensate for insufficient factual data and/or lack of preparation.

• Combat is part of a mixed strategy. You fall victim to the classic good cop / bad cop technique. Combat is replaced by cooperation. You are surprised positively and lower your guard, and then give too much away.

• Your combative approach is met with a counter-combat because you have sent combative signals or acted in a manner that has caused the other party to lose confidence in you.

• You want to get even by retaliating.

• You are in a highly competitive environment allocating scarce resources.

When Combat Is Used Unintentionally

During a negotiation, some delegates unintentionally switch styles. To them, combat is a natural reaction when they feel insecure, threatened, inferior, or stressed. The pressure is too much. This may happen because of differences in age, bargaining equity, or experience, or when the negotiator is unprepared, under time pressure, or has sent signals that cause fear or anxiety in the other party.

If the combat is unintentional, the non-combatant should send clear messages and openly demonstrate how undesirable the outcome of combat would be. At the same time, provide an alternative to combat and demonstrate how you can achieve a better outcome for both of you by means of a different presentation: *I think this negotiation is heading in an undesirable direction. If we go on like this, the whole deal is going to fall apart. I suggest that instead we take a look at how . . .*

Dealing with negotiators Who Don't Want SMARTnership

A negotiation is a game in which no one wants to lose face. It is a psychological game between two people, and your behavior will undoubtedly affect the other party. Subconsciously, we mirror each other, and, consequently, you will generally get the treatment you deserve. The wider the gulf between you and your opponent, the more important it is to show respect, to listen, and to try to understand her arguments and objections. While this does not mean you have to share your opponent's viewpoint, you will be more successful if you can keep your ego in check and avoid becoming competitive and / or combative. Do not view negotiation as a verbal fight in which your tongue is quicker and your snappy choice of words more provoking. You are not negotiating in front of an audience who will applaud your clever comebacks.

Many negotiations fall apart during bargaining because the parties become locked in verbal combat. Negotiations grind to a halt because the delegates are attempting to score points off of each other. They make snide comments at the expense of the other party and try to throw them off balance with derogatory remarks. Pressure usually triggers counterpressure. High-pressure tactics usually result in the other party's adopting a defensive position. More often than not, verbal infighting will intensify. Since neither party wants to lose, one-upmanship often threatens to destroy the entire bargaining process. In the long run, this is an unproductive negotiation style.

There are individuals, companies, and entire cultures that use combat as their preferred negotiation style choice. Through attacks and provocations, they hope to stress out and paralyze their opponent. Their opening is aggressive and will feed into the counterpart's sense of insecurity. These delegates will create a negative climate of negotiation using tactical moves such as threats, bluffs, humiliations, and other psychological influences intended to disarm their opponent and cause them to lose their effectiveness. For these combatants, cooperation is a signal of weakness and an open and positive attitude is alien.

If you recognize how dirty tricks are used in negotiation, you will then be better prepared to neutralize combative moves. If the combative opponent fails to reap the benefit of combative tactics, you may pave the way for a more positive and constructive solution.

Do not confuse combat with an unmovable position. Firmness can open the way for subsequent cooperation. If you are firm in the substance of your position without compromising your ability to establish an open, positive climate, you will cause the combatant to realize that fighting is more trouble than it is worth. A solution founded in cooperation may better serve the combatant's interests.

Combative negotiators run the risk of getting attention for their demands only from weak partners, who are forced to take what is offered. The combative negotiator runs a risk when he moves forward too harshly. In the end, he has run through all of his possible partners, leaving companies that he has run aground in his wake. They may not have had the chance of investing in new technology, product development, human resource development, or quality. If he does not find new partners, the combatant may be forced to undertake the job of getting his old subsuppliers back on their feet.

Sitting Opposite the Combative Negotiator

For some negotiators, combat is the first and only style choice. They do not see the value of solutions with two winners, and they are either unaware or do not believe that ethics and fair play will advance their objectives. Delegates with low bargaining equity see only two alternatives: cave in and lower the price, or get angry and end the negotiations, telling the buyer: *That's it. We've got nothing more to say to each other.*

You have more effective options. But before you choose your path, pause to analyze why your opponent is staking everything to win by resorting to combat. If you recognize how dirty tricks are used in negotiation, you will then be better prepared to neutralize combative moves. If an opponent fails to reap the benefit of combat, you may pave the way for a more positive and constructive solution.

If you find yourself in a negotiation climate in which you suspect that your opponent is likely to employ unfair and highly combative tactics, do not become hampered by your principles. A high degree of morality, based on American norms and values, may constitute a handicap in some international contexts. In order to achieve SMARTnership, you must be open to seeing both sides of the negotiation. You must become as familiar with unfair tactics as you are with fair tactics. If the other party goes down this path, you must know how these tactics work, what he hopes to achieve, and how you can neutralize his moves.

If you are met by combat, attempt to maneuver the other party into a more constructive and positive direction. If this cannot be done, take on the fight that the other party has initiated. If you have no alternative or if you are dependent on the other party, you have no choice but to meet the other party's challenge.

Example: Jasmine Lays a Trap

You are about to negotiate the financial terms in an offer that you have made. All the technical discussions on specifications and performance have been settled in a calm and constructive framework, and you are expecting the negotiations to be concluded in the same unruffled atmosphere. After a few minutes of general conversation, however, the buyer heatedly exclaims: *I'm sorry, but we can't accept your offer. You're just too expensive.*

This outburst is common in many negotiations. The person who has initiated the proposal (in this case, the supplier) is cut off by the buyer, Jasmine, who rejects the offer and demands concessions or changes to the proposal.

The supplier, Tomas, needs additional information to be able to assess the buyer's demands. So he asks: *Expensive compared to what?*

Jasmine: Your competitors.
Tomas: Could you elaborate on what you are saying and give me some reasons why you find us too expensive?
Jasmine: You must lower your price, or else we won't have a deal.
Tomas: Our quotation includes a number of different components. Could you please specify which of them you feel is overpriced and what you think the price should be?
Jasmine: It serves no useful purpose to go on negotiating. You seem to have misunderstood the conditions and the competition in the market. Tomorrow, at the latest, we want a new offer with better prices and conditions. This ends today's negotiations.

How Does Tomas Respond?

He must keep calm and not let himself be provoked into hasty emotional reactions. If he feels that the pressure is getting to be more than he can handle, he should ask for a break. If he does not, chances are that he will walk right into Jasmine's trap!

Before you choose a response, analyze the reason for the combative stance. In deciding how to respond, choose among the following tactics:

Silence: Respond with silence. Do not let yourself be provoked. Do not let your emotions govern your actions. Try to maintain equilibrium between sense and sensibility. Even if the other party is wrong, avoid further discussion. In this way, you can avoid the attack-and-defense spiral of gambits and countermoves that can escalate into a situation in which the whole thing falls apart. Remember that the combative negotiator is powered by adrenaline. He will not listen to you until he has finished his tirade.

If your silence does not yield the desired result, you can delay the negotiation. Suggest scheduling another session and make it clear to the other party that you think it is counterproductive to continue negotiating at the moment. This is a method that lives up to the adage *be mild in manner, but firm in substance.*

Questions: Ask questions to test the other party and make her realize the dangers of continued combat. Break the pattern of one-way communication. If you can shift the dynamic to two-way communication, you can win her trust, because she may start listening to you and realize that your proposals are stronger than hers.

Naivete: Pretend to be naive. Intentionally misunderstand, ask counter-questions, and ask for the other party to repeat all their arguments. Wear the other delegation down.

Combat: Go into battle to beat the other party if your own position is strong and if you are able to pay the price. This is only recommended after you have tried all other strategies and only if you do not want anything to do with the other party in the future.

Substitution: Switch negotiators if you suspect any personal conflicts, or if you think the personal chemistry isn't working.

THE EXAMPLE OF THE TEN ORANGES

In a room, there are ten oranges in a bowl. In two adjacent rooms, there are two groups who assign their delegates the task of collecting the ten oranges. The negotiators enter the room at the same time and discover that they have been assigned the same task, but that there are not enough oranges for both of them. They face a conflict.

Combat

If they choose combat, threats and harsh words will soon be heard. Verbal combat may turn into physical combat. Neither group feels certain of winning, nor can they be sure how the other group will feel about winning through combat. Therefore, both negotiators reject combat as a style choice.

Concession

Concession means that the negotiators avoid conflict, but leave all the oranges to the other party. The loss of bargaining equity is unacceptable because both negotiators want to achieve good results. Therefore, they reject concession as a style choice.

Stalling

Stalling means that the negotiators will leave the room to go have coffee with their group—perhaps the problem will solve itself, your group could give you new directives, or maybe the other party will cave in. Negotiation has not changed the situation because the conflict is still there. Stalling could have been advantageous if the negotiators had chosen to take advantage of this option by trying to obtain more information.

Compromise

Compromise will mean a division of the ten oranges. However, each negotiator wants more than five oranges for his group. It becomes easier to convince his group to accept a compromise. In this case, you need clever arguments. Perhaps you tell the other party: *Yesterday you took all the oranges. You have already received what's due to you. But I'll be a nice guy, and let you have two.* Later on, two may become three or possibly four.

The other party also knows how to argue, and says: *It's quite true that we took them all yesterday. You didn't want any then. If you had wanted the oranges today, you should have told us in advance. Naturally, we assumed that the oranges were for us.*

The offer of compromise does not lead to any solution that is acceptable to the delegates. Neither of them wants to look like a loser. Both of them want all ten oranges.

Cooperation

Cooperation means that they try to solve the problem together. Before they can do so, however, they need more information. When are the oranges to be used, and what are they going to be used for? The two negotiators do not know, and they ask their groups. Later, the negotiators return to the room. The oranges are to be used immediately. One group needs the oranges for juice, the other for marmalade. Now, the solution seems clear: one group will squeeze the juice out of the oranges and then give the remainder to the other group, who can now make marmalade.

By honestly disclosing their intentions to each other, the parties established that their needs were not contradictory and that both parties could have their needs met. This way, both parties feel like winners.

The reason the conflict became solvable was because the communication became two-way. As long as the negotiators are inclined to argue and attempting to manipulate, the pieces of the puzzle that are necessary for an optimal resolution will not be revealed. When communication becomes two-way, the key questions are asked and the answers are provided that will allow the negotiators to find completely new solutions to the conflict.

Take aways

- What is your primary negotiation style?
- Use compromise if you are in a combative negotiation.
- Don't be afraid of combative behavior. Unpleasant, but easy to handle.
- Be aware of the manipulative combative negotiator.
- Only cooperation will generate NegoEconomics.
- Be ready to spot cooperation.

CHAPTER 9

Sealing the Deal: The Second
5 Phases of the Negotiation Process

This chapter examines the second 5 phases of the negotiation process. In this half of the process, the deal is made, performance is undertaken, and the parties either agree to continue to work together or go their separate ways.

Phase 6 Bargaining
Phase 7 Concluding
Phase 8 Confirming
Phase 9 Implementing
Phase 10 Continued Relations or Divorce

Phase 6: Bargaining

Up until this phase in the negotiation process, the parties have been focused on cooperating to create NegoEconomic value. Now, in these phases of the negotiation, the emphasis shifts to distributing the value that has been created between the parties. The interpersonal dynamic between the delegates might also transition. During these phases, the delegate may style shift as well, making use of compromise, stalling, or even unilateral concession in order to come away from the table with a division that results in both parties being satisfied with the outcome, if not agreement on how to divide the NegoEconomics sum that has been agreed upon in phase 1. It is your job to find an overall solution that will meet the needs of the other party and solve his problem at the lowest possible cost to you.

You also have to be aware of how to spot a behavioral change from your counterpart, if he moves from SMARTnership into zero-sum.

Making an Opening Offer

You may safely assume that an opening offer is subject to negotiation. Make it a habit to reply along the following lines:

- *That wasn't quite what I had in mind.*
- *That's more than what we contemplated.*
- *Can you do any better than that?*
- *Look at your numbers again, and see if you can't come up with a better solution.*

You will discover that often a simple challenge like that expressed in these examples will create the possibility of honest bargaining that results in a better deal. If you take this approach, be prepared for the other party to respond:

- *What did you have in mind?*
- *This is something we can discuss, but then you must . . .*

The discussion should continue to build on the agreed-upon principles: *If you increase the quantity, we will see if we can do something about the price. Can you increase the quantity of your order by 25 percent?* Once you have made the offer, wait for the buyer's reply in order to get confirmation that a larger quantity is something that can be discussed before you go on: *In that case, I can reduce my price from $10.00/lb. to $9.35/lb.*

If your opening offer is too high or too low, the other party will not take you seriously. It may be difficult to know in advance where the other party will draw the line. The traditional rule is: supplier go high, buyer go low. You must have something with which to bargain. Keep in mind that high or low does not necessarily have to be related to price, but could pertain to other variables. Be sure that you can state the grounds for your proposal and any concessions that you may have to make. This sounds simple and obvious, but in practice it is often difficult. You will run into various problems.

The situation can be addressed in several ways.

- When preparing for a negotiation, find out what is acceptable to the other party. Obtain information about the prices for alternative solutions and about the useful effect of your offer. Withhold your offer until you believe the time is right.

- Make a dual price offer by saying: *I understand that the costs can be somewhere between $125,000 and $150,000.*
- Quote alternative prices.
- State a low price for your basic offer and structure your deal so your profit will be made on ancillary products, services, and extra orders that you know the buyer will want. Your profits will be made on spare parts and service provisions.

Determine the Threshold of Pain

An opening offer is a trial balloon you send up to get the other party's response. Research conducted by my company on how negotiators determine their offers shows that you may safely assume that negotiators who offer 500 when you're looking for 1,000 are aiming to arrive at 750. If the goal is 750, the **threshold of pain** will normally be somewhere between 750 and 1,000. If you accept this bargaining without any counteroffers and alternatives, you have to divide the difference between the bids by two, then divide that figure by two, and you'll have the other party's likely **threshold of pain**. Don't place your opening offer on his threshold of pain, but between your opening offer and his limit.

Offer 955. Avoid round figures. Don't go down from 10 percent to 9 percent; instead, require 9.25 percent. Don't go down from 1,000 to 900; instead, demand 955. Take small steps. Big steps indicate wide margins for maneuvering and create hope for further concessions. Odd figures indicate that you've calculated your offer very carefully.

Your opening offer: 1,000
Your next offer: 955
Threshold of pain of the other party: 875
Actual target of the other party: 750
Counteroffer of the other party: 500

Compromise is normally reached halfway between the two offers. Few negotiators take advantage of this insight, and they end up aiming too low. There might appear to be some kind of justice in dividing things equally. Nobody loses out; divisions other than 50/50 would entail an obvious loser.

You do not have to be high or low on price to have considerable room for negotiation. You can feed conditions into the negotiations that you know the other party will wish to change or negotiate. Each change calls for a counter concession on the part of the other party: either he must pay more or abandon other demands to get you to modify your offer.

You must be able to state your grounds for concessions you make. If you change your offer without being able to explain how or why, you will not be perceived as a serious negotiator. It is also important to keep in mind that when using concessions, you might be tripped up by cultural differences. Your counterpart will always expect that there is something else to be had. The other party may begin to doubt what the real price is, and speculate about whether he received more or less compared to others. Living according to this rule can best solve this problem: never give away anything without getting something back.

Package Deal versus Salami Negotiation

When you make your offer, cover all the details of the agreement. Aim for a package deal. If you do not do this, you run the risk of a **salami negotiation** in which you discuss the issues piecemeal, one-by-one, until each individual term has been clarified. A salami negotiation makes it easier for the other party to block compromise that is adverse to her position and opens up the possibility for counterclaims.

Package the Offer

In some transactions, the issues are intimately linked and can't be effectively negotiated separately. The price is a function of quality, quantity, conditions of payment, delivery terms, and other ancillary contract provisions. A buyer shouldn't become fixated on the price. He must look at total costs and what he gets for his money.

Avoid these kinds of negotiations by listening, discussing, and taking note of the other party's demands. You can discuss the various components of the deal without making decisions one by one. When you have heard all the demands and feel you have a clear overview of the entire negotiation, make an evaluation on the merits. Then you can make a new offer, a package, knowing what conditions are subject to modification and where you might find asymmetric value. In your new package offer, make modifications to accommodate the other party where it makes sense to do so. His demands are probably negotiable, and you do not have to accommodate him on every issue.

It must be clear to you that there is a need or problem behind the other party's request for the accommodation. More often than not, you can meet his need by means of another solution than the one demanded.

If the other party accepts the new proposal, the negotiation is over, and you have accomplished your mission. If he rejects the proposal, you have not made any unilateral concessions or lost ground. If the package is rejected, the individual components are taken up for discussion one by one, and new alternatives and openings are searched for.

On some of the points where you agree, you can conclude, as there is no longer a need for further discussion. If you have managed to get all of the demands out in the open, you don't run the risk that exists if partial conclusions are made in a salami negotiation.

Using Salami Tactics

When your counterpart fails to offer a package deal, you can respond using the salami tactic in which you discuss the issues piecemeal, one-by-one, until each term has been clarified. A salami negotiation may allow you to block compromise that is adverse to your position and opens up the possibility for counterclaims.

Example: Genevieve Gets Hit With the Salami

When using the salami tactic, Arnold, the buyer, will start by discussing a rather negligible issue. Arnold wants to reduce the transport costs, arguing that Genevieve's competitors are not charging for freight. Arnold also indicates that this is the only demand he is going to make. Genevieve, the supplier, finds it easy to agree to this if her expense is minimal. Arnold goes on to talk about the conditions of payment. On this issue, Genevieve's costs are higher. Once again, however, she gives in when Arnold tells her that her competitors have agreed to these conditions. Genevieve hopes that this will suffice so that she can get the deal, but Arnold does not relent. He continues to make demands until he finally demands a price reduction.

Arnold manages to negotiate the profit margin all the way down to rock bottom, but he still does not relent. He then demands a free service contract for the upcoming year. When Genevieve finally puts her foot down says *no*, Arnold replies: *This is definitely my last demand. You shouldn't turn down the deal just because you don't want to give me a year's service free of charge.*

Genevieve does not know when Arnold will stop making demands. Because she has given in too easily all along the way, without demanding anything in return from Arnold, he has maintained or even increased his bargaining equity, and she has given up everything. Instead, Genevieve should have embarked upon a package negotiation.

Note that the supplier can also use the salami tactic. His intention will generally be to camouflage a high final price.

Keep the following points in mind:

- Work toward package solutions and avoid being hit with the salami.
- Concessions must always be mutual in order to avoid distortions in the respective positions of strength in the negotiation. Avoid giving without getting something in return.
- Before making your offer, you must have reached agreement about modifications of conditions that may yield asymmetric value—for example, higher quantities might trigger a lower price.
- Find out whether the other party can accept your counterclaims before presenting your concessions.

When assessing your concessions, you should examine how much they will cost you and how much they will be worth to the other party. There are many concessions that cost you nothing, but which will yield a considerable value to the other party. Do not hand over these concessions for nothing; make sure you get something in return. If, for instance, you shorten the time of delivery without this costing you anything, what is it worth to the other party? Can he reduce his costs or risks? Will he get his revenue more quickly? Perhaps you can get a better deal than you had originally envisioned. Attempt to lock in the other party, and ensure that all requirements and demands have been tabled.

When you make your offer, do not surrender all your room to maneuver too soon or in one round of discussion. Your negotiation space should never be put on the table all at once. Test the other party and do not meet all his demands without some additional back and forth. If you give up everything all at once, your counterpart will raise his expectations believing that there is more to be had. The negotiation will go another few rounds rather than being brought to conclusion.

Mistakes in Discussing the Options

- Interrupting the other party
- Failing to develop your answers
- Putting a new and costlier proposal on the table
- Sending vague signals

Interrupting the Other Party

You interrupt the other party by rejecting his proposal. More often than not, you don't know what is behind the proposal. You know even less about the needs and requirements of the other party and why they have proposed the terms now under consideration. The person who interrupts to say no typically has no idea what he is turning down. If you do this, you will never find out whether the proposal that was presented may signal an opening that would have given you an advantage. You are likely interpreting all demands and objections as threats. You should, instead, ask probing questions in order to obtain more information before interrupting.

Example: Determining Who Will Do the Installation

Buyer: If we buy this equipment from you, we want to install it ourselves.

Supplier: Oh, no. That's against our policy. Furthermore, I don't think you have the know-how to do it. Our offer is a package deal. You can't break out the installation component.

Buyer: We want to be in charge of installation. We can manage it.

Supplier: This is something I can't even discuss. The installation is included in the package.

The supplier and the buyer are talking in circles without making any headway. If, instead, the supplier had been working with questions, the negotiation could have developed differently.

Buyer: If we buy this equipment from you, we want to do the installation ourselves.

Supplier: Why is that so important to you?

Buyer: Because of our contract with the labor union. We have workers who do not have enough to do right now. We will get into trouble with the union if we bring in your people to do the installation.

Supplier: In that case, who would be responsible for the installation?

Buyer: We thought that you would still manage the installation, but you could hire our crew. You would develop the design and the specifications. The responsibility would rest with you.

Supplier: How many workers are we speaking of?

Buyer: Four or five, I imagine.

Supplier: How much did you expect us to pay for these people?

Buyer: You can hire them for $32 an hour.

In this second scenario, NegoEconomic value is created. The example also demonstrates another common mistake: in the first scenario, the buyer never developed his requirements. He demanded the right to do the installation using his own staff, but failed to explain to the supplier why this was so important to him. If the negotiation is to work, it is important that the parties provide each other with detailed information. If you do not do this, you run the risk that the potential asymmetric value will be lost.

Failing to Develop your Answer

Instead of a curt "no," make it clear what is good and what is unacceptable in your counterpart's proposal. You should explain why you cannot accept certain provisions. Your responses will enable him to work with his proposal in order to develop it and get it closer to something you can accept.

If you simply answer "no," your counterpart is forced to guess what you want. She may misunderstand your needs and become argumentative, forcing you back into the argumentation phase. If neither party will open up and ask questions, the negotiation will become deadlocked because of insufficient information.

Some negotiators will hide their needs and leave it to you to guess what is behind their demands. They want the entire pie, but have no idea how big it is. Their demands are serving as trial balloons. In cases like this, it is important not to rush into an agreement out of frustration due to insufficient information.

Putting a New Proposal on the Table

If the other party rejects your proposal and doesn't give you an opening for further discussion, do not produce a new proposal. Instead, send the ball into the court of the other party: *I can see that our proposal does not suit you. Tell me what an acceptable solution would look like.* If you respond immediately with a new proposal, you appear to be too interested and insecure. You are likely to make unnecessary and unilateral concessions, and an imbalance in negotiations will arise.

Sending Vague Signals

Instead of sending clear signals, some negotiators send vague signals even in the face of considerable differences. It can be difficult to understand that a statement like: *Your price seems to be a bit too high. Could you do anything about the price?* is actually a serious demand and that the price gap is substantial. This negotiator fears conflict. He is afraid to express himself clearly, and confuses clarity with combativeness. He finds it difficult to distinguish the substance from the people. This behavior is typical of inexperienced or unsophisticated negotiators and acts as a serious handicap when dealing with more skillful negotiators.

SMARTner Tip for the Advanced Practioner: Mistakes Made in Purchasing Negotiations

The two most common mistakes in purchasing negotiations are unilateral concessions, and the offhand or too hasty acceptance of an offer that is within the budget or below the negotiation limit that you had in mind.

A supplier is authorized to lower his price by 12 percent. The buyer demands 10 percent. The supplier immediately accepts, because the proposal is below his limit of authority. The supplier is fixated on volume and afraid to test boundaries.

The first offer made is usually **not** the best offer. Testing the boundaries normally does not cost anything, but the potential gain is considerable for the negotiator who shows restraint and manages to reduce the demand of the other party. When negotiators hastily accept an offer, they completely miss out on any potential gain.

The buyer who easily, and without any resistance, managed to get the price reduced by 10 percent is likely to feel disappointed. He knows now, he should have asked for more—the win came too easily. He asks himself what might he have had? Additionally, now he has lost all confidence in the supplier's price terms and conditions. The way that the supplier hastily surrendered control of the negotiation allows the buyer to feel that he has the upper hand. For psychological reasons, it is important to negotiate and put up resistance, although the bid may be fully within your mandate of acceptable outcomes.

The negotiation may take only a few minutes after the parties have spent hours getting to know each other. Before the final phase, the seller may have spent several days getting final acceptance of his offer. Why, then, stress about a conclusion and risk the entire negotiation? It is essential to take sufficient time to reach a conclusion. Many negotiators spend too much time arguing and too little negotiating.

Avoid Negotiating in Writing

Whenever possible, choose personal negotiations over written ones. While a written *summary* of the terms of your finished deal will prove to be extremely valuable, a written *negotiation* is to be avoided. Negotiating by mail and email is usually difficult. You lose oral communication and can neither reinforce nor clarify your message. You cannot see and gauge the reaction of the other party, and the written word is easily and often misinterpreted. Written words can easily be misunderstood and cannot be clarified through body language. You'll miss the signals sent by the other party while they are listening to you, and you can't clarify and correct misunderstandings quickly.

What is written cannot be changed. The other party reads and rereads, analyzes and tries to understand, but you are not on hand to explain and answer questions. If you cannot meet face to face, use the telephone as a fallback position.

There are some situations when negotiating in writing may be effective. Negotiations in writing will work if used correctly, when prior to a negotiation you need supplementary information, or if you are negotiating in parallel with several parties. Written negotiations can save time and money, and may mean that the other party is better prepared when he arrives at the negotiating table.

If you are the supplier, you are often forced to submit your offer in writing in advance, but you should not send out quotations randomly. An offer should be well anchored and established in a dialogue with the buyer before it is sent. The best strategy is to make the quotation function as a summary of previous agreements. Often this is difficult, but you can and should always insist on meeting with the buyer before adding your signature to the offer.

The buyer may demand written explanations and supplementary comments from you prior to a meeting. In this way, he collects valuable information and can use it to pit competing suppliers against each other. The supplier may try to solve the problem by insisting on a personal meeting, something that the buyer can refuse or prevent by supplying incomplete answers.

Phase 7: Conclusion

When you know that you can present a package that will satisfy the needs of the other party, it is time to conclude the deal. You will know you have reached this point when:

- All the **demands** are on the table.
- You have **locked in** the other party.
- It is possible for the other party to make a decision. He has the authority to proceed and the necessary documentation. All the people required for a decision are present.

- The other party has completed their conversations with your competitors, the regulatory authorities, and so forth. If not, the other party is probably not in a position to conclude.
- Time pressure can sometimes expedite a decision. The other party is able to meet the deadline. Conclusion is often reached before the deadline has expired. The consequences of a postponement become clear.

Do not be in a rush to conclude. Your bargaining equity will suffer if the other party perceives you are too eager to conclude. The other party may choose to drag out things, put you under time pressure, and force you to make further concessions that will very often be unilateral.

Negotiations are decisions with uncertainties. Your information about the other party's alternatives and his assessment of them in the long- and short term is limited. Your understanding is insufficiant as to where the other party draws the demarcation lines between:

1. a brilliant agreement
2. a good agreement
3. a reasonable agreement
4. an agreement with which he can live
5. an unsatisfactory agreement that he wants to discontinue as quickly as possible
6. an agreement that he will reject

Does the other party have the authority to conclude?

Your purpose is a steady progression toward the conclusion of the negotiation. It is best to avoid a simple acknowledgment of a new offer or a one-word response from your opponent. If you allow this to happen, you are surrendering your bargaining equity to the buyer. Postpone any attempt to conclude until you are certain the other party has the authority to complete the transaction and conclude the deal.

Do not make concessions if the other party does not have the authority or is not ready to sign the agreement. The risk of your offer being passed on to your competitors is too great. In situations like this, the negotiation begins to resemble an auction. The other party simply takes note of your offer, passes it on to your competitor, listens to him, and returns to you. You are now expected to make even more concessions.

Lock in the Other Party

Before you attempt to conclude, lock in the other party by encouraging him to put all his conditions on the table: *Provided I find a solution that gives you what you want, do we have a deal?* This enables you better to assess how far you should go and what choices are available. This is also called the listening, summarize, lock technique.

Choose a Method of Conclusion

When you recognize that the appropriate time has arrived, you must choose your method of concluding the deal. There are many possible ways to bring the negotiation to a conclusion:

a. Frame Your Package

Summarize the demands of the other party, lock him in, and present your package. You can choose between giving the other party everything he demands, or testing the boundaries and giving him some, but not all, of what he wants. Summarize and point out the risks involved in delaying things. You may wish to include a threat, but employ this tactic with extreme caution. If the other party trusts you, he will perceive the risks as genuine. If he does not trust you, he will, rightly or wrongly, believe you are bluffing. Here, you show the strength of your bargaining position. Which party has more ability to influence the outcome of the transaction? If one of you has an advantage over the other and consequently wields more power over the result, this fact will affect the dynamic of the conclusion.

b. Submit New Alternatives

If you cannot manage to lock in the other party, or if new demands emerge, you should continue negotiating. Submit new alternatives. If you are asked to assume additional costs and risks, do not give more; rather, give the same thing in a different manner. Modify your offer or rearrange the concessions you have made. Structured differently, your package might look more attractive. The new concessions might be more valuable than the old ones. Quality improvements might be more valuable than a price reduction.

Do not feel bound by previous verbal agreements. If a verbal agreement is not directly accepted, and you do not have an offer on the table with a stated expiration, you are no longer bound by your previous offer.

If he rejects your first offer, you will have to develop a new offer, explaining the advantages of the new terms. You must show how a new package accommodates the demands or needs that the other party has stated. Point out the risks involved in postponing a conclusion. It may be helpful to ask the other party to summarize their demands one last time, as this method will not be effective unless you are clear on all of the demands and requirements of the other party.

c. Include a Threat in Your Summary

Take It or Leave It should be used only after you have first tried to reach a conclusion by other means. It can be difficult to determine how to use this tactic in a convincing manner. Due to its harsh nature, you can essentially only use it once throughout the entire negotiation process and still be taken seriously. The method is fraught with risk. If you use this approach, the dynamic of the negotiation will change and from that moment forward will be governed by the bargaining equity of the parties. If you play this card, your counterpart will be provoked. Instead of surrendering and entering into the agreement you have offered, he may turn it down to see how much you can handle. He wants to show you that he has stronger bargaining equity. Before you use the Take It or Leave It tactic, mentally prepare yourself for the best *and* worst possible outcomes. You should use this tactic only if you are ready to carry out the threat, walk away from the table, and break off negotiations.

Example: Take It or Leave It

The offer we are presenting has been structured to meet all the requirements you have stated, and this is as far as we can go on this transaction. If you delay the negotiation further, we will not make you a better offer. Because we have other orders coming in, there is a possibility that we can't guarantee these delivery dates and pricing if we do not firm this up immediately.

d. A Trial Balloon

If you are negotiating with a number of people and you suspect that they are disagreeing among themselves, you might test the waters by offering an informal proposal. If you have a good relationship with one of the people across the table or if you believe the team is not in alignment, this tactic can give you valuable information about what it will take to reach a conclusion.

e. Wait for the Other Party to Make a Move

Another tactic is to allow the negotiation to become stymied and wait for the other party to make a move. This is not advisable if there is a risk that a competitor may get his hand in. However, if the delay will increase risks and costs, take advantage of the opponent's offer.

If the other party has submitted an offer, your next move might be to tie him to it by demanding an option, that is, you have the right, but not the obligation, to take advantage of the offer. The other party is then under an obligation to stick by his offer for as long as the option remains open.

f. Insist on a Counterbid

You might ask for a counterbid, a bid that you would either consider accepting or a bid that would form the basis of further negotiations. If the other party feels that the conclusion is based on his ideas, it might be easier for him to agree.

g. Accept Your Opponent's Demand

If you believe that the disagreement between you and your opponent is minimal, you might make a unilateral concession to your opponent by accepting his demand. What you get in return for your concession is the agreement.

h. Withdraw the Offer

The hardest line of all is to threaten to withdraw an offer you have already made or to significantly modify the terms through a price increase or extension of the delivery time. This tactic should only be used if you have alternatives available. In order to avoid sounding threatening when you withdraw the offer or raise the price, you can do it by using a summation technique. Summarize the offer made, but as you restate the provisions, consciously raise the demands. The other party will protest saying: *But previously you said...* The disingenuous bluffer queries what he has been saying, but after a moment, continues with a statement along the lines of: *Well, if I have said that, I guess I will have to stand by it.* The other party, entirely erroneously, now believes that he has pressured the negotiator into giving more than he could really afford.

Documentation

Always review the negotiations immediately afterwards, interpret your notes, discuss with your colleagues what transpired, analyze results, and establish new objectives. Assess your own performance and that of your colleagues.

Forward any additional documentation after the meeting. Provide a full set of documents, highlighting the most important points in an accompanying letter. Document everything you have agreed to in writing. If disagreement occurs later on, your documentation will become highly valuable.

Phase 8: Confirmation

Once a conclusion has been reached, all that is needed to finalize the transaction is the formal signing of the agreement. Most negotiations have not been completed until the document has been executed, so be careful not to celebrate your victory too soon.

Most negotiations, big and small, are not complete until there is a formal confirmation of the agreement reached between the parties. A written document avoids future problems and conflicts. In obtaining the confirmation, there can be unpleasant surprises. In order to reduce the risk of these unpleasant surprises arising, don't be naive. Insist upon written confirmation as soon as the agreement has been reached.

Is the Signed Confirmation Identical with the Verbal Agreement?

If, in your opinion, the confirmation signed by the other party is not identical with the agreement you have previously reached, several possibilities could have created the disconnect:

- The other party is attempting a bluff.
- You have been at cross-purposes with the other party throughout the proceedings, and consequently opinions differ as to what you have agreed to. (This is a common situation.)
- Both parties differ in their interpretations of the language of the agreement

This problem can be avoided if, at the end of each session, you remember to close with a summary of the agreement made or the results achieved during that session. This is particularly important when you are negotiating in a language other than your native language, or if the formal agreement is drafted by people other than those present at the negotiating table. It is also important to take written notes throughout the negotiation. Before leaving one point for another, summarize the present position. If you ask the other party to summarize, you can more clearly ascertain how she perceives the issue and the resolution.

The Other Party Embarks on New Negotiations

If, when you meet to sign the agreement, the other party has changed his mind and refuses to stand by the verbal agreement, you are forced to reopen the negotiation. If you have already celebrated the closure of the agreement, begun production, and placed you own orders, your bargaining equity is weakened.

Example: The Buyer Drafts the Contract

Following a tough negotiation with the purchasing department of a major customer, you finally reach an agreement. The buyer undertakes the drafting of the contract. You start making preparations for production. You order the raw materials and schedule the job internally. When you meet again to discuss the details of specifications, the buyer says: *Since this is an important deal, I have asked our management group to take a look at the proposal. By and large, they like what we have done, but a few points must be modified for them to approve the agreement. For one thing, they want to. . . .*

This surprise may cost money. You are faced with the following alternatives:

- Grant the additional concessions required and hope that you have sufficient margin in your budget, or that the customer is prepared to pay for these extra costs.
- Insist that you already had a deal based on your oral agreement and demand compensation for the modifications required by the customer. The buyer may assert that you have misunderstood him. He claims that what you had was only a draft proposal. The burden of proof is on you to show finality of the previous agreement.
- Take a brief time out and then reopen the negotiation. Ask for more time to consider the new requests. Find out whether it is possible to cancel your orders for raw materials. Does the customer have any alternative, or is he dependent on this order to meet his obligations? When you know your negotiating position and your alternatives, you can make a new offer and continue negotiating. Look at it as a new negotiation with a new set of conditions. Do not let yourself be provoked by the tactical

gambit made by the customer. Instead, choose to view this new negotiation as a purchasing signal.

• Walk away from the whole transaction.

The next step is to implement the agreement reached. Here you will discover what it is worth and whether the preceding negotiation can be considered successful or not.

Phase 9: Implementation of the Agreement

The outcome of the negotiation and implementation of the transaction depend heavily on the interpersonal dynamic rather than on price, quantity, and the other conditions. Keep all people affected by the bargain, but who were not present at the meetings, informed of the provisions and objectives of the negotiation. Provided both parties are satisfied, the probability of implementing the agreement will be good. If one of the parties feels that he was the loser in the transaction, there is a serious risk that this emotion will threaten the progression of the entire agreement.

Both Parties Must Be Satisfied

• Both parties should be able to sell the benefits of the financial result when presenting the agreement to their own organization. It is not a question of dividing gains, costs, and risks equally, but rather, it is a matter of allowing the other party to have an agreement in which the short- and the long-term gains are sufficient enough to make the agreement worthwhile. The deal should be better than any of the alternatives. Assist the other party in formulating the arguments he can put forward internally when presenting the agreement to his or her organization.

• Neither party should feel cheated, insecure, or manipulated by clever tactical moves. Both parties must be satisfied that they have managed the negotiations well. No one should get worse conditions than those granted to other customers in a similar situation.

• Neither party thinks that they have lost face in the course of the negotiation.

• Interpersonal relations between the parties remain positive. Doing business and socializing with the other party should be perceived as a pleasant and rewarding experience.

What Happens If One of the Parties Feels That He Is a Loser?

If one party walks away from the deal feeling like a loser, they will want to retaliate. Sooner or later when the bargaining equity is reversed, the loser will seek revenge:

- He does not complete his part of the agreement, and it becomes worthless.
- He makes things difficult any way he can, such as by imposing extra costs or lessening the goodwill of the negotiations
- He bad-mouths his opponent whenever he can.
- He does not renew the agreement.

One day in the future, when you need him, he will take advantage of the altered bargaining equity and retaliate.

The transaction has not been completed until money and goods have exchanged hands and the contract provisions have been fully performed. No one feels good about a partner who is only pleasant and personable on the day the agreement is signed and on the day it is to be renewed. People feel abused or taken advantage of when the other party is friendly only on those occasions when there is a mission to be accomplished and when the opponent is clearly benefiting from the exchange.

Dealing with Non-Performance

Among the more difficult zero-sum games is the final adjustment of projects, claims, and disputes. The parties have not been able to fulfill the promises they originally made. The actual events have reduced the expectations of both parties. The picture is further complicated by unexpected extra expenses that nobody wants to bear and by losses that were never anticipated. Now, in addition to money, failure, blame, and responsibility are all at stake.

Forcing someone to pay money is tricky, but getting him to claim responsibility and acknowledge that things went wrong is much more difficult. Hard questions emerge: how is the agreement to be interpreted? All negotiators have to stand by their promises. Does that mean that what sounded like a promise was merely an objective? Is this a lie? Was a chance truly taken, a chance that did not make it, or was it just bad luck?

If they are able to tone down the question of who is right and who is to blame, each party can help the other save face. Is it more important to reach an agreement that works well, or to be proven right at any cost?

It is essential to keep in mind that your signals may be misconstrued. If you tone down the legal discussion, there is a risk that the other party may believe that you have no legal arguments. Therefore, he may think that he may be able to leave the battlefield victoriously and, consequently, he will pursue the legal battle vigorously.

As long as they get more from you than they think they can get elsewhere, they will probably be happy to agree to your plan. But how will they react when they are told that they are getting one-tenth, while you are keeping nine-tenths for yourself? Will they feel cheated, because you have kept your own profits from the project a secret?

Debrief Your Experience

When you have completed a negotiation, take time to look back and relate the experience to your preparations. Most likely you will find errors in your preparations that you would have avoided if you had spent more time and attention preparing.

By analyzing your own negotiating, you increase your awareness of how you and your opponent are functioning, what signals and moves get a positive reception, and why certain initiatives tend to deadlock negotiations and thus ruin communications and relations. Through your self-analysis, you will realize ineffective behavior that you can avoid in the future.

Follow-up analysis on negotiations is an excellent way of improving negotiation skills. Make it a habit to set aside time for analysis. Unfortunately, such analysis is not typical, and therefore negotiators and their organizations rarely benefit from the experience they gain in the field.

Phase 10: Continued Relations or Divorce

At some point, you will reach an intersection where the agreement expires by its own terms and must be renewed or a different path must be taken.

Provided you have kept a good personal relationship, and the agreement has functioned as both parties intended, it is likely that the agreement will be renewed, assuming the underlying need still exists. Certain parts of the agreement might have to be renegotiated, and a number of external threats may have entered the picture.

Examples: External Threats

- New individuals have assumed key positions, and they may have different sources, or contacts, or different views as to how the needs should be met. Business is done based on relationships with people.
- New technical solutions have emerged that better accommodate existing needs.
- Other suppliers have provided more advantageous pricing.
- The regulatory or political climate has changed.
- Economic conditions have changed.

Negotiators tend not to take the issue of renewal of the agreement or termination of the relationship seriously. Ending the relationship can be difficult and painful, especially if only one of the parties wants to step away from the agreement. When one of the parties has decided to end the relationship, the interaction between the parties often becomes strained. Both players will go for unilateral solutions that serve their own interests. When this happens, the resulting agreement will involve a winner and a loser, and neither party is motivated to maintain a positive relationship with the other party. The injured party will likely seek revenge.

Example: Timely Divorce Settlement

A consumer goods company hires an advertising firm to market its products. The parties conclude a three-year agreement. During the contract period, the advertising firm will receive a commission of 25 percent of the revenue generated. The managers of the firm believe they will be successful. During the first two years, they make a great effort to participate in commercial trade shows and undertake other initiatives to reach the customer base. They know that it takes time before the orders start coming in. They invest a great deal of money in marketing. During the third year, the consumer goods company is acquired by an international industrial group. This group has its own sales channels, and it gives notice to the advertising firm that it wants to terminate the agreement. The efforts made by the advertising firm have not generated any orders, but many proposals have been sent out and are under consideration. By the end of the third year, they have invested more than $100,000, but have not closed a sale. The prospecting efforts of the advertising firm will instead benefit the group that acquired the consumer goods company.

When the three-year agreement was negotiated, a typical mistake was made: The divorce settlement was never written into the agreement. When the dynamic is positive and cooperative, the parties are more inclined to agree to generous termination provisions than will be the case when the divorce is pending. In order to protect its investment, the advertising firm should have included a provision along these lines:

In the event of nonrenewal of the agreement at the end of the three-year period, a commission on all customer contacts and offers made or presented before the expiration of the agreement period and which lead to orders being placed after the expiration of the agreement shall be payable to us. In the event of nonrenewal notice being given to us, we shall prepare a list of the above contacts/offers within 30 days.

Build In Options

When you conclude an agreement, you don't know what the future will look like:

- You've purchased a machine, but you don't know how much maintenance it will require to operate smoothly. Can you handle the maintenance yourself or would you have to take out a service agreement?
- You don't know how extensive maintenance is going to be or what a reasonable price would be. You decide to operate the machine for one year before taking a service agreement.
- You rent premises, not knowing how long you will need them. You sign a lease for 12 months with an option to renew.
- You are going to purchase oil for the winter, but you do not know how cold it is going to be. You purchase 80 percent of last year's consumption. If this winter turns out to be colder, you can always buy more.

In all of these situations, you need to have an option, that is, a right, but not an obligation, to continue to buy additional quantities at prices and conditions that have already been fully negotiated. The option is binding on the supplier's part, as he guarantees that he will continue to supply goods and services at prices and on terms that are agreed to on the front end. What will happen if you don't have an option for future maintenance, and it turns out that you need assistance? The price for maintenance has risen by 30 percent. Since you have become dependent upon the supplier, he may force you to accept this price increase.

Take aways

- Always know your threshold of pain.
- Be aware of the salami tactics.
- Avoid negotiation in writing—including emails.
- A written agreement is not the end of the negotiation—it's the beginning.

CHAPTER 10

How Big Is My Piece?
How the NegoEconomic Value
Is to Be Divided

At the end of the negotiation, when the NegoEconomic value has been identified and the principles and solutions of the agreement have been given clear contours, the delegates could move to a tougher type of negotiation in which the parties test the leverage of each other (Figure 10.1). An effective negotiator uses cooperation to build relationships and trust, as well as to create asymmetric value. Zero-sum games are sometimes used to negotiate about the division of the asymmetric value that has been created, if the Rules of the Game do not clearly describe how to split that value.

Sharing the Pie

Sooner or later, you will have to agree about the division of the pie, in which case you might face a zero-sum game that you do not want to lose. When it is time to determine how the pie is to be divided, you may face a dilemma: you want to act with the openness necessary to have constructive dialogue, produce mutual trust, and gain insight into the needs of the other party, but at the same time, you do not want to seem too eager, expose your position, or sell yourself short.

The Theory behind the Division of Value

The notion that two parties can increase their wealth by means of a rational division of labor is not in any way new. The idea was first

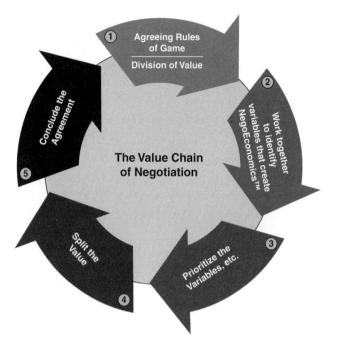

Figure 10.1 Effective communication, trust, and fair play are essential elements to progress through the Value Chain of Negotiation.

advanced by Adam Smith at the end of the seventeenth century, and was further developed by David Ricardo. The theories advanced by these two economists showed that nations, companies, and individuals could increase their wealth by creating asymmetric value.

Two American scientists, W. Edwards Deming and Josef M. Juran, developed theories in the 1940s about how added value could be created through long-term relations with suppliers. The goal was to obtain perfect production with delivery on time. Eventually, the entire industrialized world adapted these ideas in one way or another. New concepts were found such as business process reengineering, outsourcing, and strategic alliances. Shortly thereafter, the public sector followed, and companies experienced:

- Increased competition
- Introduction of new buy/sales systems
- Disappearance of trade barriers
- Birth of a common currency in Europe
- Opening up of new frontiers

Companies realized the benefits of chasing the added value. Competition became much tougher, and companies struggled to remain a step ahead of their competitors. Even greater skills were required of negotiators, technicians, project managers, and business developers to keep competitors at arm's length. With companies under intense pressure to remain on top, it became obvious that two pairs of eyes and ears could see and hear better than one pair. Two minds could more easily see the synergies.

The Division Does Not Have to Be Equal, But It Does Have to Be Fair

In a SMARTnership, it is easier to arrive at a shared view of the best presentation and distribution of responsibility than of how to share the pie. The world is not full of idealists who share things 50/50. Many negotiators are taught not give away more than they need to. Our employers demand that we go for optimal gain. Even if the negotiation starts out in cooperation, it is very likely to get tough when the pie is to be shared.

But how is the pie to be divided? When sharing the NegoEconomic value, negotiators also share the expectation that if they cannot have more than half, they are certainly not going to accept less than 50 percent.

Cooperation and SMARTnership do not presuppose an equal division of the NegoEconomic value that has been created during the negotiation process. Sometimes 50/50 is the appropriate division; other times, it is 30/70 or 90/10. As a negotiator it is your job to ensure that you get to keep the greatest possible share of the asymmetric value generated. At the same time, however, you have a duty to keep the other party satisfied.

The 50/50 distribution can take place in a fair manner, but it assumes that the value of all the efforts and divisions of risk are equal, and it does not test whether the other party will settle for less. If your opponent thinks that 30 percent of the profits is a good deal and is more than any other alternative would give him, why should you give more away than necessary? Do not hesitate to test the boundaries in a SMARTnership.

But where is the borderline between good business and greed? Is it determined by market forces, so that it is always right to take what the market will bear, or are there higher ethical values or other business considerations that you should keep in mind? Who, in that case, has the right to determine the limits for others? How far into the gray area can you move before you cross the ethical boundaries into exploitation of other people's difficulties? There is no simple answer to this. As a negotiator, you are constantly forced to make up your mind and take responsibility for your own actions.

To make sure that your counterpart feels fairly treated, the following criteria need to be met:

- He must be able to manage and develop his business within the terms reached in the negotiation. He must continue to be a good and valuable partner.
- The result must offer him a better solution in relation to his other alternatives; a deal that he cannot afford to miss; a deal he would wish to uphold and protect.
- He must feel that it is a good deal and that he has performed well in the negotiation. He should feel that he has succeeded in his task.

Example: Leveraging the Differences

Ricardo and Lupe are planning to produce a public seminar, and they have taken the following steps:

- Agreed on the presentation, contents, timetable, and distribution of responsibilities.
- Agreed on the admission fee to be paid by the participants.
- Estimated the number of participants.
- Looked at the expenses involved in marketing, administration, facility, meals, preparations, documentation, and fees for the instructors and arrived at a cost estimate.
- Subtracted their costs from their projected revenue and determined how much money they think they are going to make.

They now need to ask themselves the following questions:

- Are we satisfied with this net amount? If not, how can we arrive at a higher net amount?
- Should we increase the seminar fee and run the risk of making it difficult to sell the seminar? Are we willing to continue negotiating with the other party if we have differences in how much risk each of us is willing to take? How will we settle conflicting views on the price consciousness of the customers?
- How can we reduce the marketing costs? Should we spend more money on marketing to get more participants? Should we try to use two instructors instead of one so that we can accommodate more people per seminar? We are uncertain whether or not it is possible to recover those costs by taking on more participants.
- Should we relocate the seminar to reduce expenses for location?

- In order to get more participants, should we grant a discount if we have more than two participants from one organization?
- Could the administration be handled at lower cost?

Their joint assignment is to create the biggest possible pie to divide. In the course of the discussion, Lupe and Ricardo discover that there is a disagreement between them as to their level of willingness to take risks. They have grown apart concerning some of the central issues. Have they ruined the basis of further cooperation?

On the contrary—the differences between their assessments and viewpoints facilitate a SMARTnership. It is not the intention of either party to convince the other that he or she is right, and the other is wrong. Instead, Ricardo and Lupe need to use the differences to locate the NegoEconomic value in the transaction. They now have the necessary knowledge to formulate a solution that meets the needs of both parties.

One possible scenario is that the party more willing to take the risk offers the prudent party a guarantee that, regardless of the outcome, he will have a secure income. The risk-taker will be allowed to keep all the gains that arise if his assessments turn out to have been correct.

Division and the Trust Factor

When threats, bluffing, emotional blackmail, and manipulation are used to divide the NegoEconomic value that is realized, trust and the willingness to cooperate are affected. It is the exceptional circumstance where both effort and risk fall equally to the parties. Often disagreement arises concerning the assessment of different efforts. Negotiators who are out to get more, invest a great deal of energy in bragging about their own efforts, costs, and risks and in belittling the efforts, costs, and risks of the other party. The "get more" negotiator implies that the rewards of his opponent should be reduced.

How does the other party perceive this? She immediately recognizes that she is in danger of receiving the smaller share of the asymmetric value, and that she is also expected to accept that her efforts, costs, and risks are less valuable. The original conflict about the division of the pie has grown into an even larger issue. Now the parties are fighting about the value of their respective contributions. They are in danger of losing at the tangible and the psychological level. Both parties find this difficult to accept, and the gap between them widens. In verbal combat, they rely on strength and cutting remarks rather than substance in order to "win."

Example: Backed into a Corner

Scenario 1:

> *Supplier*: If you handle the installation, we will save installation costs in the neighborhood of $500,000.
>
> *Buyer*: I can agree to that.
>
> *Supplier*: In that case, we will reduce the price by $250,000.
>
> *Buyer*: No, you must reduce it by $500,000.
>
> *Supplier*: No, that won't work. We must share the asymmetric value.
>
> *Buyer*: No! If you save $500,000 because you don't have to pay for the installation, then we should be credited with the full $500,000 for doing the installation ourselves.

Because the buyer knows the amount of the asymmetric value, it's only natural that he thinks he is entitled to all of it because he has agreed to undertake the installation. However, if the supplier gets no share of the gain, he feels at a disadvantage. He sees no benefit from cooperating and may change his strategy.

In the dialogue above, the supplier has been both too naive and too open. He played his cards in the wrong order, and didn't withhold any information. Handling the situation differently might achieve a more favorable result.

Scenario 2:

> *Supplier*: Do you think you might be able to do the installation work, and if so, what would be the cost?
>
> *Buyer*: We have the capacity to do the installation, but it will cost us between $400,000 and $450,000.

Supplier now knows there is an extra $50,000 to $100,000 on the table. He suggests to the buyer that he undertake the installation, and that this will lead to a price reduction of $400,000. If he manages that, they can divide the entire difference of $100,000. At the same time, the buyer gets the $400,000 reduction that he thinks is fair. If the buyer's installation costs are only $350,000, and he gets a reduction of $400,000, he gets an *extra* $50,000.

Scenario 3:

Playing poker can be worthwhile, provided the negotiators are not too greedy.

> *Buyer*: Of course we can do the installation work, but it would cost us about $600,000.
>
> *Supplier*: Then it is not a good idea. It is better that we do the installation.

This would result in a $600,000 reduction in the price. The buyer's actual cost might be as low as $350,000. He then gets the $600,000 reduction, plus the $250,000 he saved by bluffing. That is $850,000 the greedy buyer would have made. You can see why the supplier assumed the installation and did not reduce the price. The door is now shut, and the parties do not take advantage of leaving the installation to the buyer in order to reduce costs. The potential asymmetric value is left on the table.

The parties do not negotiate about the issues. The buyer should ask: *But what expenses do you have?* He must get an answer. Each party must check his own calculations to see if they are correct or whether in their greed they have attempted to bluff each other too flagrantly.

If the buyer manages to extract the information that the extra cost to the supplier is only $500,000, he can respond: *Let's do the math one more time, so I can check whether we can handle it after all.*

It is very important for somebody who unsuccessfully attempts a tactical trick to know exactly what his next move is going to be. Absent planning for the fallback position, the door slams shut, and the asymmetric value is lost.

Negotiate about the Division in Advance

Example: Guaranteeing the Investor's ROI, but…

A manufacturing company plans to invest in a heat-recovery plant, but they are uncertain about the conditions under which the investment would be profitable. The suppliers with whom they have negotiated will not offer a binding estimate on future financial results, but instead refer to operational performance from similar plants. The only guarantees these suppliers are willing to give are the normal guarantees against flaws in the material and errors in manufacture.

These suppliers cannot meet the needs of the investor. They will not guarantee the heat recovery volume. Instead, they limit themselves to selling the machine to be used for recovering heat.

Another supplier is contacted. He guarantees a rate of heat recovery that insures that the investment will pay for itself in 30 months. If the investor does not achieve this result, the supplier guarantees full financial compensation or supplementary components to the plant until the guaranteed return on investment (ROI) has been achieved.

This supplier meets the needs of the investor by guaranteeing a rate of heat recovery. In return, the supplier insists on being given a service and maintenance contract for the plant for a five-year period at a fixed rate agreed in advance. Furthermore, the supplier demands that if the plant is more profitable than the amount of the guarantee, the "excess profit" must be divided on a 50/50 basis between the supplier and the investor.

Demanding Something in Return

The supplier meets all the requirements of the investor, but asks for something in return for the costs and risks that may arise. This proposal can make both parties winners. To the investor, it entails no risks. He will have to determine whether the guaranteed recovery after deducting the annual maintenance charge is high enough, and whether he is willing to relinquish any extra profits to the supplier for five years. This calculation will have to be related to the proposals made by the other suppliers.

The supplier needs to be sure that the performance of the plant is reliable. He insists on being in charge of maintenance, so that he can make sure that the equipment is operated in the appropriate manner. He is not competing on the basis of price, but rather by providing the investor with a full guarantee of profitability.

The central question concerns the scope of the annual guaranteed recovery volume after deduction of the maintenance charge. If the investor sets the guarantee number too low, the excess profit that is to be shared 50/50 will be too much. Another important point of negotiation will be whether a profit division of 50/50 is reasonable. Both parties are required to be generous when dividing the profits, or the disadvantaged party will not go along. The size of this share will be the subject of a negotiation in which the parties test each other's boundaries.

The Zero-sum Game for Known Stakes

If both parties are aware of what is at stake in the negotiation, this increases the risk of one party feeling like a loser. The loser compares his results with those of the other party, and all solutions that give the other party more than 50 percent of the pie are perceived as unfair. The result will be more palatable if the size of the stake remains unknown. If your opponent cannot compare his result with yours, then the risk that he will feel like a loser will be reduced.

When Nobody Knows What the Stakes Are Going to Be

When parties disagree, both sides spend a lot of time and energy adjusting available documentation so that it supports their point of view. Some negotiators are not above slandering the other party's honor and good name. They encourage strife and costly conflict. The fact that the pie they are about to divide will be reduced does not seem to put a damper on them. Instead, they focus only on whether the other party is getting a higher percentage than they are getting.

Instead of arguing about who can best predict an organization's profits and becoming competitive, good negotiators talk about how profits ought to be distributed and what initiatives could be taken to enlarge the pie the parties are about to share. Instead of negotiating about percentage shares, the parties should agree on a reasonable division of profits. This might get both options on the table.

Example: Determining the Relative Worth of an Advance

A supplier has demanded that 30 percent of the purchase price must be paid in advance. This advance is worth $100,000 to her. The buyer claims that none of the other suppliers have asked for an advance, and he adds: *Our policy is not to give any advances. If you demand an advance, the deal is never going to happen.*

The supplier, who is not a very clever negotiator and who has a very rigid framework within which to operate, gives in. The result of this concession is that her costs on the transaction go up by $100,000. How much does the buyer gain? Let us assume that his interest costs are somewhat lower than that of the supplier, and that his gain is $70,000. In this zero-sum game, the parties collectively lose $30,000.

By means of a more skillful negotiation technique, the $100,000 that the supplier negotiated away might have been utilized in an alternative manner, yielding higher profits for the buyer. A better solution for both parties would have been a unilateral price reduction of $80,000. The supplier would have earned another $10,000, and the buyer would have saved $20,000.

The supplier might have had even better alternatives. She might have been able to include a one-year service contract at no additional cost—a factor that might have been more valuable to the buyer than better payment conditions.

Some suppliers who are facing demands intensify their defensive strategy when they come under pressure. They do not believe the buyer's gambit that the competitors have not asked for an advance. Instead, they raise counterarguments: *Today, everybody asks for an advance—if we don't get an advance, we have to raise our prices.*

A typical solution to this type of verbal combat is a reduction of the advance from 30 percent to 10 or 20 percent. Doing so ensures that both parties share the loss, albeit a smaller one. However, they are now stuck in a behavior pattern that will govern the interpersonal dynamic of the remainder of the negotiations. Argument is used to counterargue and a tough attitude is mixed with slick, tactical moves. The negotiation will dissolve into a poker game, and both parties will become extremely suspicious of each other.

Returning to the example and the request for an advance, the supplier could reply: *Some of the benefits created by the advance payment can be passed on to you by way of a lower price. We can look at the financing terms and the amount of the advance because both will affect the price.* The supplier keeps the door ajar for a discussion.

The buyer listens and asks: *How much is the advance worth to you?*

The need for openness and honesty becomes crucial here. If the supplier can be open and honest, and reply: *Around $100,000*, then the buyer knows the value of the supplier's demand. This enables the buyer to relate the value of the advance to his gain of $70,000. It eats up more than it yields, so he tries to see whether other requirements would give a better yield. He recognizes the opportunity to exploit the difference between the interest costs of the two parties. Instead, he offers a higher advance if he gets a share of the asymmetric value: *We can raise the advance by 50 percent, but then you have to come down on your price by...*

Take aways

- Be generous—it could be ok that your counterpart gets more of the NegoEconomics than you.
- Always demand something in return.
- Identifying the NegoEconomics is the easy part. When the division is happening, it becomes difficult.
- Negotiate the division of the value before looking for it.

CHAPTER 11

Dealing with Stress, Threats, and Bluffing

Negotiations and Stress

My ancestors, the Vikings, were a wild bunch and once ruled most of Northern Europe. Imagine a short-legged, stubby-fingered little Viking running in the forest, with a wild beard flying and metal helmet precariously balanced on his head. Suddenly he meets a rival Viking from an enemy tribe. My ancestors only had two ways of reacting. Run away or draw the sword and fight. The modern negotiator is vulnerable to the same two primitive behaviors – fight or flight.

How the Body Reacts to Stress

Dealing with thousands of professionals in negotiations throughout the years has led me to believe that we all become stressed at different stages. Just like my ancestor a long time ago became stressed, so do you today, for the same reasons as people did 1,000 years ago.

When your body perceives stress, adrenaline is released into the blood stream. This is a physical defense mechanism that increases your preparedness for fight or flight. The ability of the blood to coagulate is also increased. While this is occurring, your intellect is blocked. You are no longer capable of thinking rationally, and your creative and critical cerebral functions are blocked. When you can no longer make rational decisions, you act instinctively. This is a defense mechanism that you have inherited from primordial times. You are constructed for survival.

The stress involved inhibits your ability to think logically. The rational part of the brain was developed at a later stage than other parts and provided with the ability to curb instinctive reactions. But menacing circumstances may still block your rational thought processes.

If you are forced to negotiate under stress, your effectiveness will be reduced. A certain stress level can be useful. It gives you energy and increases your ability to perform. But the threshold between useful and harmful stress varies from one person to another. Many of the events that occur in connection with negotiations easily create stress above that threshold.

Balancing Common Sense and Emotions

Your judgment is affected by your emotions. When you become insecure, threatened, or stressed, your rational thought processes will short-circuit, and you will respond emotionally by fighting or fleeing. The following scenarios illustrate the challenges of balancing common sense and emotional response:

Scenarios:

- You are waiting for some material that your employee has promised. He has forgotten his promise, and when you remind him, he replies: *Sorry, I'd forgotten all about you. I can look into the stuff for you next week.* You are angry and answer: *Just forget about it. I will manage without your help.* You make a rash emotional decision despite the fact that you could have taken the time to calm down. If, subsequently, your decision turns out to be wrong, who will bear the blame – you or your employee?
- In another context, you feel enthusiasm and excitement when you first meet a new business partner. You are both thinking along the same lines, and the personal chemistry is strong. Together you decide to collaborate on a project. It is not long before you realize, however, that you have overlooked important facts and made a premature decision. The decision to work together was made on the basis of positive feelings. However, the decision turned out to be just as mistaken as the one in the previous scenario that was based on negative feelings.
- You have been looking for a house for a couple of years. At last you find the house of your dreams. The seller has several interested buyers and puts the house up for auction. The bids go higher and higher. You are one of four interested parties. All of them are to

make a final bid in writing, and you make a considerably higher bid than you had originally planned. The seller contacts you, saying: *You've made the second-highest bid. If you want to have the house, you'll have to raise the bid by another $50,000.* Without any hesitation, you raise the bid immediately. It is difficult to negotiate with a cool head when you are passionate about acquiring a particular item that you have fallen in love with. Intense emotions will predominate over common sense.

- In a discussion, your business partner hesitates, saying: *We can't afford to accept all these conditions. The risk is too high.* Keeping a cool head, you reply: *You should, of course, do as you please, but I don't think you've made proper calculations concerning this project.* There is a serious risk that communication will grind to a halt if you do not make an effort to understand your partner's concerns. You indicate a pronounced lack of empathy in saying: *You should, of course, do as you please.* You cannot understand what your partner is saying. Ask her to expand on her line of thought. Continue to ask questions until you understand her concerns.

When your emotions get the best of you:

- Take a break. Leave the negotiation room, make yourself a cup of herbal tea, or walk around the block. If you stay at the negotiating table, the pressure generating the strong feelings will continue.
- Count to ten. Before you have reached ten, rational thinking may kick in again. You will become aware of the impact of your emotions.
- Get someone else's advice. If your arguments are not convincing to the other delegation, something is missing, and you need to let someone else step in and take the lead.
- Let your emotions work for you. Make the other party aware of what you are feeling: *I get aggravated and feel taken advantage of every time you . . . .*
- Mentally prepare for strong feelings during the negotiations and be ready to manage them. Be prepared to handle those situations in which you or the other party grows angry. Have a strategy in place to neutralize the volatility.

Keep Stress from Getting the Best of You

In a negotiation, you will never fight the other party with your fists, but you might take them on with your words. A negotiator who cannot handle the stressful situation created by the other party will be pressured into looking for any conceivable solution, usually presented in the form of concessions. If you move from negotiation to verbal combat, you run the risk of making unilateral concessions. In fleeing the table and making these one-sided concessions, negative aspects of your personality are reinforced.

Frequently taking a break is the very best tactic to re-establish equilibrium. Anticipate the stressful factors that may emerge and be prepared to handle them. This will improve your stress tolerance, and you will respond less intensely and emotionally to the moves of the other party.

Situational Stress

You are in a situation in which you run the risk of losing face and becoming the object of the other party's mistrust. You might, for instance, have left important documents at your office or made a serious error in your calculations. If worse comes to worst, you must accept your mistake and apologize. Under no circumstances should you go on the defensive. This will only aggravate the situation. If you admit to an error openly and without reservations, you will gain the respect of the other party.

Confrontational Stress

If the other party's provocation is intentional, you should take a break in the negotiations. Use the break to unwind and to re-establish equilibrium. Do not respond to the provocation, blow it out of proportion, or lose sight of the negotiation objective. Sometimes it is a good idea to change the negotiation environment or location, or to delay the conflict the other party has opened. Spend your break socializing, relaxing with the other party, and having a drink and a meal. Avoid the subject under negotiation. Meet some of the people on the other side of the table informally. You may be able to resolve the matter face to face.

Be En Garde for Stress-provoking Behavior

You need to be on the lookout for tactical moves used by combative negotiators that are intended to cause stress in the opponent:

- Interrupting the opponent, speaking at the same time he does, and challenging everything he says. (Be aware of the fact that this is not seen as stress-provoking behavior in all cultures. In France, for instance, people expect to be interrupted.)

- Demonstrating a lack of interest, avoiding eye contact with the opponent, or by making notes while he is speaking.
- Suppressing body language.
- Failing to answer questions.
- Responding with standard arguments of the type: *But that's how we've always done it.*
- Discussing only one delegation's proposal instead of examining both sides'.
- Being condescending.
- Not being punctual.
- Acting with superiority.
- Using threats to create insecurity and exert pressure.
- Using silence.

Managing Stress

Stress is a health hazard. It is very important that you maintain a healthy lifestyle, with a good physical and mental constitution, a rewarding family life, hobbies, and time for relaxation. Be aware of performance anxiety. A transaction that does not happen, does not have to be equivalent to a failure. Do not demand that you succeed every time. Some situations are hopeless.

Methods are available to reduce stress. Tenseness and heart activities can be controlled by willpower. Meditation and yoga are time-honored methods that have found their way into the world of business. Biofeedback is a method in which, by means of simple instruments, you teach yourself about the thoughts and situations that affect muscle tension and heart activity in a negotiation. You learn how to recognize your body's stress signals before you make a bad decision.

The Pressure of Time

Time is a central factor in all negotiations. It determines your expectations, restricts your room for negotiation, often costs money, and is a limited resource. If you are short of time, it is important is to utilize the available time in the best possible manner.

- Use an agenda; make sure that the other party receives it in advance so that he can prepare, and so that decisions can be made with reference to the agenda.
- Have written, preliminary negotiations.
- Make sure that both you and the other party have sufficient authority.

- Be well prepared.
- Agree on a schedule for various partial decisions. It is important not to let the other party know whether or not you are under time pressure, as it might then be easy for him to take advantage of your situation.

All negotiations have a deadline. Running late can be expensive, risky, or impossible. If a negotiator knows the other party's deadline, he can take advantage of it to press through a decision or concession. Using time pressure as a tactic is effective because:

- Most negotiators lower their expectations. They start negotiating against the clock to try to force an agreement to a conclusion.
- Often decisions are only made when delegates have reached their deadline.
- Competitors who cannot deliver fall by the wayside.
- It has the effect of a hidden threat. A delay can lead to increased costs, increased risks, or can enable competitors to get back in the picture.
- Time to prepare, investigate, or develop alternatives is limited.

Do not inform the other party of the details of your timetable. Make sure you have plenty of time in foreign markets, where the negotiation pace may be very different.

Change the Subject

To avoid taking up a position on the demands of the other party, shift the negotiation to a completely different issue. For instance, the buyer insists that the offer be reduced by 5 percent. Listen and take notes. Instead of expressing an opinion on the demand, say: *I see we have forgotten to agree on the time of delivery. In order to avoid any problems with the delivery, we should find a suitable date.* If this gambit is not made by the head of the delegation, but by an accompanying member, it works even better. The buyer lets go of the price issue, and the parties can agree on the practical details concerning delivery.

Shifting the focus in this way will often be combined with presenting the other party with a choice: *We can deliver during the third or fourth week of November.* The buyer chooses the alternative that suits him best. If he decides about the time of delivery, the supplier can interpret his delivery choice as an acceptance that the price demanded is okay.

Watch Out for Good Cop-Bad Cop

The classic situation with the good cop and the bad cop exists in many variations. Its application is not by any means limited to the negotiating table, but is part of the toolbox of any negotiator in a zero-sum game.

First, the bad guy is in play, assuming a hard and intransigent stance. The negotiations lead nowhere and have to be discontinued. In situations in which you do not have good alternatives, or are forced to reach an agreement with the other party, you have to put up with this treatment. You may go on round after round. You will likely end up pressed for time and deeply frustrated. At the same time, your own organization will be expecting to see results. The pressure affecting you from all sides will increase your inclination to accept a deal that meets your minimum requirements.

When the bad guy has hammered you long enough, you unexpectedly meet the good guy. The bad guy is no longer there. The negotiation can be informal and even begin in the street, in the elevator, or in a restaurant. Often the good guy has not participated in the previous negotiations, and appears to be quite surprised that no agreement has yet been reached. He says that they are interested in reaching an agreement and expresses his regrets that his colleague has shown such an antagonistic attitude. He is ready to take on the responsibility for anchoring an agreement. He sees no major obstacles as long as you make some concession.

Faced with this unexpected possibility to achieve a solution to your negotiation problems, you lower your guard and make a unilateral concession. It is now or never that an agreement is to be reached, and you are really feeling the pressure. You cannot bear to play the waiting game, nor do you have the courage to do it.

There are many situations in which negotiators play this game. The role of the good guy can be played by the CEO, while the human resources manager can be the bad guy. The secretary of the local trade union can be the good guy, while the people from the trade union center are the bad ones. The people from the home office are bad, while the local agent is good. The delegation leader at the negotiating table is the good guy, while the others are bad.

In a situation in which you are dependent on the other party, it would be enough for them to dictate their demands. This may be harmful to the personal relations, however. You might feel defeated and want revenge. By having the good guy come onto the stage near the end of the negotiations, they improve their relationship with you and reduce the risk of future acts of vengeance on your part. Their bad negotiator will be a pawn that they can sacrifice.

When you come across the bad guy, try not to let yourself be provoked. Biased allegations, personal attacks, and lies are used to upset you. Respond with silence. Interrupt the negotiation, but leave the door ajar for new contacts. Do not react in an unplanned emotional manner by slamming the door. Refrain from bringing your own bad guy to the table. Do not let the negotiation turn into a battle for power.

Beware of Corporate Policies

Printed provisions and corporate policies can also take on the role of the bad cop. The other party makes reference to existing laws, to the management decrees, and to regulatory requirement, and claims that there is no way that these rules can be altered. He shows great understanding for your demands, and promises that he will find out whether an exception can be made or a way around can be found. It would make things easier if you were to accept a few of his demands. You lower your expectations and make minor concessions to help him so he will be more inclined to help you.

If you are exposed to this tactic, you must stay **icy cold** and sit tight. If the other party has designed his gambit in this manner, it is generally because he is very interested in reaching an agreement with you. You can win the initiative by staying silent, thereby pressuring the other party into making the next move. Take advantage of the opening he is offering. Your position is probably strong, and you have a good chance of getting a satisfactory agreement if you see through his tactic and stay calm and collected.

Having the Authority to Take Action—Or Not

Ensure that you have considerable authority. However, at the negotiating table, it is sometimes advisable to act as though you have none. Do not make decisions without taking the necessary time to consider them. Quick decision-making is not necessarily a matter of status. Show self-discipline, impose narrow limits upon yourself, and aim high.

Bluffing and Threats

Bluffing, sometimes referred to as "the tactic of the weak," replaces facts and logical reasoning. A blue chip company with a respectable facade is not a guarantee of honesty and integrity at the negotiating table. The higher the stakes, the higher the risks some negotiators are willing to run.

If you choose to bluff, you should keep in mind that it will affect your credibility. If your bluff is called, you must expect to be perceived as unreliable for the remainder of the negotiation.

Bluffing is used to test and pressure the other party. If you do not have the courage to test the other party, or if you are not quite sure how to handle bluffing games, you might cave in. A more effective approach is to assess the other party in silence, and try to determine how much of what he is saying is true.

Bluffing Games

- **Time pressure:** *We must finish this deal before the boss leaves on Friday... We find it difficult to keep to the time of delivery... A price rise is on its way... We will not have the next meeting of the purchasing committee until three weeks from today.*
- **Competition:** *The competitor's price is 8.5 percent lower... We have other offers that are just as good, but the competitor provides service free of charge for one year.*
- **Deny facts:** *We haven't received your invoice... We haven't made any agreement that entitles you to an additional debit... Anderson promised me that you would....*

Anticipate Threats When Bluffing Occurs

To intensify the pressure on the other party, bluffing may be combined with a threat: *Your competitors have promised that the price will stay firm for 18 months. If you do not make us the same offer, we can't go on doing business with you.*

If the threat is to work, the threatened party must perceive the threat as credible and assume that it will be carried out. To use threats successfully, you must be prepared to carry out your threat if the other party does not give in. Otherwise, the threat will be an empty one, and you will lose credibility. When you lose credibility, there is a risk that the things you present and the obstacles you raise in the future might not be taken seriously. If you are forced to carry out the threat, you must have alternatives available to you that are nearly as good. If your gambit fails, you always need to have a retreat position or your next step ready and prepared.

Threats constitute an uncertain tactic. When faced with a threat:

- Delegates become obstinate.
- Negotiators begin to play power games.
- The climate deteriorates, which in turn means that communication suffers.

- Threats are perceived as combative, and combat only provides short-term solutions.
- Relations become disturbed.

These negative effects can be avoided if you refrain from phrases like: *Either you'll let us have...or we will have to...* Instead, you should use phrases like "if...when" or "what if."

Sometimes it is useful to let the media make the threats as a kind of trial balloon, in connection with which you deny having made a threat.

Example: Threats and the Media

A newspaper article reads: *Big Industry Ltd is forced to discontinue operations in Denver, if stalemate isn't resolved by month end.*

Big Industry responds: *Our board of directors has not yet discussed the question, but it is certainly a possibility.*

The governor's secretary of economic development says: *The matter is being looked into. At the present time, I have no further comment.*

The mayor says: *I will inform the secretary of economic development of the issue. A closure of the plant isn't acceptable because all these workers will lose their jobs. The state must to be able to ____.*

The trade union says: *Our bargaining position remains unchanged. We expect the secretary of economic development to uphold his previous promises to us. He is responsible for finding an acceptable solution.*

Instead of ending up in opposition to the trade unions and the mayor, Big Industry points to a common enemy, in this case the secretary for economic development. At the same time, Big Industry denies that their board of directors has discussed the question.

Do not burn all your bridges. Many conflicts lead to open combat if, by your threats, you push the other party into a corner in which they have no opportunity to act and no new openings, and have a serious risk of losing face. They will choose combat, and you could potentially risk the entire deal.

How to Handle Threats and Bluffing

Avoid creating deadlock. If you are interested in resolving the negotiation, leave the door ajar so that new negotiations can be opened. If the other party is misrepresenting the facts and you disclose this in front of colleagues, he will lose face and try to retaliate. Instead of accusing the other party of lying, you can point out that his tactic will not help him and suggest that he will benefit from choosing an alternative.

There are situations in which an unqualified statement may yield a good result. The following are strong words: *I don't like this type of negotiation, and I don't intend to go along with the conditions you've made. I'm convinced that we'd both be better off if we cooperate. So instead, I suggest...*

The ground rule when you are being threatened is to stall, but keep a communication channel open. Ask questions instead of becoming defensive.

Time may be on your side when the other party is issuing threats. Threats are a desperate move on the part of a negotiator who believes himself safe with a strong hand to play, but an urgent need to reach an agreement. The issuing of threats also indicates that the negotiator has run out of good arguments, thus signaling that he has lost his bargaining equity in the negotiation.

Make it clear to the other party that you would rather pay the price than be part of his threats. Relate his threat to how much he will benefit from following your ideas and let him choose. Remember that this response may be interpreted as a threat made by you, and that you must be prepared to carry it out if necessary.

Example: Hoodwinked by a Very Shrewd Buyer

A government representative of the department of transportation in a country in Southeast Asia is in the market for a large number of buses. An invitation for bids is sent to all the known suppliers, except one – a European manufacturer he wants to buy from. The European manufacturer makes a major effort with the representative to be allowed to submit an offer. To begin with, the representative is never in his office, and he does not respond to her emails or return her calls. The manufacturer does not give up, but remains persistent. At last, she manages to arrange a meeting. The representative explains: *We're not interested in you. European prices are much too expensive.*

The manufacturer argues and says: *That is not the case.* She promises to make a very competitive offer, if the representative will let her submit a bid.

The representative replies: *I'll let you have a chance.* He shows her the bids submitted by the competitors. *They are way over the existing budget*, he says, *and we have told your competitors to recalculate their bids. Any supplier who wants to be in on the final negotiation must reduce his bid by at least 10 percent.* In this way the representative influences the importer as she calculates her bid.

The bus manufacturer meets with the production manager with whom she has worked in the past on similar important bids. The manufacturer takes a hard line and manages to lower the factory's asking price. This can be done because equipment utilization at the bus factory is operating beneath optimum production capacity. The manufacturer prepares a quotation. She has made serious cuts in her margins. The quotation is 10 percent below the bids the importer was shown by the government representative.

The government representative reacts with silence when the manufacturer shows him her bid. He does not contact the manufacturer again. The manufacturer thinks that the government representative has no more interest in her bid. She has spent a lot of time and energy working on this deal, and she does not want to quit. Finally, she establishes a dialogue with the representative, who tells her that the new quotations submitted by her competitors are 2.5 percent below her bid. The government representative hints that if she reduces her price by another 3 percent, he can guarantee that the transportation director will sign the contract. Once again, the manufacturer calls on the production manager. They agree that they do not want to lose the deal when it is only a matter of 3 percent. A new offer with prices that are 3 percent lower is emailed to the government representative. A contract negotiation meeting is convened.

The head of marketing from the bus factory and the manufacturer show up to sign the contract. The government representative gives his congratulations and expresses the hope that the manufacturer can meet the requirements to be made in connection with the contract negotiations. The manufacturer is stunned, as she thought that the transaction was already completed. The reality is that the manufacturer has been hoodwinked, and her profitability in the deal has been squeezed to nothing.

The government representative says that the contract is hers if she can offer the same financing terms as those of her competitors. Following tough negotiations, the representative obtains the manufacturer's concession on the relevant financing terms.

Then several other issues are taken up for negotiation. The representative makes a number of small and insignificant concessions, setting her up to secure his demands. Finally, the deal is landed, and the representative states that the contract will be constructed in accordance with the laws of her country.

The representative has the transportation director sign the contract with several terms left blank and then formally conveys it to the manufacturer at the next meeting. On the occasion of this meeting, the representative asks the importer how much the extended credit costs the bus manufacturer. The factory's head of finance is called, and he says that it costs $3.5 million. The representative then says: *Our country has a very high liquidity rate. The director wants to go back to your original conditions of payment, which did not provide for financing.* He picks up the contract, already signed by the director, fills in the missing financial term and deducts $3.5 million from the bid price already agreed upon.

The representative's negotiation was based on bluffing and lies. He intended to get the manufacturer involved in a combative negotiation. The manufacturer was fighting to be allowed to join the bidding process. She was fighting for her chance to sit at the negotiating table. She had invested time and money in the transaction and did not want to walk away. However, she lacked the courage to show initiative in the negotiation process, and so the government representative remained in the superior position throughout. Step by step, the representative forced her down to a price level that, at the end of the day, leaves her with no profit on the transaction.

Take aways

- Listen and understand your stress signals in a negotiation. Act. Don't react.
- Prepare, if you want to use any of the tools in this chapter. Don't act spontaneously.
- Define your negotiation strategy prior to your negotiation, but prepare your NBA (Next best alternative).
- Understand tactical gambits conducted by the opponent in a zero-sum game.
- Use breaks – use breaks – use breaks – use breaks.

CHAPTER 12

Make the Pie Bigger and Nobody Loses

T he following case study brings together all the concepts that have been discussed in this book in a single real-world example. It illustrates how these ideas are used in combination and in phases to achieve optimized outcomes for negotiators who are brave enough to venture into the land of SMARTnership and NegoEconomics. The mutual gains solutions that were achieved in this case were enabled by the trust factor.

Theory in Practice: The Not So Drywall

Acme Construction, a national leader in civil engineering and heavy industrial markets, has forged a long-standing relationship with Benton Manufacturing, a producer of high-quality construction materials. The two companies meet annually to negotiate terms for a new procurement agreement. Acme Construction purchases approximately 70 million drywall boards from Benton Manufacturing. Contract negotiations typically focus on purchase price, cash discounts, and payment terms, while product quality and procurement quantity remain relatively fixed inputs. On average, a piece of drywall board costs anywhere from $5.00 to $5.20 per unit, depending on the thickness of the board.

The standard deal-making objective for Acme Construction is to negotiate procurement terms that will yield the most value for their investment, while Benton Manufacturing seeks the optimal price for their products. Since both companies negotiate with competing goals, where one company is striving to minimize expenses and the other is

SAM: Strategy Assessment matrix

	Less Critical	More Critical
More Critical	High Impact **Medium Risk**	High Impact **High Risk**
Less Critical	Low Impact **Low Risk**	Low Impact **Medium Risk**

Figure 12.1   Always tailor your negotiation strategy based on the value you bring to the other party. Those with the most power have the greatest flexibility to assert their will.

attempting to maximize the profit margin, representatives from each company rarely pursue mutually beneficial deals. Instead, each party attempts to carve out a bigger piece of the existing pie, leaving the other party with the smaller portion.

Prior to the most recent round of negotiations, the board of directors at Acme Construction had directed procurement specialists to find ways to reduce construction material expenses. Acme executives devised an overall procurement strategy based on the organization's position as an industry leader and the international buying power that accompanies a strong market position. At the bargaining table, Acme negotiators demanded that suppliers reduce wholesale pricing or risk losing business to overseas competition.

When Acme Construction sought to leverage their zero-sum strategy against Benton Manufacturing, they insisted on a wholesale price of $4.80/unit nearly 14 million dollars ($14.000,000) less than what Benton was requesting. Acme negotiators argued that they could seek out cheaper foreign suppliers and that the organization's reputation would encourage other construction companies to import materials. As a result, foreign suppliers would strengthen their distribution networks and further undercut Benton Manufacturing on price. In order for Acme Construction to win the argument and receive such a significant price reduction, Benton would have to yield a sizeable portion of profits from the sale of drywall materials.

Abandoning Zero-Sum for a Bigger Pie

Faced with a zero-sum challenge, Benton executives were forced to choose between forgoing profits and dropping a major client. Typically, wholesale suppliers would elect to absorb the loss in order close the deal. They would view it as an opportunity to generate some short-term revenue and, by providing a valuable customer with a substantial price reduction, the manufacturer might negotiate for a higher-than-average price in future transactions. At the very least, the manufacturer would be able to move product and keep their manufacturing facilities in operation.

Therefore, rather than conceding to Acme's zero-sum tactics, Benton executives sought an entirely new approach with a slight shift in perspective. Benton recognized that past deals had focused solely on the production costs associated with drywall materials, which would help to determine the fair market price that Benton asked their customers to meet. In order for Benton Manufacturing to request that price and provide Acme with substantial savings, Benton executives would need to consider the cost of drywall materials from the perspective of their commercial customers.

Benton analysts studied the major expense inputs for a typical construction project, including transportation and fuel costs, man-hours and payroll expense, and the cost of drywall compared to other building materials. But most importantly, Benton executives looked at how drywall materials were handled and installed on-site. The research team eventually honed in on a total cost of ownership analysis of drywall materials, estimated at $22.50 per board. Based on their preliminary findings, Benton Manufacturing was able to develop a negotiation strategy that would seek to lower Acme's drywall materials expense at the back end—in other words, at the point of drywall installation, rather than at the point of wholesale purchase.

Back at the bargaining table, Benton executives were able to introduce the plan to their counterparts at Acme. The presentation hinged on a simple but critical question: is there any way we can bring down the cost of *installing* individual sheets of drywall? By posing the question in this manner, Benton executives sent a clear message that they were interested in fulfilling Acme's demand for lower cost materials. Benton's negotiation strategy had the dual advantage of shifting focus away from the win-lose, zero-sum approach to a more cooperative model focused on common goals (Figure 12.1). If the two companies were able reduce installation expenses, then Acme Construction could justify paying the fair market price that Benton was seeking, yielding a win-win outcome.

Breaking It Down: Sharing Information

In an effort to address the installation question, the two parties made an effort to acquire more accurate construction data. Acme researchers examined the company's operational procedures, devising a step-by-step breakdown of drywall materials handling from receiving to the installed, finished product. The research demonstrated that much of the drywall material was damaged and destroyed on-site due to improper handling. Once delivered to the construction site, drywall materials needed to be unloaded from the trucks, moved about the site, and cut to fit before final installation. At each point of contact, the fragile sheets might end up with broken corners or cracked edges, and those sheets had to be discarded.

Furthermore, the size of a full sheet of drywall required at least two crewmembers to handle it, making it a cumbersome and time-consuming task to haul drywall materials around the construction site. And finally, the research revealed that careful handling was essentially a low priority for construction crews because they considered drywall to be an inexpensive, disposable material. Out of a typical procurement lot, the three mishandling factors—excessive handling, unwieldy size, and a collective disregard for materials—proved to be the cause of at least 40 percent of the waste on a typical Acme Construction project. Acme Construction clearly had internal issues to address. More importantly though, Benton had successfully pinpointed an area where substantial savings could be made, and the plan that their executives had developed not only outlined practical cost-reduction goals, but it also enabled Benton Manufacturing to take the lead in the cooperative strategy.

The collaborative project, a relatively simple plan spearheaded by Benton negotiators, was designed to reduce the need for on-site handling. Innovative material delivery systems and simplified handling methods would be implemented to curtail waste and ultimately drive down construction costs. Beginning with manufacturing, Benton introduced a new line of half-sized drywall sheets to make on-site handling more efficient. And, to further reduce the need for excessive handling, Benton offered to test a pilot program supplying Acme Construction with custom-cut drywall sheets. Working closely with Acme architects and engineers, Benton's design experts would review the construction blueprints to develop a streamlined drywall materials delivery system. Essentially, Benton Manufacturing would fabricate custom drywall pieces in the factory. Then, the custom-cut sections would be individually packaged and delivered along with a predetermined number of full- and half-sheets, so that Acme crewmembers could install materials in the order received.

Where past projects would have required the coordinated effort of 30 to 40 crewmembers to unload, haul, place, and install large sheets of drywall, the new system not only alleviated the handling burden for crewmembers but also reduced waste from mishandling. These innovative and streamlined handling procedures would not have been possible for Benton and Acme to develop independently. However, the collaborative effort to reduce drywall material expenses provided the companies with the incentive to innovate and the means to calculate the risks and the benefits involved.

As a result of the more cooperative strategy, Acme Construction was able to order roughly the same quantity of drywall materials at a wholesale price similar to past procurement deals. Moreover, with the implementation of innovative manufacturing and a more efficient delivery system, Acme was able to reduce on-site waste and increase productivity. The net benefit amounted to about $10 per board in value-added savings, considerably way more than the price discount that Acme executives had originally demand. With a cooperative effort aimed at common goals, both parties benefited from the deal.

Final Challenge: Dividing the Added Value

Before finalizing the procurement deal, negotiation executives had to discuss how the savings would be divided. An equal split would seem like the most expedient and equitable solution, but corporate negotiations rarely follow this simple course of action. A simple 50/50 split often shows a fear of additional bargaining and could end up benefiting one of the parties disproportionately. Instead, it is a better approach for executives to run hard bargains and ultimately reach deals through concessions. Collaborative efforts aimed at common goals are the ideal way for negotiators to increase the size of the pie, but when it comes to dividing the added value, a more hard-line, zero-sum approach is necessary.

When it came time to distribute the added value from the drywall procurement deal, Acme Construction was able to bargain for the larger share. At first, negotiators at Benton offered to give up 60 percent of the $800,000 savings, retaining only 40 percent after the deal. They argued that new approaches to manufacturing and materials delivery warranted compensation for investments. Acme negotiators fell back on their strong market position to justify a claim for closer to 70 percent of the value-added savings. By taking advantage of bargaining equity made possible by their size and market dominance, Acme executives were able to bargain for a greater share of the value.

If Benton executives had wanted to push the issue, Acme negotiators could have reinforced their power position with the threat of taking their business to the international market with cheaper labor costs. Faced with the pressure of global competition, Benton negotiators accepted the 70/30 deal to deliver drywall materials to Acme Construction's upcoming projects. Although Benton Manufacturing did not win the lion's share of the added value, their executives could conclude knowing that they were able to generate profits from the deal and improve their product line.

Cooperative deal-making is relatively simple. It starts with good chemistry between parties and thrives on constructive, sincere discussions. Negotiations of this type tend to be fueled by an open exchange of information, where integrity and fairness are as valuable as the information contributed. Under the right conditions, cooperative deals can effectively multiply the overall value of a deal. It is important to look beyond the traditional measures of unit price and short-term profits. Although working closely with their counterparts to increase the overall value in a deal is the necessary first step in the bargaining process, the most resilient executives, like those at Acme Construction, will not shy away from capturing the greatest share of the bigger pie for their firm.

Restoring Trust to the Marketplace: It All Starts with You

I have the privilege of meeting thousands of interesting, exciting, intelligent people every year around the world. Sometimes after one of my presentations, one of these people will approach me and say something like: *I agree with your philosophy and thinking about the creation of NegoEconomics, openness, and trust. But how do I change my counterpart so that they will work with me in a spirit of cooperation?*

Changing other people's thinking and attitude is usually very hard. You can't really change the mindset of your counterpart. The only person in the room whose mindset you can change is your own.

It all starts with you. Like the FitzGerald chieftain who chanced his arm by putting it through the Door of Reconciliation at the cathedral in Dublin, you might need to be the first to sacrifice something. You might need to take the initiative in showing trust. Perhaps you are the one who should test the ice—to make sure it does not break. Openness and honesty most often mirror openness and honesty. But be careful not to become naive. Be aware that you are not actually negotiating quantity, delivery dates, finances, or time. The only thing you negotiate, regardless of industry or business, is information. "I will show you mine, if you will show me yours."

A great leader can change an industry overnight and continue to be a successful negotiator. How? He knows what he is looking for.

Think what you can change right now in your behavior. Put down this book and make a brief list of the things you can change in your practices and habits. Ask yourself: What issues can I be more open about? How can I change the way I open a negotiation? What variables do I need to put a cost or value on? I am sure that if you give yourself ten minutes to think this through, you will come up with a to-do list of things that are within your control, that will change the dynamic of your next negotiation.

The world needs people like you—people who are brave, willing, and able to change the way we have been conducting business for the last 300 years. People who see the benefits of changing the world from a place of distrust and zero-sum-oriented negotiation to something more beneficial for all of us—the spirit of SMARTnership.

My mission is a simple one: make the world a better place to live and make the world of business more prosperous and rewarding. I am doing this not because it sounds good. I am doing this to make a contribution to the commercial marketplace—you become wealthier when you help other people become wealthier.

In your next negotiation, consider opening your meeting by saying to your counterpart, "I am here today to help you reduce your costs, limit your liabilities, reduce your risks, and at the same time increase your profits! Are you interested in that?" If they indicate their interest, continue by saying, "And furthermore, I expect you to help me reduce my risk, limit my liabilities, contain my costs, while at the same time improve my profits!" Who can resist an opening like that?

It all starts with you!

Notes

Preface

1. Risk Response Network Insight Report, *Global Risks 2013 Eighth Addition* (Cologny, Switzerland: World Economic Forum, 2013).

2 Behavioral Economics in Deal-making

1. Daniel Kahneman, *A Perspective on Judgment and Choice: Mapping Bounded Rationality* (Washington, DC: American Psychologist 58 (9), 2003) 697–720.
2. Walter Mischel, Ebbe Ebbesen, and Antonette Raskoff, *Cognitive and Attentional Mechanisms in Delay of Gratification* (Washington, DC: American Psychology Association, 1972) 204–218.
3. Justin Kruger and David Dunning, *Unskilled and Unaware of It: How Difficulties in Recognizing One's Own Incompetence Lead to Inflated Self-Assessments* (Washington, DC, The American Psychology Association, 1999) 1121–1134.
4. Keith Campbell, Constantine Sedikides, *Self-threat Magnifies the Self-Serving Bias: A Meta-Analytical Integration* (Washington, DC, The American Psychology Association, 1999) 23–43.
5. Daniel Yankelovich, *Profit With Honor: The New Stage of Market Capitalism (The Future of American Democracy Series)* (Harrisonburg, Virginia: R.R. Donnelley, 2006) 114.

3 The Trust Factor: The Keystone of NegoEconomics

1. Harold Macmillan, *Biography of Harold Macmillan* (Cosford, UK: The National Cold War Exhibition).
2. St. Patrick's Cathedral, *The Doors of Reconciliation* (Dublin, Ireland: St. Patrick's Cathedral).
3. Edelman Insights, *2012 Edelman Trust Barometer: Global Deck* (New York: Edelman, 2012), 5.

4. See also, The Economist, *Busted Trust* (New York: The Economist Newspaper Limited, 2012), 1–2.
5. "The iEconomy," *NYTimes.com: Business Day*, http://www.nytimes.com/interactive/business/ieconomy.html?smid=pl-share.
6. Dr. Pat Lynch, *Trust: A Personal Value Essential to Organizational Success* (Long Beach, California: Business Alignment Strategies, 2010), 1–2.
7. Søren Kierkegaard, *Either/Or* (Copenhagen, University bookshop Reitzel, 1843).
8. William Shedd, *Quotes on Ships and the Sea* (Arlington, Virginia: Richer Resources Publications, 2008) 14.
9. 2011 National Business Ethics Survey, *Workplace Ethics in Transition* (Arlington, Virginia: Ethics Resource Center, 2011).
10. Brad Blanton, *Radical Honesty: How to Transform your Life by Telling the Truth* (Stanley, Virginia: Sparrowhawk Publishing, 2000).
11. Scott Dahl, *Ethics on the Table: Stretching the Truth in Negotiations* (Washington, D.C., Arnold & Porter, 1989) 173, 194–195.
12. Terry Carter, *Ethics by the Numbers* (Washington, DC: ABA Journal, 1997).
13. Paul Ekman, *Telling Lies* (New York, W.W. Norton & Company, 1992).
14. Dan Ariely, *Why We Lie* (New York: Wall Street Journal, 2012).
15. Dan Ariely, *The (Honest) Truth About Dishonesty* (New York: HarperCollins Publishers, 2012).
16. Ariely, *Why We Lie*.
17. Daniel Kaufmann, *Rethinking The Fight Against Corruption* (New York City, NY: The Huffington Post, 2012).
18. Network of Global Agenda Councils 2012–2013 report, *Global Agenda Council on Anti-Corruption* (Cologny, Switzerland: World Economic Forum, 2013).
19. Network of Global Agenda Councils 2012–2013 Report, *Global Agenda Council*
20. Network of Global Agenda Councils 2012–2013 Report, *Global Agenda Council*
21. Network of Global Agenda Councils 2012–2013 Report, *Global Agenda Council*

6 Creating a Culture of Trust and Openness

1. Dick Lee and Delmar Hatesohl, *Listening: Our Most Used Communication Skill* (Kansas City, Missouri: Terra Nova Coaching, 2012).
2. Constantine von Hoffman, *Secrets of Successful Business Negotiation* (Framingham, Massachusetts: CSO Magazine, 2010), 5.
3. Gary W. Noesner and Mike Webster, *Crisis Intervention: Using Active Listening Skills in Negotiations,* http://www.au.af.mil/au/awc/awcgate/fbi/crisis_interven2.htm (1997).

Index